Recommender Systems

Recommender Systems: A Multi-Disciplinary Approach presents a multi-disciplinary approach for the development of recommender systems. It explains different types of pertinent algorithms with their comparative analysis and their role for different applications. This book explains the big data behind recommender systems, the marketing benefits, how to make good decision support systems, the role of machine learning and artificial networks, and the statistical models with two case studies. It shows how to design attack resistant and trust-centric recommender systems for applications dealing with sensitive data.

Features of this book:

- Identifies and describes recommender systems for practical uses
- Describes how to design, train, and evaluate a recommendation algorithm
- Explains migration from a recommendation model to a live system with users
- Describes utilization of the data collected from a recommender system to understand the user preferences
- Addresses the security aspects and ways to deal with possible attacks to build a robust system

This book is aimed at researchers and graduate students in computer science, electronics and communication engineering, mathematical science, and data science.

Intelligent Systems

Series Editor: Prasant Kumar Pattnaik

This series provides a medium for publishing the results of recent research into the applications, tools and techniques of Intelligent Systems, including a wide range of relevant topics. The audience for the book series consists of advanced level students, researchers, and industry professionals working at the forefront of their fields. It will present books focused on the development of advanced intelligent environments, Generic Intelligent Tools, Techniques and Algorithms, applications using Intelligent Techniques, Multi Criteria Decision Making, Management, international business, finance, accounting, marketing, healthcare, military applications, production, networks, traffic management, crisis response, human interfaces, Brain Computing Interface; healthcare; and education and learning.

Interoperability in IoT for Smart Systems
Edited by Monideepa Roy, Pushpendu Kar, and Sujoy Datta

Recommender Systems
A Multi-Disciplinary Approach
Edited by Monideepa Roy, Pushpendu Kar, and Sujoy Datta

For more information about this series, please visit: www.routledge.com/Intelligent-Systems/book-series/IS

Recommender Systems

A Multi-Disciplinary Approach

Edited by
Monideepa Roy,
Pushpendu Kar,
and Sujoy Datta

CRC Press
Taylor & Francis Group
Boca Raton London New York

CRC Press is an imprint of the
Taylor & Francis Group, an **informa** business

Designed cover image: © Shutterstock

First edition published 2023
by CRC Press
6000 Broken Sound Parkway NW, Suite 300, Boca Raton, FL 33487-2742

and by CRC Press
4 Park Square, Milton Park, Abingdon, Oxon, OX14 4RN

CRC Press is an imprint of Taylor & Francis Group, LLC

© 2023 selection and editorial matter, Monideepa Roy, Pushpendu Kar, and Sujoy Datta;
individual chapters, the contributors

ISBN: 978-1-032-33321-2 (hbk)
ISBN: 978-1-032-33322-9 (pbk)
ISBN: 978-1-003-31912-2 (ebk)

DOI: 10.1201/9781003319122

Typeset in Times
by Apex CoVantage, LLC

Contents

About the Editors

Dr. Monideepa Roy did her bachelors and masters in mathematics from IIT Kharagpur and her PhD in CSE from Jadavpur University. For the last 11 years, she is working as an associate professor at KIIT Deemed University, Bhubaneswar. Her areas of interest include remote healthcare, mobile computing, cognitive WSNs, remote sensing, recommender systems, sparse approximations, and artificial neural networks. At present she has seven research scholars working with her in these areas and two more have successfully defended their theses under her guidance. She has several publications in reputed conferences and journals. She has been the organizing chair of the first two editions of the International Conference on Computational Intelligence and Networks CINE 2015 and 2016 and ICMC 2019, and she has organised several workshops and seminars. She also has several book chapter publications in various reputed publication houses as well as an edited book under Taylor and Francis. She has also been an invited speaker for several workshops and conferences in machine learning and recommendation systems. She is also a reviewer for several international journals and conferences.

Dr. Pushpendu Kar is currently working as an Assistant Professor in the School of Computer Science, University of Nottingham (China campus). Before this, he was a Postdoctoral Research Fellow at the Norwegian University of Science and Technology, the National University of Singapore, and Nanyang Technological University. He also worked in different engineering colleges as a lecturer and in the IT industry as a software professional. He has more than 12 years of teaching and research experience as well as one and a half years of industrial experience at IBM. He has completed his Ph.D. from the Indian Institute of Technology Kharagpur, Master of Engineering (M.E) from Jadavpur University, and Bachelor of Technology (B.Tech) from the University of Kalyani in Computer Science and Engineering. He was awarded the prestigious Erasmus Mundus Postdoctoral Fellowship from the European Commission, the ERCIM Alain Bensoussan Fellowship from the European Union, and SERB OPD Fellowship from the Dept. of Science and Technology, Government of India. He has received the 2020 IEEE Systems Journal Best Paper Award. He has received four research grants for conducting research-based projects, three of them as a Principal Investigator (PI). He also received many travel grants to attend conferences and doctoral colloquiums. He is the author of more than 50 scholarly research papers, which have been published in reputed journals and conferences, and in IT magazines. He has also published two edited books. He is also an inventor of five patents. He has participated in several conference committees, worked as a team member to organize short-term courses, and delivered a few invited talks as well as Keynote Lectures at international conferences and institutions. He is a Senior Member of IEEE and a Fellow of the Higher Education Academy (FHEA), UK. He has been recognized as a High-Level Talent by Ningbo Municipal Government, China. Dr. Kar mainly teaches Computer Networks and programming-related modules and his research areas include Wireless Sensor Networks, Internet of Things, Content-Centric Networking, Machine Learning, and Blockchain.

Sujoy Datta has done his MTech from IIT Kharagpur. For the last 11 years, he has been working as an Assistant Professor in the School of Computer Engineering, at KIIT Deemed University. His areas of research include wireless networks, computer security, elliptic curve cryptography, neural networks, remote healthcare, and recommender systems. He has several publications in various reputed conferences and journals. He has co-organised several workshops and international conferences in the capacity of Organizing co- chair and Finance Chair, as well as several workshops and seminars. He has several upcoming book chapter publications as well as an edited book by Taylor and Francis. He has also served in various committees in the roles of examination observer and assistant controller for exams. He has guided several undergraduate students in their final year projects and thesis. He has also filed and has been granted several patents in his name. He loves to travel and discover new and offbeat places.

Contributors

Anjali Agarwal
Amity Institute of Information
   Technology

Mansheel Agarwal
Amity University
Kolkata, India

N S Agbeb
Department of Electrical/Electronics
   Engineering
Kenule Beeson Saro-Wiwa Polytechnic
Bori, Rivers State, Nigeria

Debajyoty Banik
Kalinga Institute of Industrial
   Technology

Soumya Sankar Basu
Department of Computing, College
   of Business Technology &
   Engineering
Sheffield Hallam University
Sheffield, United Kingdom

Bikram Pratim Bhuyan
School of Computer Science
UPES
Dehradun, India

Swarup Chattopadhyay
Machine Intelligence Unit
Indian Statistical Institute
Kolkata, India

Anjan Chowdhury
Center for Soft Computing
   Research
Indian Statistical Institute
Kolkata, India

Keshav Dahal
School of Engineering and
   Computing
University of the West of Scotland
United Kingdom

Ajanta Das
Amity Institute of Information
   Technology
Amity University Kolkata
Newtown, Kolkata, India

Sujoy Datta
School of Computer Engineering
Kalinga Institute of Industrial
   Technology
India

Shreya Dey
School of Computer Engineering
Kalinga Institute of Industrial
   Technology
India

Subrata Dutta
Dept of Computer Sc. &
   Engineering
National Institute of Technology
Jamshedpur, Jharkhand, India

Kuntal Ghosh
Machine Intelligence Unit
Indian Statistical Institute
Kolkata, India

Arindam Giri
Dept of Computer Sc. &
   Engineering
Haldia Institute of Technology
West Bengal

K T Igulu
Department of Computer Science
Kenule Beeson Saro-Wiwa
  Polytechnic
Bori, Rivers State, Nigeria

Pushpendu Kar
School of Computer Engineering
The University of Nottingham
Ningbo, China

Supreet Kaur
Manav Rachna University
Faridabad, India

Manish Kumar
Manav Rachna University
Faridabad, India

Tapas Kumar
Manav Rachna University
Faridabad, India

Md Ashifuddin Mondal
Department of Computer Science and
  Engineering
Narula Institute of Technology
Kolkata, India

Shweta Mongia
Manav Rachna University
Faridabad, India

Sarmistha Neogy
Dept. of Computer Sc. & Engineering
Jadavpur University
Kolkata, India

F E Onuodu
Department of Computer Science
University of Port Harcourt
Rivers State, Nigeria

Hukam Singh Rana
School of Computer Science

University of Petroleum and Energy
  Studies, Bidholi campus
Dehradun, Uttarakhand, India

Zeenat Rehena
Department of Computer Science and
  Engineering
Aliah University
Kolkata, India

Monideepa Roy
School of Computer Engineering
Kalinga Institute of Industrial Technology
India

Arkajit Saha
School of Computer Engineering
Kalinga Institute of Industrial
  Technology
India

N R Saturday
Department of Computer Engineering
Rivers State University
Port Harcourti, Rivers State, Nigeria

Ananya Singh
School of Computer Engineering
KIIT, Deemed University
Bhubaneswar, India

Shriya Singh
School of Computer Engineering
KIIT, Deemed University
Bhubaneswar, India

T P Singh
School of Computer Science
UPES
Dehradun, India

Ravi Bhushan Thakur
Dept of Computer Sc. & Engineering
National Institute of Technology
Jamshedpur, Jharkhand, India

Foreword

"If you build it, they will come."

Ever since the fictional character of Ray Kinsella uttered that expression in the 1989 film *Field of Dreams*, it has almost become a business mantra for many startups and other new technology innovations. Given that there are many visionaries in the technology area who can design and build new technologies without any forethoughts on whether their products will have customer acceptances or not, and even though many new innovations eventually luck out on this, for the rest of us there is no option other than following what Sam Walton had said, "There is only one boss. The customer. And he can fire everybody in the company from the chairman on down, simply by spending his money somewhere else." But how do we know what a customer wants without having a crystal ball? We can perhaps use the following quote from Bill Gates for some guidance: "Your most unhappy customers are your greatest source of learning." One of the fundamental principles of recommendation engines is to learn from the customer directly and make recommendations in the future so that we do not have many "unhappy customers."

The ultimate goal of a recommendation engine is to predict what the customer may like or at least feel useful and make suggestions accordingly. Unfortunately, it is not an easy task. More often than not, the recommendation engine has to make a recommendation with very little or no information whatsoever. If the recommendation turns out to be wrong the customer may completely ignore any future recommendations or may even get irked or antagonized by the recommendations.

The information that is used by a recommendation engine is often stored in a customer vs. product preference matrix called a utility matrix. Consider the utility matrix for one of the major online retailers who might have over a quarter billion customers worldwide and carry about quarter billion different products on their catalog. The utility matrix for such a retailer would be in the order of 10^{16} entries. However, most of the entries of such a huge table will be blank because most customers would be using and may provide feedback for only a few hundred products. It is not necessary to predict every blank entry in a utility matrix. Rather, it is only necessary to discover some entries in each row that are likely to be of high relevance to the customer.

In most applications, the recommendation system does not offer users a ranking of all items but rather suggests a few that the user should value highly. It may not even be necessary to find all items with the highest expected ratings, but only to find a large subset of those with the highest ratings. Even for a simpler subset of problem like that the recommendation engine needs to do it so efficiently that even for such a large matrix it can make these recommendations almost in real time and on the fly, as when the customer is browsing and searching for a product online. Amazon first used the idea of the item-wise collaborative filtering approach along with the traditional customer-wise collaborative filtering approach, which made unpacking and retrieving information from large utility matrix over a very large and distributed data servers really feasible. The journal, *IEEE Internet Computing*, recognized the 2003 paper called "Amazon.com Recommendations: Item-to-Item Collaborative Filtering," by then Amazon researchers Greg Linden, Brent Smith, and Jeremy York with the "Test of Time" honor during its 20th anniversary celebration in 2017.

Without a utility matrix, it is almost impossible to recommend items. However, acquiring data from which to build a utility matrix is often difficult. There are two general approaches to discovering the value users place on items.

We can ask users to rate items. Movie ratings are generally obtained this way, and some online stores try to obtain ratings from their purchasers. Sites providing content, such as some news sites or YouTube, also ask users to rate items. This approach is limited in its effectiveness, since generally users are unwilling to provide responses, and the information from those who do may be biased by the very fact that it comes from people willing to provide ratings.

We can make inferences from users' behavior. Most obviously, if a user buys a product at Amazon, watches a movie on YouTube, or reads a news article, then the user can be said to "like" this item. More generally, one can infer interest from behavior other than purchasing. For example, if an Amazon customer views information about an item, we can infer that they are interested in the item, even if they don't buy it. Some of the recent research works deal with this idea of "implicit feedback." Many recent research works deal with interpreting the "implicit feedback" from customers using deep neural networks.

Development of recommender systems is a multi-disciplinary effort which involves experts from various fields such as artificial intelligence, human computer interaction, information technology, data mining, statistics, adaptive user interfaces, decision support systems, marketing, or consumer behavior.

The last items in the list, the consumer behavior, is the most important item for an accurate prediction of effectiveness of a recommendation system—but often gets the least amount of visibility in research literature. Many recommendation engines fail to understand the consumer behavior and keeps on displaying the same items to the customer even after the customer has either already purchased it elsewhere or has no interest in it any longer.

The Netflix Prize is a good example to show that even one of the best algorithms leave a lot of scope for improvements. The Netflix Prize was an open competition for the best collaborative filtering algorithm to predict user ratings for films, based on previous ratings only, without any other information about the users or films. The competition was for the best algorithm that could improve upon Netflix's own algorithm by at least a specified threshold. The competition started on October 2, 2006, and by the middle of October a team called WXYZConsulting has already beaten the native Netflix algorithm by the specified threshold.

When it comes to recommendation engines, there is no "one size fits all" solution. One needs to keep the human aspects of it in the focus while trying to calibrate other parts of the algorithm. The relationships between customers and product items may be often context based, making the utility matrix more non-uniform and complex than it may appear initially. A memory-based collaborative filtering is traditionally used for computing the "similarity" between users and/or items. However, a model-based collaborative filtering takes the solution a bit further by using different models for different sub-groups within the utility matrix.

Often a hybrid approach with a machine learning model along with a knowledge graph-based ontology might be the best solution when we have too little data or data is not reliable enough. Knowledge graph-based approaches have been shown to be particularly useful for a cold start for a new product or a new customer with no information on either being available for the utility matrix. Even when customer feedback might be available, sometimes they might be difficult to rely upon. A hybrid approach with knowledge graph and with both memory-based and model-based collaborative filtering can often cover the full life cycle of a product from its inception to maturity to when the product is no longer preferred anymore and can be discontinued.

In this anthology you will find several chapters covering different facets of the problem of recommendation engines, such as how to get user feedback using mood detection based on facial feature recognition to various frameworks for recommendations engines using swarm intelligence and IOT-based systems, as well as different methods related to content-based and collaborative filtering and their comparisons for efficacy using deep neural network, TensorFlow and other techniques. I am sure they will take you further down the road for choosing or building your own recommender systems for your particular problem.

Maharaj Mukherjee, PhD
IBM Master Innovator for Life
Chair, IEEE Region 1 Central Area
Member, IEEE USA Awards Committee
Member, IEEE USA Region 1 Awards Committee

Preface

A recommender system, or a recommendation system, is a subclass of information filtering systems that predicts the "rating" or "preference" a user would give to an item. They are primarily used for commercial applications. They are most commonly recognized as playlist generators for video and music services like Netflix, YouTube, and Spotify; product recommenders for services such as Amazon; or content recommenders for social media platforms such as Facebook and Twitter. These systems can operate using a single input, like music, or multiple inputs within and across platforms like news, books, and search queries. There are also popular recommender systems for specific topics like restaurants and online dating. Recommender systems have also been developed to explore research articles and experts, collaborators, and financial services.

There are many types of algorithms that have been used in building recommender systems, and they each have their own unique set of features. When building a recommender system, a good knowledge of the working of the algorithms will help the developer in choosing the correct type of algorithm for their application.

People use social networks to understand their health condition, so the health recommender system is very important to derive outcomes such as recommending diagnoses, health insurance, clinical pathway-based treatment methods, and alternative medicines based on the patient's health profile. Recent research that targets the utilization of large volumes of medical data while combining multimodal data from disparate sources reduces the workload and cost in healthcare. In the healthcare sector, big data analytics using recommender systems have an important role in terms of decision-making processes concerning a patient's health.

The application of recommender systems can also be extended to more crucial areas like healthcare and defense. The health recommender system (HRS) is becoming an important platform for healthcare services. In this context, health intelligent systems have become indispensable tools in decision-making processes in the healthcare sector. Their main objective is to ensure the availability of valuable information at the right time by ensuring information quality, trustworthiness, authentication, and privacy concerns. In the past few years, the machine learning and artificial intelligence communities have done significant work in using algorithms to identify patterns within data. These patterns have then been applied to various problems, such as predicting individuals' future responses to actions and performing pattern-of-life analyses on persons of interest. Some of these algorithms have widespread application to Department of Defense (DoD) and intelligence community (IC) missions. One machine learning and artificial intelligence technique that has shown great promise to DoD and IC missions is the recommender system. Here the recommender systems can be used for generating prioritized lists for defense actions, detecting insider threats, monitoring network security, and expediting other analyses. In addition, while designing such a system, it is important to know the security and safety features that need to be addressed. This book brings together the research ideas and experiences of academicians and industry experts in building robust and reliable recommender systems for critics' applications.

Since developing recommender systems requires the efforts of various disciplines and has a varieties of applications, by compiling the experiences of experts from various domains, this book is aimed at being a comprehensive handbook for developing a recommender system from scratch and is suitable for readers from a wide cross-section of specialization. Recommender systems are, at present, primarily used for commercial applications; the main aim of this book is to provide students, researchers, and solution providers with the steps needed to design recommender systems for critical and real-time applications like healthcare and surveillance. It also addresses the security aspects and ways to deal with possible attacks to build a robust system. It familiarizes the readers, who wish to design a recommender system from scratch, with the steps to create such a system. It is expected to empower the readers to do the following:

- Identify and describe a recommender system for practical uses
- Design, train, and evaluate a recommendation algorithm
- Understand how to migrate from a recommendation model to a live system with users
- Utilize the data collected from a recommender system to understand user preferences
- Apply the knowledge to new settings.

This book presents a multi-disciplinary approach to the development of recommender systems. Different types of algorithms for recommender systems along with their comparative analysis have been done. The book also presents the research findings of experts in various fields of computer science in the role of building recommender systems for various types of applications. Some examples are handling the big data behind recommender systems, using marketing benefits, making good decision support systems, understanding the role of machine learning and artificial networks, using statistical models, etc. The book also presents two case studies of the application of the recommender system in healthcare monitoring. The book shows how to design attack-resistant and trust-centric recommender systems for applications dealing with sensitive data.

The book has presented an in-depth discussion in the following chapters, which cover various aspects of recommender systems.

- **Comparison of Different Machine Learning Algorithms to Classify Whether or Not a Tweet is about a Natural Disaster—A Simulation-Based Approach**

    This chapter discusses the use of various machine learning algorithms to classify whether or not a tweet is about a natural disaster and compares the results of classification algorithms in order to identify the best one for analyzing Twitter data. This chapter also discusses the role of social media (presently, Twitter) in a natural disaster or emergency situation along with current research works as well as challenges faced by researchers in this field.

- **An End-to-End Comparison among Contemporary Content-Based Recommendation Methodologies**
  This chapter reviews a substantial number of articles and gives a final judgment on which algorithms should be adopted and tweaked in particular ways in order to have a more trustworthy environment. It also discusses some ideas for future development of this field based on choices made by users of any other evolving culture in whatever form it may take.

- **Neural Network-Based Collaborative Filtering for Recommender Systems**
  This chapter analyses different algorithms developed and used in the collaborative filtering (CF) based recommender systems and compares their performances in selecting the best algorithm.

- **Recommendation System and Big Data: Its Types and Applications**
  In this chapter, various recommendation systems are discussed and their application in various sectors are compared.

- **The Role of Machine Learning/AI in Recommender Systems**
  This chapter covers the machine learning algorithms that are associated with recommender systems. It also highlights the hybridization of these algorithms and how robust solutions are achieved from them.

- **A Recommender System Based on TensorFlow Framework**
  This chapter aims to examine TensorFlow recommenders in implementing a recommender system. This chapter discusses how to build a recommender system based on deep learning.

- **A Marketing Approach to Recommender Systems**
  This chapter examines recommender systems: their classes, their characteristics, and how they can be used for marketing. It also discusses recommender systems that facilitate massive, detailed, and cost-effective data acquisition; one-to-one marketing analysis; market basket analysis; more informed, personalized, and adaptive recommendations; one-to-one marketing analysis; personalization and adaptation; niche targeting analysis; and improved merchandising and atmospherics.

- **Applied Statistical Analysis in Recommendation Systems**
  This chapter provides a thorough literature overview of what is commonly regarded to be the most popular statistical approaches to recommender systems. It lays attention on the statistical basis of the techniques rather than their computing details. This chapter discusses in detail the major statistical methods used in different recommender systems.

- **An IoT-Enabled Innovative Smart Parking Recommender Approach**
  This chapter proposes an IoT enabled and network-based smart parking recommender solution, RecoPark. The proposed system enables cars to find a parking space automatically across cities and reserve them on the move. Optimal usage of parking space is rewarded to encourage disciplined usage of the system.

- **Classification of Road Segments in Intelligent Traffic Management System**

  This chapter presents a framework for an intelligent traffic management system and discusses the different components of it. It also presents road segment classification techniques using different machine learning approaches based on traffic density and average speed.

- **Facial Gestures-Based Recommender System for Evaluating Online Classes**

  This chapter discusses creating a model to track and recognize students' postures and gestures throughout the class duration to measure student engagement with the material and teaching techniques of their professors.

- **Application of Swarm Intelligence in Recommender Systems**

  This chapter discusses the advantages of the applications of Particle Swarm Optimization algorithms for developing more complex recommendation systems using multi-agent frameworks.

- **Application of Machine Learning Techniques in the Development of Neighborhood-Based Robust Recommender Systems**

  This chapter evaluates and discusses the utility of traditional network clustering techniques such as Louvain, Infomap, and label propagation algorithms for the development of neighborhood-based robust recommender systems. It also looks into and incorporates a modality-based network clustering method to make another neighborhood-based robust recommender systems.

- **Recommendation Systems for Choosing Online Learning Resources—A Hands-On Approach**

  This chapter is a hands-on approach which describes, step by step, the process of developing a recommendation system for choosing online resources.

We are thankful to all our authors for their excellent contributions, which led to the compilation of such an excellent resource for anyone who is interested in developing their own recommendation systems. A special thanks to Dr. Maharaj Mukherjee of IBM for kindly writing such a valuable foreword for us.

We also thank our series editor, Dr. Prasant Kumar Pattnaik, from the school of computer engineering, KIIT DU, for his excellent support and suggestions throughout our venture.

Finally we are thankful to Dr. Gagandeep Singh and Ms. Aditi Mittal from Taylor and Francis for providing their timely inputs for the smooth execution of the entire project.

(Editors)
Monideepa Roy
Pushpendu Kar
Sujoy Datta

1 Comparison of Different Machine Learning Algorithms to Classify Whether or Not a Tweet Is about a Natural Disaster
A Simulation-Based Approach

*Subrata Dutta, Manish Kumar, Arindam Giri,
Ravi Bhushan Thakur, Sarmistha Neogy, and
Keshav Dahal*

CONTENTS

DOI: 10.1201/9781003319122-1

1.1 INTRODUCTION

In the growing field of artificial intelligence, researchers are mostly focusing on utilization of the available data and the upcoming data in future. Social media has too
much data and, hence, it can be utilized in various fields to get the best out of it,
such as a) getting feedback of a newly launched product or movie, b) knowing public
opinion in an ongoing election, c) review of a restaurant using comments/feedback
posted by various user, etc. Analysis of user tweets/comments/feedback/reviews by
using machine learning and/or deep learning technique is called sentiment analysis.
[1-2] Basically, sentiment analysis is performed to know the concern of the public.
Similarly, when a natural disaster takes place or in any emergency situation, social
media produces too much information, and by performing sentiment analysis over
that information, some necessary action can be taken for the wellness of mankind.
Researchers are working so that information available over social media could be
utilized to its full capacity.

In any emergency situation, especially in the case of a natural disaster, it is very
difficult to maintain communication because of disturbances due to the heavy impact
of that incident at a particular location.

In the past, most communications were done via televisions, radios, and newspa-
pers, which are affected during disaster period. It was also very difficult to get timely
and accurate information because communication was one way. To get the actual
scenario of any incident, two-way communication plays an important role. This is
why social media outperforms other communication media.

Social media such as Facebook, Twitter, etc. allow their users, irrespective of
their location and role, to share text information, pictures, and videos related to
any news. At the same time, the data available over social media are real time
data and can be utilized to get the current status of a particular location regarding an event. These data can be utilized by concerned authorities, which is an
important factor in reducing the impact of an incident by taking proper mitigat-
ing actions.[2-3] In this technological world, we get some news earlier from
social media than from traditional sources. The main objective of this chapter is
to analyze the sentiment of various tweets and check whether or not it is about
a natural disaster.

The remainder of the chapter is organized as follows. Section 1.2 includes
related works. In Section 1.3, we discuss various challenges faced by researchers
in this area. Section 1.4 discusses the dataset used in simulation. In Section 1.5, we
outline the methodology of data classification using machine learning. Section 1.6
provides results and discussions. Finally, Section 1.7 includes the conclusion and
future work.

1.2 RELATED WORK

The influence of neighborhood equity on disaster situational awareness is investigated in hurricane by Zhai et al. 2020.[4] In Zou et al. 2018, Twitter data is mined
and analyzed in disaster resilience.[5] The authors try to find common indexes
from Twitter data so as to manage emergency situations. Human mobility patterns

during disasters are detected in Wang and Taylor 2014.[6] Potential use of social media in hurricanes is mentioned in Guan and Chen 2014 and Kryvasheyeu et al. 2016.[7-8] Research work in Wang et al. 2019 reveals that socially vulnerable communities had more influence than other factors in Hurricane Sandy.[9] Bayesian networks classifiers are used in sentiment analysis of Twitter data during natural disaster in Ruz et al. 2020.[10] This research demands the superiority of Bayesian classifier over support vector machine and random forest. The authors in Yang et al. 2019 proposed a credibility framework of Twitter data in a disaster scenario.[11] The framework is tested using a number of Twitter keywords. In order to generate Twitter Situational Awareness (TwiSA), sentiment analysis and topic modeling are used in Karami et al. 2020.[12] The TwiSA was used during the 2015 South Carolina flood to manage huge tweets and find people's negative concerns. A real-time disaster damage assessment model using social media is proposed in Shan et al. 2019.[13] In order to provide credible information about disasters, the Zahra et al. 2020 proposed an automatic identification of eyewitness messages on Twitter.[14] Based on different sources of tweets, the authors classify tweets and find associated characteristics. Analysis of Twitter data is used during the 2015 Chennai flood through random forests, naïve Bayes, and decision tree. The research in Nair et al. 2017 reveals that random forests gives best result.[15]

1.3 CHALLENGES

1.3.1 DATA COLLECTION

The importance of data can never be neglected in data analysis and data mining. The more data, the more information can be gathered. In the present application, we needed text data. As we worked on disaster tweets, we focused only on Twitter data extraction. We could access Twitter data by purchasing from private vendors or using Twitter application programming interface (API) to extract the data.[16] Most researchers prefer APIs for data extraction. But data extraction is restricted through this method. There is also restriction on the number of calls made for data extraction using a particular account. Also, most of the social media data (including Twitter) are unstructured, so it is very difficult to extract data. Unstructured data does not follow any particular pattern so that specific keywords could be used to extract the relevant data of any incident.

1.3.2 DATA AUTHENTICATION

As we analyze social media data, where every individual is allowed to share data, there is no proper authentication or verification of data. So in a case of emergency, incorrect data may lead to danger of human lives. Beyond emergency situations, sometimes rumors also spread over social media, which indirectly become responsible for violence in society. So detecting fake news or posts in social media is still a very big challenge. Due to an increase in fake news, concerned authorities are working hard to deal with such situations.

1.4   THE DATASET

We took a dataset from a Kaggle competition,[17] in which 5329 samples were used as training data and 2284 samples were used for model evaluation (i.e., out of 7613 samples, 70% were used as training data and 30% were used as test data). Some of the samples were manually verified to check the correctness of the sample dataset. The dataset contains fields such as ID, keyword, location, text, and target. The ID is a unique identity; the keyword (may be empty) is an important key from the tweet; text (most important field for our analysis) is the actual text of tweet; and the target is our dependent variable (i.e., 1 represents tweet is about a real disaster, 0 means tweet is not about a real disaster).

A sample dataset is shown in Figure 1.1. The number of tweets per class is shown in Figure 1.2(a), and the percentage of each class is shown in Figure 1.2(b). The number of tweets for the top 10 locations is shown in Figure 1.3. The number of tweets according to location in an entire dataset on a map is shown in Figure 1.4. The number of tweets for each class for top 10 locations is shown in Figure 1.5. Word clouds for disaster tweets are shown in Figure 1.6. Word cloud for non-disaster tweets are shown in Figure 1.7. Flesch-Kincaid readability test analysis [18] is shown in Figure 1.8 and Figure 1.9, and sample data after preprocessing is shown in Figure 1.10.

Id	Keyword	Location	Text	Target
1	NaN	NaN	Our deeds are the reason for this earthquake may Allah Forgives us all	1
4	NaN	NaN	Forest fire near La Ronge Sask Canada	1
23	NaN	NaN	What's up man	0
24	NaN	NaN	I love fruits	0
25	NaN	NaN	Summer is lovely	0
26	NaN	NaN	My car is so fast	0
28	NaN	NaN	What a goooooaaaaa!!!!	0

FIGURE 1.1   Sample dataset.

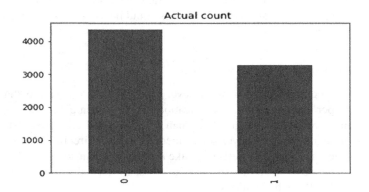

FIGURE 1.2A   Number of tweets per class.

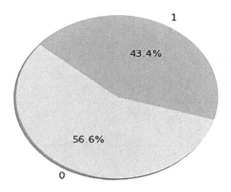

FIGURE 1.2B Percentage of each class.

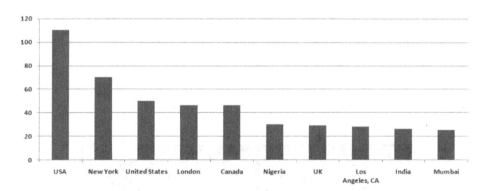

FIGURE 1.3 Number of tweets for 10 top locations.

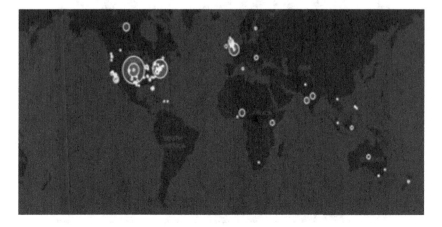

FIGURE 1.4 Number of tweets according to location in the entire dataset on a map.

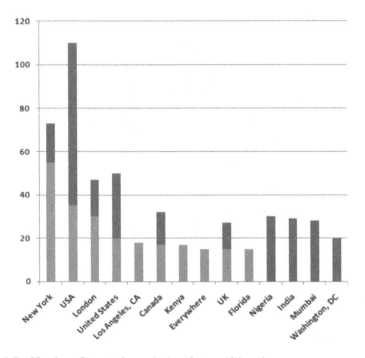

FIGURE 1.5   Number of tweets for each class for top 10 locations.

FIGURE 1.6   Word cloud for disaster tweets.

FIGURE 1.7   Word cloud for non-disaster tweets.

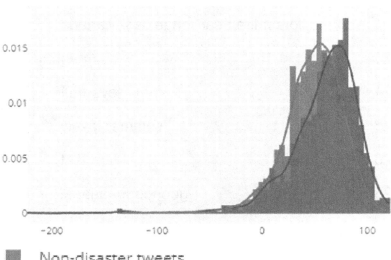

FIGURE 1.8   Flesch-Kincaid readability test.

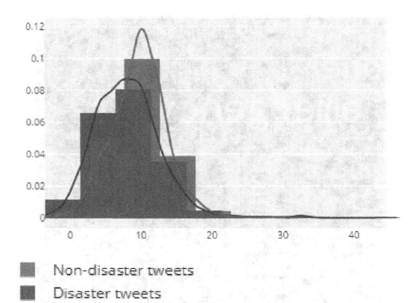

FIGURE 1.9   Flesch-Kincaid analysis of data.

id	Clean_all_text	target
1	deed reason earthquake may allah forgive	1
4	forest fire near ronge sask canada	1
23	man	0
24	love fruit	0
25	summer lovely	0
26	car fast	0
28	gooooooooaaaaaal	0

FIGURE 1.10   Sample data after preprocessing.

Two formulae for evaluating the readability of text—usually by counting syllables, words, and sentences—are Flesch Reading Ease and Flesch-Kincaid Grade Level.

1.4.1 FLESCH READING EASE

In the Flesch Reading Ease test,[19] higher scores indicate material that is easier to read; lower scores mark passages that are more difficult to read. The formula for the Flesch Reading Ease score (FRES) test is:

206.835-1.015*(total words/total sentences) – 84.6 (total syllables/total words)

1.4.2 FLESCH-KINCAID GRADE LEVEL

These readability tests are used extensively in the field of education. The Flesch–Kincaid Grade Level Formula presents a score as a US grade level, which makes it easier for teachers, parents, librarians, and others to judge the readability level of various books and texts. It can also mean the number of years of education generally required to understand this text, which is relevant when the formula results in a number greater than 10. The grade level is calculated with the following formula:

0.39*(total words/total sentences) + 11.8*(total syllables/total words) – 15.59

Scores can be interpreted as shown in Table 1.1.

TABLE 1.1
Flesch–Kincaid Readability Test Summary

Score	School level	Notes
100-90	5th grade	Very easy to read. Easily understood by an average 11-year-old student.
90-80	6th grade	Easy to read. Conversational English for consumers.
80-70	7th grade	Fairly easy to read.
70-60	8th & 9th grade	Plain English. Easily understood by 13- to 15-year-old students.
60-50	10th to 12th grade	Fairly difficult to read.
50-30	College	Difficult to read.
30-10	College graduate	Very difficult to read. Best understood by university graduates.
10-0	Professional	Extremely difficult to read. Best understood by university graduates.

1.5   METHODOLOGY

The methodology adopted while applying machine learning in analyzing Twitter data is depicted in Figure 1.11. As stated earlier, we have taken dataset from a Kaggle competition,[17] in which 5329 samples were used as training data, and 2284 samples were used for model evaluation (i.e., out of 7613 samples, 70% used as training data and 30% as test data). We divided our experiment into two sections: model learning and testing.

1.5.1   MODEL LEARNING/TRAINING SECTION

Model learning/training consists of data preprocessing, feature extraction, and executing algorithm for classification [20].

1.5.1.1   Data Preprocessing

This is done on three columns (keyword, location, text). Then data cleaning was done by expanding the contraction, removing accented character, converting text to lower case, removing digits, splitting into tokens, and, finally, lemmatization and stop word removal.

1.5.1.2   Feature Extraction

Term frequency-inverse document frequency (TF-IDF), a technique used to convert text into word vectors, was used; finally, we got the matrix with dimension $m*n$, where m represents the number of samples in our dataset and n represents the number

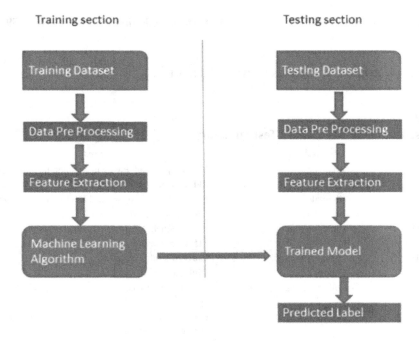

FIGURE 1.11   Methodology adopted for applying machine learning for analyzing Twitter data.

of features in the dataset.[21] We tuned some of the parameters of TF-IDF, such as n_gram range and max_feature to get good feature vector.

1.5.1.3 Classification

With feature vector obtained in the last step as input, machine learning classification algorithms were used, and we got a trained classifier/model as an output of this step. Some algorithms used here were logistic regression, K-nearest neighbors, nearest centroid, Gaussian naïve Bayes, Multinomial Naïve Bayes, linear support vector machine (SVM), decision tree, and random forest.

1.5.2 EVALUATION/TESTING SECTION

This phase consisted of data preprocessing, feature extraction, and label prediction. Data preprocessing and feature extraction were conducted in the same way as was done in the training phase. Feature vector obtained was given as input to a trained model/classifier (as obtained in the training phase), and a label for each sample was predicted as an output.

The simulation set up used for classifying Twitter data is given in Table 1.2.

1.6 RESULTS AND DISCUSSION

After analyzing the results of different machine learning classifier algorithms obtained after the simulation process, we found that logistic regression gave good accuracy with TF-IDF word embedding technique. We have presented our score, which is an average of five executions. Obtained result are presented in Table 1.3.

We used the following eight algorithms in this experiment: logistic regression, K-nearest neighbor (KNN), nearest centroid, Gaussian naïve Bayes (GNB), Multinomial Naïve Bayes (MNB), SVM, decision tree, and random forest.

For further analysis we split the training data (i.e., 70% of the original dataset) into various subsets such as 25%, 50%, 75%, and 100%. These individual subsets were used for training the algorithms and tested on the same test data (i.e., 30% of the original dataset). The results are presented in Table 1.4.

TABLE 1.2
Simulation Parameters

Parameter	Value
Programming language	Python 3.0
Library used	NumPy, pandas, Matplotlib, re, NLTK, sklearn, LIME, warnings, Seaborn, Plotly, statistics, textstat, PyLab, spaCy, GeoPy, folium
IDE	Jupyter Notebook
Processor	Intel core i5 2.4GHz, 2.10GHz
Memory	8GB RAM
System type	64-bit OS, x64-based processor

TABLE 1.3
Result Obtained by Various Classifiers

Algorithm	Class	Precision	Recall	F Score	Accuracy
Logistic regression	0	78	88	83	79
	1	81	67	73	
KNN	0	69	92	79	72
	1	81	47	59	
Nearest centroid	0	80	80	80	77
	1	74	73	74	
GNB	0	70	90	79	72
	1	79	50	61	
MNB	0	76	91	83	78
	1	84	61	71	
SVM (Linear)	0	78	85	81	77
	1	77	69	73	
Decision tree	0	77	74	76	72
	1	67	70	69	
Random forest	0	75	89	81	76
	1	80	61	69	

TABLE 1.4
Accuracy Obtained by Varying Training Dataset Sizes

Algorithm	25%	50%	75%	100%
Logistic regression	73	75	78	79
KNN	70	70	71	72
Nearest centroid	73	75	76	77
GNB	70	70	71	72
MNB	73	76	77	78
SVM (Linear)	73	75	76	77
Decision tree	70	70	71	72
Random forest	71	74	75	76

We also experimented on a word embedding technique called count vector-izer,[21] and the results are presented in Table 1.5. By making word clouds, we dug deeper into the feature set and got to know the important keyword or tokens, which play an important role in classification. Figure 1.12 shows a word cloud of important features that we used in our experiment.

Further we used a technique called Local Interpretable Model-Agnostic Explanations (LIME), which was used to explain the predictions of any regression or classifier by approximating it locally with an interpretable model.[17] Figure 1.13 explains predictions of the chosen classifier (logistics regression) to determine if a document is about a disaster or a non-disaster based on LIME. The bar chart in Figure 1.14 shows various

TABLE 1.5
Results Obtained by Various Classifier Using Count Vectorizer

Algorithm	Class	Precision	Recall	F Score	Accuracy
Logistic regression	0	79	86	83	79
	1	79	70	74	
KNN	0	68	91	78	71
	1	78	44	56	
Nearest centroid	0	76	86	81	76
	1	77	63	70	
GNB	0	70	91	79	73
	1	80	49	61	
MNB	0	77	89	83	79
	1	81	66	73	
SVM (Linear)	0	78	81	89	76
	1	73	70	71	
Decision tree	0	78	78	78	75
	1	70	71	71	
Random forest	0	76	86	81	77
	1	77	65	70	

FIGURE 1.12 Word cloud of important features used in the experiment.

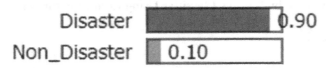

FIGURE 1.13   Predictions of the chosen classifier.

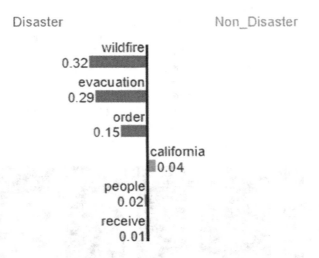

FIGURE 1.14   Bar chart of various positive and negative keywords for the disaster class.

positive and negative keywords for the disaster class obtained; the model interpretation for a particular example is in Figure 1.12. Color indicates which class the word contributes to (blue for disaster, yellow for non-disaster).

1.7   CONCLUSION AND FUTURE WORK

We analyzed the use of Twitter data and realized that Twitter is a community where people post the status of the current situation of their surroundings. Social media platform such as Twitter can be used for communication during any kind of natural disaster and emergencies. These Twitter data can be used in getting information related to public opinion by using various machine learning techniques.[21] In this chapter, we analyzed Twitter data related to natural disaster, and we found that logistic regression is able to classify a tweet, whether or not it is about natural disaster, with an average accuracy of 79%. Twitter data can be used to build an application that can be helpful in natural disasters or other emergencies. The biggest difficulty we found is the authenticity of data available over Twitter or any other social media platform. As future work, we will try to analyze all types of data (such as images, videos, etc.) available over social media platform like Twitter and other platforms. We would like to find the importance of the data in a particular scenario and action that may be taken based on the data, if any. In addition, we will try to improve the accuracy of current work.

REFERENCES

[1] J. Kersten and F. Klan, "What happens where during disasters? A Workflow for the multifaceted characterization of crisis events based on Twitter data," *J. Contingencies Cris. Manag.*, vol. 28, no. 3, pp. 262–280, 2020.

[2] N. Pourebrahim, S. Sultana, J. Edwards, A. Gochanour, and S. Mohanty, "Understanding communication dynamics on Twitter during natural disasters: A case study of Hurricane Sandy," *Int. J. Disaster Risk Reduct.*, vol. 37, p. 101176, 2019.

[3] B. Abedin and A. Babar, "Institutional vs. non-institutional use of social media during emergency response: A case of Twitter in 2014 Australian bush fire," *Inf. Syst. Front.*, vol. 20, no. 4, pp. 729–740, 2018.

[4] W. Zhai, Z.-R. Peng, and F. Yuan, "Examine the effects of neighborhood equity on disaster situational awareness: Harness machine learning and geotagged Twitter data," *Int. J. Disaster Risk Reduct.*, vol. 48, p. 101611, 2020.

[5] L. Zou, N. S. N. Lam, H. Cai, and Y. Qiang, "Mining Twitter data for improved understanding of disaster resilience," *Ann. Am. Assoc. Geogr.*, vol. 108, no. 5, pp. 1422–1441, 2018.

[6] Q. Wang and J. E. Taylor, "Quantifying human mobility perturbation and resilience in Hurricane Sandy," *PLoS One*, vol. 9, no. 11, p. e112608, 2014.

[7] X. Guan and C. Chen, "Using social media data to understand and assess disasters," *Nat. Hazards*, vol. 74, no. 2, pp. 837–850, 2014.

[8] Y. Kryvasheyeu et al., "Rapid assessment of disaster damage using social media activity," *Sci. Adv.*, vol. 2, no. 3, p. e1500779, 2016.

[9] Z. Wang, N. S. N. Lam, N. Obradovich, and X. Ye, "Are vulnerable communities digitally left behind in social responses to natural disasters? An evidence from Hurricane Sandy with Twitter data," *Appl. Geogr.*, vol. 108, pp. 1–8, 2019.

[10] G. A. Ruz, P. A. Henríquez, and A. Mascareño, "Sentiment analysis of Twitter data during critical events through Bayesian networks classifiers," *Futur. Gener. Comput. Syst.*, vol. 106, pp. 92–104, 2020.

[11] J. Yang, M. Yu, H. Qin, M. Lu, and C. Yang, "A Twitter data credibility framework—Hurricane harvey as a use case," *ISPRS Int. J. Geo-Information*, vol. 8, no. 3, p. 111, 2019.

[12] A. Karami, V. Shah, R. Vaezi, and A. Bansal, "Twitter speaks: A case of national disaster situational awareness," *J. Inf. Sci.*, vol. 46, no. 3, pp. 313–324, 2020.

[13] S. Shan, F. Zhao, Y. Wei, and M. Liu, "Disaster management 2.0: A real-time disaster damage assessment model based on mobile social media data—A case study of Weibo (Chinese Twitter)," *Saf. Sci.*, vol. 115, pp. 393–413, 2019.

[14] K. Zahra, M. Imran, and F. O. Ostermann, "Automatic identification of eyewitness messages on Twitter during disasters," *Inf. Process. Manag.*, vol. 57, no. 1, p. 102107, 2020.

[15] M. R. Nair, G. R. Ramya, and P. B. Sivakumar, "Usage and analysis of Twitter during
      2015 Chennai flood towards disaster management," *Procedia Comput. Sci.*, vol. 115,
      pp. 350–358, 2017.

[16] M. Martinez-Rojas, M. del Carmen Pardo-Ferreira, and J. C. Rubio-Romero, "Twitter
      as a tool for the management and analysis of emergency situations: A systematic litera-
      ture review," *Int. J. Inf. Manage.*, vol. 43, pp. 196–208, 2018.

[17] M. T. Ribeiro, S. Singh, and C. Guestrin, "' Why should I trust you?' Explaining the
      predictions of any classifier," in *Proceedings of the 22nd ACM SIGKDD International
      Conference on Knowledge Discovery and Data Mining*, 2016, pp. 1135–1144.
      https://www.researchgate.net/publication/305342147_Why_Should_I_Trust_You_
      Explaining_the_Predictions_of_Any_Classifier

[18] P. Misra, N. Agarwal, K. Kasabwala, D. R. Hansberry, M. Setzen, and J. A. Eloy,
      "Readability analysis of healthcare-oriented education resources from the American
      academy of facial plastic and reconstructive surgery," *The Laryngoscope*, vol. 123, no.
      1, pp. 90–96, 2012.

[19] P. Jacob and A. L. Uitdenbogerd, "Readability of Twitter Tweets for second language
      learners," in *Proceedings of the 17th Annual Workshop of the Australasian Language
      Technology Association*, 2019, pp. 19–27. https://aclanthology.org/U19-1003

[20] S. Karmaniolos and G. Skinner, "A literature review on sentiment analysis and its foun-
      dational technologies," in *2019 IEEE 4th International Conference on Computer and
      Communication Systems (ICCCS)*, 2019, pp. 91–95.

[21] K. S. Kalaivani, S. Uma, and C. S. Kanimozhiselvi, "A review on feature extraction
      techniques for sentiment classification," in *2020 Fourth International Conference on
      Computing Methodologies and Communication (ICCMC)*, 2020, pp. 679–683.

2 An End-to-End Comparison among Contemporary Content-Based Recommendation Methodologies

Debajyoty Banik and Mansheel Agarwal

CONTENTS

2.1 INTRODUCTION

As we set our feet in this world of recommender systems, it's really important for us to understand why we need recommender systems. With the growth of technology and an increase in the scale of artificial intelligence (AI), machines are now capable of providing us with a list of movies which seem exactly in sync with us. Before we start comparing different recommender systems, we should, first and

DOI: 10.1201/9781003319122-2

foremost, understand a very basic model of a content-based movie recommendation. Once we understand how it works, we will quickly dive into the technical terms related to it, so that all my non-tech friends get to understand the various algorithms with ease too.

2.1.1 WHY DO WE NEED RECOMMENDER SYSTEMS?

Living in such a beautiful a country as India, I will definitely start out by giving an insight into a little apparel store in the area where I reside. My mother would always go to a sari store, and the salesman there would try to "recommend" saris to my mom, which surprisingly matched her taste. That was the very primitive idea I had of recommender systems before I even started school. The world evolved and so did the stores around us. What we had in a physical environment started changing to what we now call a massive chain of multi-national companies who will do anything to bind in their customers. A very loved field for tech-seekers, machine learning became the salesman in this platform readily adapting to the booming e-commerce led by hotshots like Amazon, Walmart, Myntra, Ajio and Wish.

A recommender system (Figure 2.1) is not just important to multi-media companies but is also required to connect similar people and create a cohort in this ever-increasing world of possibilities. I started out by giving a very general instance of where a recommender system was in use before it was even introduced. I would conclude by maintaining that it's a really important factor in user engagement and integrity and, therefore, inducing people to often switch careers and bring in more ideas about how the algorithms can be made more robust and trustworthy.

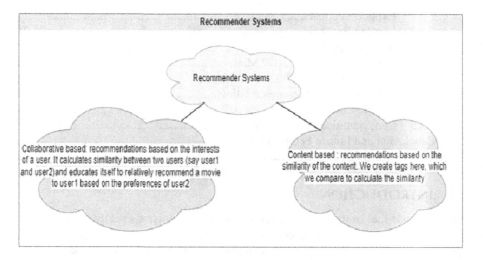

FIGURE 2.1   Classification of the recommender system.

2.2   A VERY BASIC CONTENT-BASED MODEL

A content-based recommendation system basically involves an inbuilt search engine in itself that enables it to weigh certain items and predict the overall measurement of the movie to be recommended based on the overall weight calculated.[1-2]

We will now understand the working of the system with the help of an example. Suppose we have a super set A consisting of all the possible movies in the given platform. Now we have another set, B, consisting of all the movies that a user has watched and given us some information about, such that $\forall B \in A$ and $|B| << |A|$, which makes sense as we're taking a considerable amount of data for training our recommendation model. We also introduce another set, C, consisting of the movies the user has yet not rated, $\forall C \in A$ and $|C| << |A|$ and a function f(x) that can also be referred to an interest function of the user, which denotes a positive (1) or a negative (0) value and helps us to derive another function g(x), which will estimate the value of f(x) for every element of the set A to effectively recommend appropriate content to the user based on his or her personal choice.

Now the whole game of recommendation depends upon classification and regression wherein we take into account the user's ratings and the content of a limited number of training data sets to educate our estimation function and then try to match it best to the user's interest function before a movie is recommended to him or her. This chapter discusses the recently used algorithms, extensively working in these two main domains, and tries to incorporate the machine learning techniques to either make the user's ratings more trustworthy or to expand the whole data set of the information we have about the movies set B from different resources to match the user's interests better.

Before we move on to understanding how the recent methodologies have affected the contemporary content-based recommendation system, we must know how we prepare and present the data so as to feed into our user rating estimation or the item analysis model.

2.3   DATA REPRESENTATION

Now that we know we need a robust and accurate data set so as to provide an appropriate estimation of the user's ratings, we need to know how we source in and work through this data. Usually, the data used in the field of content-based recommender systems is real time data like books, interviews, movies, authors, plays, etc., which we cannot give our model directly. We must now move forward and dive into how we manage and organise this data in an efficient manner as the more incorrect the data sets we have, the lesser will be the chances of our estimation matching with the interests of the users. We don't want to waste our time deriving theoretical data that will not be of any use to the practical circumstances.

The biggest question that we have in mind is if this data should be generated or manually fed by some technician. Both have their own pros and cons; for example, if we try to get really automated, we might not get a proper description of a particular item from a computer-generated data set. On the other hand, if we let the human mind map put the data for us, it will be really subjective, which again will not help us increase the percentage of integrity of the estimation function in any form. Keeping this in mind, we have two different methods in which there will be an unbiased approach to represent the data in a way that we get the advantages of both the fields without trusting one blindly. They are discussed in the following sections.

2.3.1 STRUCTURED DATA

When we talk about structured data, we mean the relational tables that we have in a properly constructed data set. They have a known data model or, in other words, a data schema. We have an attribute defined for every item and can also differentiate among them using an identification trademark called the primary key.

2.3.2 UNSTRUCTURED DATA

Almost every data that does not follow a fixed database schema can fall into this category. It includes all the lengthy unrestricted texts and multimedia, even if they have an underlying structure, like a bit of grammar. In unstructured data, it is common to represent multimedia data using textual descriptions.[3] Although in the usual case this requires human intervention, this representation allows us to analyse multimedia data which usually has a much greater size than its textual description and requires complex and time-consuming analysing techniques. Furthermore, as noted before, the modern techniques of pattern recognition from multimedia data are still in their infancy and do not always produce satisfying results.

We also have another data set that we call a semi-structured data, which is almost in the shape of a data schema and breaks the rules of regular data by containing some multimedia data for some of its attributes. This representation is really important for movies—the topic of our chapter—which doesn't follow a strict data schema and consists of mostly an amalgam of regular and multimedia values that we need to break down in order to provide the data set to our recommendation model. In information extraction and data mining, semi-structured data is usually partitioned in structured and unstructured data and then treated using different techniques for each kind of data.

The strict structure of structured data allows us to treat every item as a n-dimensional vector, where n is the number of characteristics used to describe an item. Then we can apply well known techniques from the fields of information theory and information retrieval, such as cosine similarity and Pearson correlation, in order to measure the similarity of items. Whereas, as for the unstructured data, we cannot directly process them using simple natural language processing methods as none of the algorithms have proved so right that it has been able to crack into the complex multimedia data like graphics and pixels. So we first convert such unstructured data set to a structured form and then process it by using information extraction and pattern recognition to comprehend the multimedia and the restricted texts.

2.4 CONTENT-BASED RECOMMENDATION THROUGH USER RATINGS AND ITEM ANALYSIS

Now that we have explained how the sourcing of the data works, we must move to our concept of how user ratings and his or her profile can add with the item factors to calculate an estimated value g(x) for every movie in the set A. Now this user model can be put to work to compare the estimates of the unrated movies with the rated ones to correctly predict whether or not a user will like it. The many algorithms we're about to discuss in this chapter deal with how a proper user model is created and how it can be used to relate this with the unrated data.

In the scenario of a movie recommender system,[4-6] what remains intact is the flowchart, which starts from having a training data set that is used to familiarise our function with the kind of movies the user likes. The number of movies we consider basing our model on also contributes to its error percentage to a rather accountable scale as the greater the data will be, the more accurate our estimation will be. For this fact to become clear, we first need to examine the different ways of rating the items in the training data.

2.4.1 EXPLICIT FEEDBACK

To gather explicit feedback from the user, the device must ask customers to grant their scores for items. After accumulating the feedback, the gadget is aware of how applicable or comparable an object is to users' preferences. Even though this approves the recommender to examine the customers' specific opinions, because it requires direct participation from the user, frequently, it is not effortless to collect. That is why there are one-of-a-kind approaches to gather feedback from users. Implementing a like/dislike performance into a net site offers customers the ability to consider the content material easily. Alternatively, the device can ask customers to insert their ratings where a discrete numeric scale represents how the consumer liked/disliked the content. Netflix frequently asks clients to rate films. Another way to acquire explicit feedback is to ask customers to insert their remarks as text. While this is a fantastic way to analyse consumer opinion, it is normally no longer handy to acquire and evaluate.

2.4.2 IMPLICIT FEEDBACK

In contrast to the explicit feedback, there is no consumer participation required to collect implicit feedback. The device mechanically tracks users' preferences by way of monitoring the carried out actions, such as which object they visited, the place they clicked, which gadgets they purchased, or how long they stayed on a web page. One ought to locate the right movements to track primarily based on the area that the recommender device operates on. Another gain of implicit remarks is that it reduces the cold start troubles that take place till an object is rated ample enough to be served as a recommendation.

2.5 COMPARING AND ANALYSING

Several technical laureates came forward with different ways of improving this basic architecture so as to improve our experience of a developed and sometimes integrated system. We basically divide our genres into these broad classifications wherein we state the comparison among different techniques under these subtopics and, therefore, state the advantages and disadvantages of each.

2.5.1 IMPROVEMENT OF THE NLP MODEL

The term frequency-inverse document frequency (TF-IDF) model has been in existence since the time it has been discovered.[7] The bag-of-words model used to exist before that which failed in the proper positioning of related vectors and, hence, the accuracy of the estimation wasn't up to the mark. On the contrary, we have articles suggesting how the bag-of-words model of user tags is more suitable to a movie recommender system than an TF-IDF model. This involves splitting the available user and movie tags (author, writer, director, actors, cast, crew etc.) into tokens and cleaning them. Once we have a vectorized model, we pass the processed features into certain detailed media sources such as the ones available in Wikipedia or IMDB and then go on to create fuzzing recommendations based on how many tags appear in the resource for how many times. Alternatively, the bag-of-words representations of tags can be used together with an unsupervised dimensionality reduction algorithm, as latent semantic analysis (LSA), to represent movies. Another significant change is the use of the power of word embedding, which is used for transforming a word into a vector from a vector space with a fixed dimensionality in a way that words occurring in similar contexts are represented by similar vectors. Other than this, data can be further enriched by scraping some tags off commercial movie websites and the big hotshots of the media industry so that we can then use this information as an embedding into our model to provide more relatable recommendations as well. As aforesaid, we can even improve this whole thing by generating a training data set and using the methods of classification along with some deep learning algorithms such as recurrent neural networks (RNNs) and long short-term memory (LSTM) to finally predict a list of movies the user may find interesting.

The downside of the previously stated approaches is that we're still using a bag-of-words model, which isn't suitable for new strings and would, at some point, enlarge the length of the vectors to a state where it'll become unmanageable. It will also render many 0s this way, making it into a sparse matrix that we're trying to avoid from the very start. Additionally, word embedding, as of what we've been introduced to date, integrates all the words that have multiple meanings into a single representation, after which it's really difficult to make out the exact meaning of the word in a particular sentence. For example, the word "nursery" can mean the place where plants are harboured or the place where primary children go to study.

2.5.2 ADJUSTMENT OF WEIGHTS

A content-based recommendation system makes use of weights that are given to the factors in accordance of their importance as per the user. We, intentionally or unintentionally, provide a lot of personalized data over the web in our daily lives, and this is where the story of the weights begins. References have been made that these weighted values be extracted from a linear regression obtained from our data on social media platforms through which a similarity graph can be generated of whether or not the user would like a particular factor. Feature weighing system make it possible to incorporate different factors of an item and draw a similarity chart by calculating the weight in the following fashion:

$$S(Oi, Oj) = \omega 1 f(A1i, A1j) + \omega 2 f(A2i, A2j) + \cdots + \omega n f(Ani, Anj)$$

Where:
S(Oi, Oj): similarity function
An: the factors of item in consideration
$\omega f(Ani, Anj)$: the weights of the similarity values calculated by the function f(i,j)

Hence, feature weighting is found to be really useful as it shows a considerable improvement in the recall value and serves as a more personalized system than a pure content-based recommender. Using this takes into account the human behaviour of giving more importance to a particular factor than laying all their importance on some fixed factors incorporating both practicality and machine independence. However, if we go on assigning weights to every particular feature, the output model of our algorithm might mislead consumers to negative and rapid conclusions. The recommendation process is more heuristic, which doesn't justify the item preference for some other user. This was also improved in another research where they cited [1] the permutations and combinations technique to double check the data to improve the recommendation list created by the tradition feature weighting technique.

2.5.3 THE COLD START RECOMMENDATION

The algorithms that we've seen until now deal with a training data set that has to be of a considerable size to make better predictions. This leads us to a major problem, which is a cold start. Cold start [8-9] refers to the initial period of recommendation where the machine doesn't have much information about the user and just has a very little set to choose from. The challenge of still giving out a trustworthy list of recommendations were undertaken by many such professionals, which gave us an overview about how machine learning and its concepts can be used in a way to make the traditional algorithm work efficiently in such cases.

To avoid the cold start problem, some platforms recommend the popular movies and videos to people after which they can choose and provide ratings to increase the size of the training data set. But, even by using deep learning, we still cannot solve the cold start problem for users who don't rate many movies. Hence, a meta-learning system was introduced to solve the problem by taking only a small data set and optimising it with the help of the user search history, which will give us more personalized information about the user and will help us to recommend better movies to the new users promoting platform binding (Figure 2.2).

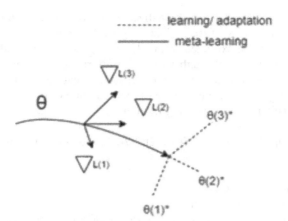

FIGURE 2.2   Diagram of the optimisation-based meta-learning algorithm.

Even though meta learning opens up a whole new world for machine learning, it comes at its own cost, quite literally. Meta learning requires a lot of simpler instructions for its training, thus it burns a hole in your pocket. Also, although it doesn't require as large a data set, it works on the historical data of a user, which is more difficult to comprehend and complex to mitigate. The existing model can show fast and efficient learning ability on simple new tasks such as moving and sorting targets, but the learning ability shown on some complex new tasks such as action cohesion is very unsatisfactory. Finally, the current algorithms are basically learning single metaknowledge, and metaknowledge is diverse, so the generalisation of the model may be affected to a certain extent.

2.5.4   Emotion Based

Till now, we have seen how we can recommend user-based choices to them through a third person perspective. But what we failed to understand is that even though we apply millions of algorithms to make our output as friendly as possible, we might never be able to break into a person's current mental state. A moody person, in this way, may never have a proper set of movie recommendations and would thus not prefer to stick to a particular platform. To solve this problem, researchers proposed a system based on the emotional and mental situation of each individual, which is bound to be strikingly different from any other consumer on the website.[10] Hence, a graph-based movie recommender system promised to integrate the user's emotions as well as his or her emotions on a single graph. Using Bidirectional Encoder Representations from Transformers (BERT) as a state-of-the-art model improved the language processing and helped our system understand the semantics of the user's activities much more deeply than any other natural language processing (NLP) algorithm, which proved to be much more effective than any other conventional systems we've talked about. Using multiple BERTs and then passing them all finally through our good old inductive graph-based matrix completion (IGMC) model, we get the final amalgamation function of emotions and ratings.

Other articles mean to take into considerations the product reviews as well as the history of purchase to demonstrate an overall outlook on the user's emotions to predict their current mood. Extracting data from Wordnet and various other psychological resources and then merging them to obtain a fuzzy emotions data, we can then introduced it to the classification model which will hand over the absolute recommendations based on our emotions.

However, the drawback of this system is that they require a lot of psychological data that are generally really personal and would thus be susceptible to copyright issues. Even if we get a safe set of data, it's really difficult to pay attention to each emotion and break it down into such a preliminary level as to comprehend it's meaning in a very high rate of accuracy.

2.5.5 CONVERSATIONAL RECOMMENDER

Last but not least, we consider the conversation factor [11-13] in our recommendation system. All our previous architectures provided us just a one-way conversation between the user (giving ratings) and the system (maintaining recommendations); now it was time to up the game and step into the field of a one-to-one conversation with the customer to dynamically refer movies at a point of time. Certain chatbots were introduced in the market along with some robust NLP algorithms to semantically understand a person's criteria.

As shown in Figure 2.3, the system worked on four major aspects: Recommend, Request, Explain and Respond. The user would first interact with an NLP model after it requests him or her, and then the processing will be done to respond and recommend to the user solving the purpose.[14-15]

The downside of this approach was that it provided a totally dynamic and unique output for every model, which made it complex for the researchers to analyse if it had an appreciative rate of success. Also, there is no such current NLP project, which can take under its responsibility and read the minds of every user in a particular way. After all, machines can never mimic our minds fully.[6,16]

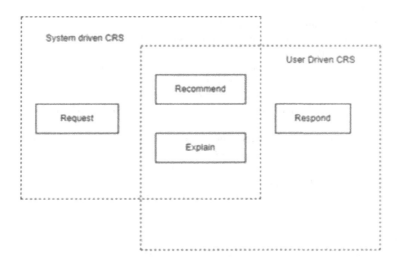

FIGURE 2.3   Simple block representation of a conversational recommender.

2.6   CONCLUSION AND FUTURE PERSPECTIVE

In this chapter, we discussed the various methods of content-based recommendation systems and did a survey over several new algorithms that have recently come into action, which provided us a clear idea about why we should or should not go for such methods before designing our very own model. It is high time we focus on more relatable recommendations if we want our lives to be easier. We still stick to the fact that no machine can read a person's mental state completely, but we can still strive to achieve as much closeness to the human mind as possible. All of the earlier mentioned algorithms show a clear indication of how far we've reached in comprehending people's choices, but it all depends on the purpose for which a recommendation system has to be created.

Personally, we can understand that recommendation systems are made for an individual rather than for a cohort; the sole purpose of mentioning emotional and conversational recommendation approaches at the end of the chapter was to convey an idea to the outside world of merging these two technical algorithms to create a hybrid one. The emotional intelligence calculator of the former can be used to integrate vectors in the graph of the NLP model the latter created, which then can be used to figure out recommendations more wisely and accurately. The main purpose of selecting these two algorithms was that they are some of the most integrity-based models and would thus be useful in making the matters simpler rather than more complicated.[17-18]

REFERENCES

1.   Debnath, Souvik, Niloy Ganguly, and Pabitra Mitra. "Feature weighting in content based recommendation system using social network analysis." *Proceedings of the 17th International Conference on World Wide Web*, 2008. https://doi.org/10.1145/1367497. 1367646

2.   Son, Jieun, and Seoung Bum Kim. "Content-based filtering for recommendation systems using multiattribute networks." *Expert Systems with Applications* 89 (2017): 404–412.

3.   Alharthi, Haifa, and Diana Inkpen. "Study of linguistic features incorporated in a literary book recommender system." *Proceedings of the 34th ACM/SIGAPP Symposium on Applied Computing*, 2019. https://doi.org/10.1145/3297280.3297382

4.   Pazzani, Michael J., and Daniel Billsus. "Content-based recommendation systems." *The Adaptive Web*. Springer, Berlin, Heidelberg, 2007: 325–341.

5.   Son, Jieun, and Seoung Bum Kim. "Content-based filtering for recommendation systems using multiattribute networks." *Expert Systems with Applications* 89 (2017): 404–412.

6.   Pan, Weike, et al. "Mixed factorization for collaborative recommendation with heterogeneous explicit feedbacks." *Information Sciences* 332 (2016): 84–93.

7.   Hospedales, Timothy, et al. "Meta-learning in neural networks: A survey." *arXiv preprint arXiv:2004.05439* (2020).

8.   Saraswat, Mala, Shampa Chakraverty, and Atreya Kala. "Analyzing emotion based movie recommender system using fuzzy emotion features." *International Journal of Information Technology* 12.2 (2020): 467–472.

9.   Lee, Hoyeop, et al. "Melu: Meta-learned user preference estimator for cold-start recommendation." *Proceedings of the 25th ACM SIGKDD International Conference on Knowledge Discovery & Data Mining*, 2019. https://doi.org/10.1145/3292500.3330859

10. Dhelim, Sahraoui, et al. "A survey on personality-aware recommendation systems." *Artificial Intelligence Review* (2021): 1–46.
11. Jannach, Dietmar, et al. "A survey on conversational recommender systems." *ACM Computing Surveys (CSUR)* 54.5 (2021): 1–36.
12. Habib, Javeria, Shuo Zhang, and Krisztian Balog. "Iai MovieBot: A conversational movie recommender system." *Proceedings of the 29th ACM International Conference on Information & Knowledge Management*, 2020. https://doi.org/10.1145/3340531.3417433
13. Sun, Yueming, and Yi Zhang. "Conversational recommender system." *The 41st International ACM Sigir Conference on Research & Development in Information Retrieval*, 2018. https://doi.org/10.1145/3209978.3210002
14. Pecune, Florian, Lucile Callebert, and Stacy Marsella. "A socially-aware conversational recommender system for personalized recipe recommendations." *Proceedings of the 8th International Conference on Human-Agent Interaction*, 2020. https://doi.org/10.1145/3406499.3415079
15. Mori, Hayato, et al. "Dialog-based interactive movie recommendation: Comparison of dialog strategies." *International Conference on Intelligent Information Hiding and Multimedia Signal Processing*. Springer, Cham, 2017.
16. Berbatova, Melania. "Overview on NLP techniques for content-based recommender systems for books." *Proceedings of the Student Research Workshop Associated with RANLP 2019*, 2019. DOI: 10.26615/issn.2603-2821.2019_009
17. Gawinecki, Maciej, et al. "What makes a good movie recommendation? Feature selection for content-based filtering." *International Conference on Similarity Search and Applications*. Springer, Cham, 2021.
18. Leng, Hongkun, et al. "Finding similar movies: Dataset, tools, and methods." 2018. DOI: 10.24132/CSRN.2018.2802.15

3 Neural Network-Based Collaborative Filtering for Recommender Systems

Ananya Singh and Debajyoty Banik

CONTENTS

DOI: 10.1201/9781003319122-3

3.1   INTRODUCTION

Recommender systems are the emerging technologies that are used in EdTech, fashion, shopping, entertainment, and marketing industries. There are different types of recommender systems that have evolved with time: collaborative filtering-based recommender system, demographic-based recommender system, content-based recommender system, utility-based recommender system, hybrid recommender system, and knowledge-based recommender system; however, collaborative filtering-based recommender system is the most extensively implemented. This chapter compares different algorithms for collaborative filtering.

Collaborative filtering is the process in which the algorithms filter data from user ratings to generate personalized recommendations for those with similar likes. This system calculates recommendations based on the user's (let's call him/her our target user) previous interaction with different items. It then finds users similar to our target user and suggests the items that the similar users have interacted with and liked based on their ratings given to those items.

3.1.1   ROLE OF AI/ML IN RECOMMENDER SYSTEMS

Artificial intelligence (AI)/machine learning (ML) is widely used in recommendation systems because AI can interpret a set of data and find unique patterns that help the system recognize what the consumer wants, and hence, it can suggest the products/services that they are highly susceptible to purchase. To be more specific, recommendation systems are a set of machine learning algorithms that offer highly relevant subjects to the users. This gives the user a sense of credibility and rapport with the system. This is important because user retention is highly desirable and, hence, is a must-have for every brand. Examples are Netflix, Amazon, and even social media platforms like Instagram. These websites use AI/ML algorithms to suggest better content, product, and services.

3.1.2 Explicit and Implicit Feedback

Recommender systems can be categorized into two types based on the feedback or data they gather, explicit feedback recommender systems, and implicit feedback recommender systems. An explicit feedback recommender system refers to the type of recommender system that gathers information directly from the user. This type of system is considered to be the best because the feedback comes directly from the user and, hence, is valuable.

On the other hand, an implicit feedback recommender system refers to the type of recommender system that gathers data or information based on the behavior of the user. This is usually speculation and pattern-based and varies with the algorithm used.

3.1.3 Ensemble v/s Joint Training

Individual models in ensemble learning are trained independently, unaware of the other models present, and their outputs are integrated during inference but not during training; whereas joint training optimizes all the factors simultaneously and takes the deep and the wide parts of the model along with the weights of their total into consideration at the time of training. To provide appropriate clarity for ensemble learning to operate, every single model size must be big (since training for an ensemble is discontinuous).

3.2 ALGORITHMS FOR COLLABORATIVE FILTERING

In this chapter, nine algorithms are compared on the dataset MovieLens 1M. In this section, all the algorithms are explained elaborately.

3.2.1 Wide & Deep Learning Algorithm

There are two components to this algorithm: a wide part and a deep part.[1] For the job of recommendation, in this method a linear model is blended with a deep neural network. This method was introduced by Google to recommend mobile applications to its users.

3.2.1.1 The Wide Component

It is regarded as a generalized linear algorithm. If one takes o as the output, i.e. the prediction, i as the input, i.e. the vector of features, p as the parameters of the model, and b as the bias, then the formula becomes:

$$o = p^T i + b \qquad (3.1)$$

Cross product transformation is defined by:

$$\phi_m(i) = \Pi_{i=1}^d i_n^{cmn} c_{mn} \in \{0,1\} \qquad (3.2)$$

Here c_{mn} is boolean

$c_{mn} = \{1$, i^{th} feature is a part of the cross product transformation
0, otherwise $\}$

In the case of binary features, a cross-product transformation is 1 if and only if all the features match the description, otherwise it is 0, e.g. if AND operation is performed on [(genre = comedy), (actor = Jim Carey)]. If both of these statements are true, then the cross product transformation is 1, and if any of these or both are false, then the cross product transformation is 0. The interactions between the binary characteristics are recorded through the step mentioned earlier, and the extended linear model gains non-linearity.

3.2.1.2   The Deep Component

This works as a feed-forward neural network or a deep neural network. The initial inputs for categorical features are attribute strings (e.g. "genre = comedy"). All the categorical features that are high-dimensional and sparse are turned into an embedding vector, which is dense real-valued and low-dimensional. These vectors are initialized randomly while the model is being trained, and their values are learnt to reduce the final loss function. These embedding vectors are fed into the hidden layers of a neural network during the forward pass. Every hidden layer carries out the computation:

$$a^{(n+1)} = \alpha(w^{(n)}a^{(n)} + b^{(n)}) \tag{3.3}$$

Here, n represents the nth layer, α represents the activation function, $a^{(n)}$, $W^{(n)}$, and $b^{(n)}$ are the activations, weights, and bias of the model at the ith layer.

3.2.1.3   Joint Training of Wide & Deep Model

The wide and deep elements explained earlier are merged as the prediction using a weighted linear combination of the logarithm of the probabilities of success/failure of the result, which is then input into a single log loss function, enabling joint training. Joint training of this model is accomplished by taking the gradients from the output and back-propagating them to the two parts of the model at the same time through mini-batch stochastic optimization. At training time, it optimizes all parameters concurrently by taking into consideration the two parts along with the weights of their sum. Instead of a full-size broad model, the wide portion simply has to supplement the deep part's shortcomings with a limited number of cross-product feature conversions. In comparison, rather than a full-size broad model, the wide component for joint training only needs to supplement the deep part's shortcomings with a limited number of cross-product attribute transformations. The model's estimate for logistic regression is given by:

$$P(Y = 1|x) = \sigma(w^T_{wide}[x, \varphi(x)] + w^T_{deep}a(1) + b) \tag{34}$$

Here, Y represents the binary class label, σ represents the sigmoid function, $\varphi(x)$ is the cross-product representation of the original feature, i.e. x, and b represents the bias. w_{wide} represents the vector containing all the wide model weights, and w_{deep} represents the weights applied on the activation a(l).

The point should be noted that the model's capacity is boosted by using neural networks for learning the non-linear interactions between embeddings rather than dot products.

Memorization is roughly described as studying the repeated co-existence of the items or traits and utilizing the relationship present in past data. Memorization via a diverse collection of cross-product feature conversions is efficient and comprehensible, whereas generalization, which necessitates more feature engineering work, is predicated on the transitive property of the relationship and investigates novel feature aggregations which have rarely or never appeared before. Deep neural networks (DNN) have the ability to adapt effectively to unknown feature aggregations with less feature engineering by learning the dense and low-dimensional embeddings for the sparse data. Both memorization and generalization are necessary for recommender systems. Using cross-product feature transformations, the wide element of the model can successfully memorize sparse feature interconnections, whereas the DNN can generalize to previously unknown feature interconnections via low-dimensional embeddings.

3.2.2 Neural Graph Matching-Based Collaborative Filtering

Neural graph matching-based collaborative filtering (GMCF) [2] takes into account two different kinds of interactions, namely inner interactions and cross interactions, which prove to be a reliable technique for using the information conveyed through interactions.

Inner interactions are interactions that occur just between two types of users (or two types of items). For example, {male, 5–10} and {Doraemon, animated} are examples of inner interactions for users and items respectively.

Cross interactions refer to interconnections of the characteristics of a user and that of an item. For example, {male, animated} and {Doraemon, 5–10} are examples of cross interactions that ask the question: would a male like to watch animated movies or would a person aged 5–10 years like to watch Doraemon movies.

In the graph matching framework, inner and cross interactions are directly represented and combined in various ways. To symbolize the user, a graph is built of a user's (or item's) features. Each feature is represented by a node, and every pairwise feature relation (or interaction) is represented by an edge.

GMCF is a collaborative filtering approach based on graph matching. Based on their inner interactions, GMCF models a user traits network and an item traits graph using a graph neural network (GNN).[3, 4] Based on cross interactions, it compares the two feature graphs at the node level and generates the final prediction result. It learns item and user features and links users' interests to the items based on their characteristics and explicitly models and collects feature interactions in a graph-matching structure, which has shown to be very effective in characteristic interaction simulation and structural information collection.

This methodology distinguishes between inner and cross connections and combines these actions in a graph matching framework, which is deemed to be more thought for a recommendation.

3.2.2.1 Graph Neural Networks

Graph neural networks make it easier to learn about things and their relationships.[2, 5–8] They use a neighborhood aggregation technique in which a node's representation is modified repeatedly by combining representations of its neighbors.

Here a graph is represented by G = (N, L), where M depicts a set of n nodes in which every node is depicted by n_i, and L is the set of edges that provide the information about the neighborhood between two nodes. A GNN acquires each node's vector representation through message transmission, which is a means of acquiring neighborhood knowledge. The message forwarding method of a node i combines the vector expressions of all of its neighbors, and the conjoined form of the node i is then created by combining n_i with the collected vector representation.

3.2.2.2 Graph Matching-Based Collaborative Filtering

This model has three steps. First, the user and item feature graphs are constructed, then a node-matching operation is performed, and finally, graph-matching is performed.

3.2.2.2.1 User and Item Graph Construction

Two graphs are created: the user feature graph and the item feature graph. In the user attribute graph, every node depicts a characteristic-value pair within the users' domain; whereas in the item feature graph, every node depicts a characteristic-value pair in the items' domain. The edges of these graphs are their inner interactions. Every node pair is connected by an edge to represent the pairwise interconnection of two features. The user feature graph is considered a complete graph because all the pairwise features are taken into account. The same operations are performed on the item attributes graph. The graphs are generated by simply partitioning the feature interconnection as edges and the matching pairs for the distinct components.

3.2.2.2.2 Node Matching-Based GNN

In this part, the model evaluates the message carrying information m_i and the node-matching information v_i for each node n_i with the user feature graph or the item feature graph. Then n_i, m_i, and v_i are fused together and a fused node is acquired. Then the fused nodes are combined together.

The message passing portion of this part uses inner interactions while the node matching portion uses cross interactions.

3.2.2.2.3 Neural Interaction-Based Message Passing

The inner interactions are simulated using a multi-layer perceptron (MLP).[9, 10] The outputs of this step are combined together and form the message carrying information. The MLP takes the input as the two nodes' embeddings and gives the output as the interaction simulation results. All of these outputs for each node are pooled using an element-wise sum.

3.2.2.2.4 Bi-Interaction-Based Node Matching

Let us first consider an example. If a user aged between 5–10 likes animated movies, then the node matching score for the node pair (5–10 years, animated) is high.

This means that a user aged between 5–10 years has a higher preference for the item attribute "animated", and thus, their embeddings must be similar. In order to make this happen, this model uses bi-interaction for the process of node matching that maintains a uniformly growing relationship between interaction modeling results and characteristic similarities.[11] Therefore, if the node matching score of a user attribute is high on an item attribute, then their feature representations are similar.

This node-matching model works by taking the element-wise product of the embeddings of a node from one graph and another from another graph. This step is performed for all the nodes in a graph with all the nodes in another graph. Then their combination is taken, which is the final output of this part.

3.2.2.2.5 Information Fusing

In addition to message passing outcomes, GMCF uses the outcomes of node-match-ing for collecting details of node-level matching while producing the merged node representations. The node-merging function has the input as the node n_i, message-carrying results m_i, and node-matching results v_i and the output is the fused node. From testing, it is evident that recurrent neural networks give the best results. Therefore gated recurrent unit (GRU) is used in this model for the fusing function. The fused node representation is GRU's final output hidden layer.

3.2.2.2.6 Node Representation Aggregation

The graph representation is composed of the fused node forms of each graph. To combine the node representations, the element-wise sum is employed.

3.2.2.3 Graph Matching

An operation of graph matching is performed between the user feature graph and the item feature graph, which gives the output as the vector form of the user's and item's feature graphs. Dot product operation is applied to the two graphs obtained, and the prediction is acquired from this result.

3.2.3 NEURAL FACTORIZATION MACHINE

Neural factorization machines (NFMs) are an extension of factorization machines, with the use of neural networks, which are both explained in the following section.[11]

3.2.3.1 Factorization Machines

Factorization machines (FMs) models the interaction between every pair of attri-butes and then adds the findings to generate the ultimate forecast.[12–14] It is a com-mon method for making optimal use of second-order feature interactions.

This technique may be used for classification and regression applications. It describes interconnections of features in sparse and high-dimensional data in an effi-cient manner. In click-through rate prediction (CTR), FMs can record the trend of click rates, which is seen when the advertisements of a category of ads are put on websites. These are well-suited for applications involving sparse and high-dimen-sional data like CTR prediction and recommendation.

FMs employ factorized interaction parameters with feature interaction weights expressed by the inner product of the hidden factor space embeddings of the two attributes.

3.2.3.2 Deep Neural Network

A deep neural network (DNN) is an artificial neural network, but it has many layers in between the input and output layers. Its elements are neurons, biases, functions, and weights. It behaves similarly to the human brain.

The recent work of He et al. 2017 provides actual proof that just combining the user and item embedding vectors results in terrible collaborative filtering outcomes. [15] To address this, one must depend on the layers of a DNN, to develop significant interconnection functions.

3.2.3.3 Neural Factorization Machine

This algorithm combines the efficacy of linear FMs with the high appearance capabilities of non-linear neural networks.[16]

3.2.3.3.1 Embedding Layer

Each feature is projected to a dense vector representation via the embedding layer. Following embedding, one acquires a collection of embedding vectors that symbolize the input characteristic vector. Just the embedding vectors for the non-zero features are included in this algorithm due to the sparsity of the input vector.

Assume that v_i is the embedding vector for the ith feature. A collection of embedding vectors is obtained, which is used to depict the input feature vector x.

$$V_x = x_1{}^*v_1,......, x_n{}^*v_n \qquad (3.5)$$

The embedding set V_x is fed to the Bi-Interaction layer.

3.2.3.3.2 Bi-Interaction Layer

It is a pooling process that combines a collection of embedding vectors into a single vector. The element-wise dot product of the two is taken in this layer.

$$f_{Bi}(V_x) = \sum_{i=1}^{n} \sum_{j=i+1}^{n} x_i{}^*v_i.x_j{}^*v_j \qquad (3.6)$$

It enables a neural network structure to capture more descriptive characteristic interconnections at a lower level.

Deepening of the shallow linear FM, modeling higher-order, and non-linear characteristics interconnections are achieved by piling together the non-linear layers above this layer, which substantially improves the FM's expressiveness.

The use of bilinear-interaction pooling encodes more useful feature interactions, considerably helping the learning of relevant information by the next "deep" layers.

3.2.3.3.3 Hidden Layers

A collection of fully-connected layers above the bilinear-interaction pooling layer is able to study higher-order interactions between features.

$$z_1 = a_1(W_1 f_{Bi}(V_x) + b_1),$$
$$z_2 = a_2(W_2 z_1 + b_2), \quad (3.7)$$
$$z_n = a_n(W_n z_{n-1} + b_n),$$

Here
n = number of hidden layers,
W_n = weight matrix for the nth layer,
b_n = bias vector of the nth layer,
And a_n = activation function for the specific layer.

Activation functions like sigmoid, tanh, and ReLU can be used to capture higher-order attributes interconnections non-linearly.

3.2.3.3.4 Prediction Layer

In this layer, the prediction is done by multiplying the output of the last hidden layer by the weight of the neurons of the prediction layer.

$$f(n) = z_n * w^T_n \quad (3.8)$$

3.2.4 DEEP FACTORIZATION MACHINES

Deep factorization machines (DeepFM) use CTR prediction in this algorithm, which is click-through rate prediction.[17] The possibility/probability of a user clicking on a specific link/something on a website is predicted.

This contains two components, namely the FM element and the deep element. The input for the FM element and the deep element is the same. If the input is categorical, then one-hot encoding will be applied to it and it is represented as a vector. Whereas, if the input is continuous in nature, then it is represented just as its value or can be converted to a discrete form, then into a vector. The input is usually high-dimensional and quite sparse. Then the outputs of the two components are summed together.

3.2.4.1 FM Component

FM stands for factorization machine.[12] It is explained in Section 3.2.3. The addition in this component is that even if the data is sparse, this component is capable of effectively extracting pairwise feature interactions.

The inner product of two features' hidden vectors is used to catch the pairwise feature interactions. The latent vectors of the features are taken as the input to this model.

The output is given by the addition of two functions. The first function is the addition of two vectors: the vector of the weights of the linear interaction of a feature and the vector of the fields/features. The second function is the inner product function in which the inner products of the two features' latent vectors and the features are taken.[17]

$$y_{FM} = (w, x) + \Sigma^d_{i=1} \Sigma^d_{j=i+1} (Vi, Vj) x_i \cdot x_j \tag{3.9}$$

The addition function represents how important the linear features are, whereas the inner product depicts the effect of the pairwise feature interactions.

FM may train the latent vector of any feature i anytime i appears in a dataset because of this adaptable architecture. As a result, characteristics interconnections that are seldom or never seen in the training data are better learned by FM.

3.2.4.2 Deep Component

This component is a deep neural network. The latent vectors of the features are taken as input in this model. The latent vectors have to be brought to be low-dimensional and should be dense instead of the initially sparse vector. To achieve this, use an embedding layer before feeding the input to the first hidden layer.

The output of the embedding layer is then inputted to the next layer of the deep neural network.

$$a^{(0)} = [e_1, e_2, ..., e_n] \tag{3.10}$$

Here e_i is the embedding of ith field and n is the number of fields.

In the next layer, the output is calculated by passing the addition of the bias of the previous layer and the product of the input and the weight of the model into an activation function.

$$a^{(n+1)} = \alpha(w^{(n)}a^{(n)} + b^{(n)}) \tag{3.11}$$

Here n is the depth of the layer, and σ is the activation function. $a^{(n)}$, $W^{(n)}$, $b^{(n)}$ are the output, weight of this model, and bias of the ith layer.

The output of this layer is a dense and real-valued feature vector. This is then fed into a sigmoid function.

$$y_{DNN} = W^{|Hn|+1} \cdot a^{|Hn|} + b^{|Hn|+1,} \tag{3.12}$$

Here |Hn| is the number of hidden layers.

The output of both the components is added and passed through a sigmoid function, which is the predicted CTR.

$$y = sigmoid(y_{FM} + y_{DNN}) \tag{3.13}$$

DeepFM is the only framework that can account for both low and high-order feature interconnections and requires no pretraining or feature engineering.

3.2.5 NEURAL COLLABORATIVE FILTERING

The neural architecture substitutes the user-item inner product in neural collaborative filtering (NCF). NCF attempts to express and generalize matrix factorization, and it employs an MLP to capture interconnections of the users and items.

In this method, the input is the specifications of the user and the item, which is then transformed into a sparse vector (that is binarized) by performing one-hot encoding.

Here the output lies in the range of 0 to 1, 0 being the unawareness of the user about the item and 1 being the interaction of the user with the item. The output layer has a probabilistic function as its activation function.

3.2.5.1 Matrix Factorization

The most common algorithm is matrix factorization (MF), which reflects the items and users into a common hidden space by employing a vector of hidden characteristics to depict an item or a user.[18] Following this, a user's interconnection with an item is represented as the inner product of their hidden vectors.

Despite MF's efficacy in collaborative filtering, it is generally recognized that its performance might be hampered by the easy selection of the interaction function-inner product. It is well known, for example, that including item and user bias components into the interaction function enhances the MF's performance for rating prediction based on explicit input. It is a quick and easy approach to producing suggestions. However, it has its limitations.

The linearity of a normal matrix factorization technique restricts the model's expressiveness, or how complicated a relationship it can describe among all of our users and products. Because items and users are modeled in the same hidden space and the result is calculated by using dot-product, one can run into circumstances where they can't show the connection between user m and user n without violating a previously established relationship between two users n and k. This implies that it might be impossible to appropriately present a new user in a hidden space in relation to all prior user depictions.

One solution might be to expand the dimensions of the hidden space, allowing more intricate interactions. This may still result in the structure being less general, i.e. overfitting more easily and taking more time to train for getting optimal outcomes.

The basic concept behind utilizing a deep neural network is to train a non-linear function in place of a linear function, with the goal of increasing the expressiveness of the structure.

3.2.5.1.1 Neural Collaborative Filtering

The embedding layer (above the input layer) is a fully linked layer and converts the sparse expressions to a dense vector. The resulting item embedding may be thought of as the hidden vector for the item in view of a hidden vector model (same for the user). The item and user embeddings are sent to a multi-layer neural design called the neural collaborative filtering layers, which routes the hidden vectors to the prediction scores. Every neural CF layer can be modified to find selected hidden patterns of the interactions between the user and the item. This structure's capacity is decided by the dimension of the ultimate hidden layer.

3.2.5.2 Generalized Matrix Factorization (GMF)

The resultant embedding vector may be thought of as the user's or the item's latent vector because of the input layer's one-hot encoding of the item ID or the user ID.

In the first layer of the neural CF, an element-wise product of the item and user hidden vectors is performed, and the result is passed to the next layer. In the next layer, weights of the output layer are applied to the output of the previous layer and the activation function is applied to the term achieved.

3.2.5.3 Multi-Layer Perceptron (MLP)

A multilayer perceptron, or an MLP, is the most fundamental type of deep neural network.[19, 20] There are buried layers of neurons, and every neuron has a non-linear activation function. These layers are closely coupled such that every neuron in every layer communicates with each neuron of the next layer, and this process continues till the neurons of the last layer.

As the NCF uses two paths to model items and users, it is natural to integrate their features by appending them. MLP is employed in order to record the interconnection of the hidden characteristics of the item and user. The use of an MLP is effective as employing only the concatenation of vectors does not provide any interaction between the hidden layers of the user and the item.

The output is given by a formula in which the activation function is applied on the addition of the bias and the product of the weight and the input vector. ReLU is used as the activation function as it performs better than tanh and sigmoid.

3.2.5.4 Fusion of GMF and MLP

GMF employs a linear kernel to describe hidden feature interconnections, whereas MLP learns the interconnection function from observations by employing a non-linear kernel.

Assume that the two models share an embedding layer and combine their interconnection function outputs. Sharing GMF and MLP embeddings may restrict the efficiency of the fused model. They should employ the same embedding size because, for datasets in which the ideal embedding size of these two methods differs greatly, this technique can fail to produce the best ensemble.

To provide the merged model with greater flexibility, enabling GMF and MLP is important (to study distinct embeddings). These two methods are integrated by appending their final hidden layer. For creating hidden structures of the user and item, this method incorporates the linearity of MF and the non-linearity of DNNs.

3.2.6 FEATURE INTERACTION GRAPH NEURAL NETWORK

This algorithm predicts the click-through rate. Here the input is the sparse feature vector which is mapped to the one-hot embedding vectors, which are also sparse. Thereafter, the embedding later and multi-head self-attention layer is used to embed the input to the embedding vectors which are dense. After that, the field embedding vectors are expressed as an attribute graph in which every node relates to a distinct attribute field and the edges allow them to interact. Modeling interaction may be simplified to customizing node interconnections on the attribute graph, which is fed into the feature interaction graph neural network (Fi-GNN), which is used to simulate the interconnections of the nodes. To predict the clickthrough rate, an attention rating layer is added to the end result of Fi-GNN.

3.2.6.1   Embedding Layer

Every field of the features is represented as a one-hot encoding vector and embedded into the field embedding vector. This lowers the dimension of the vectors, which are now dense and not sparse. The embedding vectors for an n-field feature are:

$$\varepsilon = [e_1, e_2, e_3, ..., e_n] \tag{3.14}$$

Here, e_i is the embedding vector for the field i.

3.2.6.2   Multi-Head Self-Attention Layer

From Vaswani et al. 2017, it can be inferred that the multi-head self-attention structure simulates the complex relationships between word pairings in many semantic subspaces.[21]

$$H_i = \text{softmax}_i \left\{ \left[(W^{(Q)}_i E) (W^{(K)}_i E)^T \right] \div [\sqrt{d_K}] \right\} (W^{(V)}_i E) \tag{3.15}$$

Here, the feature representations of the features can be acquired by the equation, where the term $(W^{(A)}_i E)$ represents the three parameters for the weight for the attention head I, and d represent the dimension of the specific attention head. Thereafter, in every conceptual subspace, the learned feature representations of every head can be aggregated to maintain the pairwise feature interactions. This is done by concatenating all the feature representations and applying the ReLU activation function to them.

In CTR prediction, this mechanism is used to extract the complicated connections between feature field pairs.

3.2.6.3   Feature Interaction Graph Neural Network

Every node is correlated with a latent state vector, and the graph state is made up of these node states. The multi-head self-attention layer's learned feature representations are employed for their initial node states. The nodes communicate with one another and update their statuses on a regular basis.

On every communication stage, the nodes combine the converted data streams with neighboring nodes and then update the state of the nodes using GRU and residual connections based on the combined present and past data. On a specific communication step, every node combines the information it has collected from its neighbors. The collected information is the sum of the node's altered state information.

3.2.6.3.1   Attentional Edge Weights

An attention technique is used to study the edge weights aiming to estimate the relevance of interconnections of distinct nodes. The weight of an edge between two nodes is determined by their respective field embedding vectors.

$$w(n_i, n_j) = [\exp(\text{LeakyRelu}(W_w [e_i \| e_j]))] / [\Sigma_k \exp(\text{LeakyRelu}(W_w [e_i \| e_j]))] \quad (16)$$

Here, W_w represents the weight matrix and $e_i \| e_j$ represents the conjunction or concatenation between the two embedding vectors.

3.2.6.3.2   Edge-Wise Transformation

A firm but transformed function on all the edges is impossible to simulate the adjustable interconnections, and each edge requires a specific alteration. Merely giving a different transforming weight to every edge takes up significantly more parameter time and space. Assigning an output matrix W^i_{out} and an input matrix W^i_{in} to every node n_i decreases the time and the space complexity while still achieving edge-wise translation.[22] When node-1 delivers its state information to node-2, it is first processed by its output matrix W^1_{out} and modified by node-2's input matrix W^2_{in} before it is received by node-2. The number of parameters is thus relative to the number of nodes instead of several edges, dramatically reducing space and temporal complexity while achieving edge-wise interconnection.

3.2.6.3.3   State Update

After collecting the information about the states, the nodes use GRU and residual connections to update the state vectors. The two steps are as follows:

3.2.6.3.3.1   State Update by GRU   GRU updates node n_i's state vector depending on pooled state information and its state in the previous step.[23]

3.2.6.3.3.2   State Update by Residual Connections   Additional residual connections [1, 24, 25] are provided to modify node states alongside GRU and allow for low-order feature reuse and gradient back-propagation.

3.2.6.4   Attentional Scoring Layer

The feature interactions are simulated as the nodes have already communicated with their neighbors. Each field node's final state has recorded the global information. As a result, a score is forecasted based on the end state of every field and aggregates them together using an attention method that quantifies their effect on the entire prediction. Every node's forecast rating and attentional node weight may be computed using two MLPs.

The first MLP is used to simulate the forecast rating of each field while taking into account the global information, while the second one is used to simulate the relevance of each field's effect on the entire prediction.

3.2.7   AUTOMATIC FEATURE INTERACTION LEARNING

The input to this algorithm is the sparse feature vector. Then the embedding layer puts all the attributes into a low dimensional space. Following that, all field embeddings are inputted into a new interaction layer that is designed as a multi-head self-attentive neural network. The attention mechanism combines high-order features for each interaction layer, and different types of combinations may be assessed using the multi-head methods, which translate the features into distinct subspaces. Different orders of recurrent characteristics can be described by stacking various interacting layers.

The last interaction layer's output is a low-dimensional version of the input attribute that represents high-order recurrent characteristics and is then utilized to estimate the click-through rate using a sigmoid function.

3.2.7.1 Input Layer

The attributes of the user and the item are modeled as sparse vectors that connect all the fields. If the field is categorical, then one-hot encoding is applied to its values and if it is scalar, then the value is kept as it is.

3.2.7.2 Embedding Layer

First, each categorical feature is expressed as a low-dimensional vector. When a categorical feature has multiple values, it has to be expressed by a multi-hot vector. The numerical features are also represented in the low-dimensional feature space. Thus, the end result of this layer is a collection of many embedding vectors.

3.2.7.3 Interacting Layer

This layer comes into use when both the numerical and the categorical features have been represented in a single low-dimensional space. The key-value attention method is used to identify the feature pairings that are useful.[26] The association between two features j and k under a certain attention head h is represented as:

$$a^{(h)}_{j,k} = \exp(^{(h)}(e_j, e_k))/\Sigma^M_{l=1} \exp(^{(h)}(e_j, e_l)), \tag{3.17}$$

Here, $^{(h)}(e_j, e_k) = (W^{(h)}_{Query}e_j, W^{(h)}_{Key}e_k)$ is the attention function that describes the resemblance between the two features j and k. This technique learns a new combinatorial feature from the fusion of feature j and its related characteristics (under head h). The gathering of all the combinatorial characteristics discovered in all subspaces is done by concatenating all the feature vectors from 1 to the number of heads. Typical residual connections are added to the system to maintain previously learnt combinatorial information and the first-order features. It is done by:

$$e^{Res}_m = ReLU(\tilde{}e_m + W_{Res}e_m), \tag{3.18}$$

W_{Res} represents the projection matrix if dimensions are mismatching, ReLU is an activation function which is non-linear, e_m represents the feature field, and $\tilde{}e_m$ is the combination of the feature m with its related characteristics.[25]

The expression of every attribute is transformed into a new feature depiction, i.e. representation of high-order features with an interaction layer. One may stack numerous layers with the preceding interacting layer's output, serving as the input for the following interacting layer. This allows one to represent arbitrary-order combinatorial characteristics.

3.2.7.4   Output Layer

The final output, i.e. the click-through rate prediction, is estimated by connecting all the e^{Res}_i (output of the previous layer) and passing them through a non-linear projection.

$$y = \sigma(w^T(e^{Res}_1 \oplus e^{Res}_2 \oplus \cdots \oplus e^{Res}_N) + b) \tag{3.19}$$

Here, w aggregates the combined features. It is a column projection vector, b is the bias, and all of these are passed through the sigmoid function, represented by σ.

3.2.8 L_0-Statistical Interaction Graph Neural Network

Every input of this method is regarded as a graph with nodes representing features and edges representing interactions. This algorithm has two components—L_0 edge prediction and SIGN.

3.2.8.1 L_0 Edge Prediction Model

This model examines the presence of edges on every node pair.[22] It is represented by $F_{ep}(X_n; \omega)$. ω represents the parameters of this F_{ep} model which predicts the edge. This model is based on neural matrix factorization (NMF). By factorizing a graph's adjacency matrix into node dense embeddings, MF is efficient in modeling relationships between node pairs. The gradients for optimizing this component are derived from the differences between the SIGN outputs and the desired outcomes.

The input for the prediction function of this model is the dimension d of the node embeddings' pair. The output is either 0 or 1, reflecting the connection of the nodes through an edge—1 if they are connected by an edge and 0 if they are not linked.

The embedding of a particular node n_i for the prediction of edge (v^e_i) is given by the product of the parameters (W^e) and the one-hot embedding of the node (o_i).

$$v^e_i = W^e o_i \tag{3.20}$$

The value of edge prediction should be the same for any two nodes, i.e. the value of edge prediction between nodes a and b is the same as that between nodes b and a.

3.2.8.2   Statistical Interaction Graph Neural Network

Every node n_i is first represented as an initial node embedding v_i of dimensions d (for interaction modeling), i.e. every node has node embeddings v^e_i and v_i for edge prediction and interaction modeling, respectively, to assure the optimal performance of respective tasks. The next step is to subject every node pair to interaction modeling through an additive function. Then, using a linear clustering method, every node is modified by combining all of the analysis findings between the node and its neighbors. Lastly, a linear function translates every modified node embedding into a scalar value and all of these scalar values are combined to give the output of the SIGN model.

3.2.9 ATTENTIONAL FACTORIZATION MACHINES

This model is an extension of the factorization machines. It uses a sparse format for the input attributes and incorporates every non-zero attribute into a dense vector in its input and embedding layers.

3.2.9.1 Pair-Wise Interaction Layer

This layer enlarges n vectors to n(n-1)/2 linked vectors, with each linked vector being the element-wise product of two unique vectors to express their interaction.

$$f_{PI}(\varepsilon) = \{(v_i.v_j)x_ix_j\}_{(i,j)\in Rx} \qquad (3.21)$$

Here, the output is given by taking the dot product of two vectors; x_i and x_j are feature vectors, and ε is the output of the embedding layer.

$$y = p^T \sum_{(i,j)\in Rx} (v_i.v_j)x_ix_j + b \qquad (3.22)$$

Here, p represents the weights for the prediction layer, and b represents the bias for the prediction layer. The output y gives the prediction score.

3.2.9.2 Attention-Based Pooling Layer

When condensing several elements into a single representation, this part allows various portions to contribute differently. An attention-based technique is applied to the attribute interconnections by computing the weighted sum of the linked vectors.[11]

$$f_{Att}(f_{PI}(\varepsilon)) = \sum_{(i,j)\in Rx} a_{ij}(v_i.v_j)x_ix_j \qquad (3.23)$$

Here, a_{ij} represents the attention score for the interconnection of features i and j.

An attention network has to be employed to solve the problem that some attributes have not interacted during the training. A multi-layer perceptron (MLP) is used in this network. The interacted vector of the two features is taken as the input to this network, which is defined as:

$$a_{ij} = [\exp(h^T ReLU(W(v_i.v_j)x_ix_j+b))] / [\sum_{(i,j)\in Rx} \exp(h^T ReLU(W(v_i.v_j)x_ix_j+b))] \quad (3.24)$$

Here W, b, and h represent the structure's parameters.

This layer produces an n-dimensional vector, which reduces all attribute encounters in the embedding space by ranking their relevance. The prediction score is then projected onto it. The final output of this model is:

$$y_{AFM}(x) = w_0 + \sum_{i=1}^{n} w_ix_i + p^T \sum_{i=1}^{n} \sum_{j=i+1}^{n} a_{ij} (v_i.v_j)x_ix_j \qquad (3.25)$$

3.3 DATASET

3.3.1 MovieLens 1M

MovieLens 1M includes movie ratings from users. Every data point comprises a user and a movie along with their associated characteristics.

TABLE 3.1
Information about the MovieLens 1M Dataset

Dataset	Data points	#Item	#User	#Item attributes	#User attributes	Sparsity
MovieLens 1M	1,149,238	3,514	5,950	6,944	30	95.73%

3.4 RESULTS

NCF's prediction for a specified user and item pair is given by the dot product of their associated embeddings. As a result, if an item is not encountered during the training, this model system is unable to generate an embedding for that item and is unable to access the system for this item.

It is observable that AFM's scores are lower than the other variants as it predicts all the pairwise interactions between the features and even if not all of them are meaningful, the neurons of the pair-wise interaction layer might readily co-adapt one another, resulting in overfitting.

NFM's efficiency may be increased by employing hashing methods to make it more acceptable. The usage of bi-interaction pooling detects low-level second-order attribute interconnections, which is more descriptive than the concatenation procedure. It significantly improves the subsequent NFM hidden layers in learning crucial higher-order feature interactions.

DeepFM performs better than Wide & Deep as professional feature engineering is required to be applied on the input to the "wide" component. DeepFM, on the other

TABLE 3.2
Comparison of Different Models on NDCG@10 Metric

Name of the algorithm	NDCG@10 value	Result from
DeepFM	0.8848	[2]
AutoInt	0.8931	[2]
Fi-GNN	0.9029	[2]
NCF	0.4349	[27]
AFM	0.8676	[2]
GMCF	**0.9436**	[2]
W & D	0.8869	[2]
L_0-SIGN	0.9094	[2]
NFM	0.8832	[2]

hand, needs no such specialized knowledge to handle the input because it learns directly from the input raw characteristics.

Models which directly analyze attribute interactions achieve higher prediction accuracy scores than alternate models, which suggests that the clear and direct interaction modeling is effective and promising in terms of obtaining valuable information from the features.

The three best-performing models are L_0-SIGN, Fi-GNN, and GMCF. The reason for this is their use of graph neural networks, which can preserve the data's graph structure since they only have to gain information about the interactions between the nodes rather than storing all the neurons within the graph.

Fi-GNN can describe interactions between fields as node interactions and the multiple field characteristics are represented as a graph. It can describe advanced feature interaction using a more efficient transparent and adjustable edge-wise interaction function. It can learn the edge weights expressing the relevance of various interactions that provide solid model justifications for CTR prediction.

In GMCF, using one layer of multi-layer perceptrons is enough, as using more than one may lead to overfitting. Moreover, one hidden layer is sufficient to examine the underlying interactions.

It is seen that GMCF performs the best, and the reason for this performance is the consideration of the inner and cross products. The explicit interaction modeling method appears to be promising for extracting meaningful information from characteristics and attribute interactions in order to make accurate predictions. GMCF employs MLP for representing the inner interactions within the user and item characteristics graphs, which results in robust interaction modeling capability for predictions. It distinguishes between inner and cross-connections and creates and organizes the interactions in a graph-matching framework that is thought to be more appropriate for a recommendation. The graph is constructed by partitioning feature interactions as edges and matching pairs for distinct structures, which require no more work than previous explicit pairwise interaction modeling approaches.

3.5 CONCLUSION

In this chapter, nine algorithms for collaborative filtering-based recommender systems are compared.

The data clearly represents the importance of recommender systems in our daily lives. As mentioned before, everything we buy is a result of the influence of one or more recommender systems, and hence we must not neglect the principles of their functioning. The data also shows the various types of systems that we encounter in our daily lives and their mechanisms as well. This will surely help people understand the importance, functioning, and the need for AI/ML in today's world and will encourage its use in the industry even more.

With the inner interactions, GMCF certainly does item trait learning, and with the cross interactions, it matches preferences for the recommendation. Experimental findings demonstrate that the GMCF model works quite well and beats all other models in terms of accuracy. Even when the user or item characteristics are not accessible,

GMCF can still be used. In particular, if one kind of attribute, such as user attributes, is absent, the user feature graph collapses into a single node.

Further explorations in the field of GMCF might be edge matching and sub-graph exploration.

REFERENCES

1. Heng-Tze Cheng, Levent Koc, Jeremiah Harmsen, Tal Shaked, Tushar Chandra, Hrishi Aradhye, Glen Anderson, Greg Corrado, Wei Chai, Mustafa Ispir, RohanAnil, Zakaria Haque, Lichan Hong, Vihan Jain, Xiaobing Liu, and Hemal Shah. 2016. Wide & Deep Learning for Recommender Systems. In *Proceedings of the 1stWorkshop on Deep Learning for Recommender Systems (RecSys)*, 7–10.
2. Yixin Su, Rui Zhang, Sarah M. Erfani, and Junhao Gan. 2021. Neural Graph Matching Based Collaborative Filtering. In *Proceedings of the 44th International ACM SIGIR Conference on Research and Development in Information Retrieval (SIGIR '21), July 11–15, 2021, Virtual Event, Canada.* ACM, New York, NY, 10 pages.
3. Zekun Li, Zeyu Cui, Shu Wu, Xiaoyu Zhang, and Liang Wang. 2019. Fi-GNN: Modeling Feature Interactions via Graph Neural Networks for CTR Prediction. In *Proceedings of the 28th International Conference on Information and Knowledge Management (CIKM)*, 539–548.
4. Yixin Su, Rui Zhang, Sarah Erfani, and Zhenghua Xu. 2021. Detecting Beneficial Feature Interactions for Recommender Systems. In *Proceedings of the Conference on Artificial Intelligence (AAAI)*.
5. Thomas N. Kipf and Max Welling. 2017. Semi-supervised classification with graph convolutional networks. In *Proceedings of the 6th International Conference on Learning Representations (ICLR)*, 1–14.
6. Yunsheng Pang, Yunxiang Zhao, and Dongsheng Li. 2021. Graph Pooling via Coarsened Graph Infomax. *arXiv preprint arXiv:2105.01275*.
7. Keyulu Xu, Weihua Hu, Jure Leskovec, and Stefanie Jegelka. 2019. How Powerful are Graph Neural Networks?. In *Proceedings of the 8th International Conference on Learning Representations (ICLR)*, 1–17.
8. Yunxiang Zhao, Jianzhong Qi, Qingwei Liu, and Rui Zhang. 2021. WGCN: Graph Convolutional Networks with Weighted Structural Features. *arXiv preprintarXiv:2104.14060*.
9. Peter W. Battaglia, Razvan Pascanu, Matthew Lai, Danilo Jimenez Rezende, and Koray Kavukcuoglu. 2016. Interaction Networks for Learning about Objects, Relations, and Physics. In *Proceedings of the Advances in Neural Information Processing Systems (NeurIPS)*, 4502–4510.
10. Yixin Su, Rui Zhang, Sarah Erfani, and Zhenghua Xu. 2021. Detecting BeneficialFeature Interactions for Recommender Systems. In *Proceedings of the Conference on Artificial Intelligence (AAAI)*.
11. Xiangnan He and Tat-Seng Chua. 2017. Neural Factorization Machines for Sparse Predictive Analytics. In *Proceedings of the 40th International ACM Conference on Research and Development in Information Retrieval (SIGIR)*, 35.
12. S. Rendle. 2010. Factorization Machines. In *ICDM*.
13. S. Rendle, Z. Gantner, C. Freudenthaler, and L. Schmidt-Thieme. 2011. Fast Context-Aware Recommendations with Factorization Machines. In *SIGIR*.
14. F.-M. Steffen Rendle. 2010. Factorization Machines. In *Proceedings of the 10th International IEEE Conference on Data Mining (ICDM)*, 995–1000.
15. X. He, L. Liao, H. Zhang, L. Nie, X. Hu, and T.-S. Chua. 2017. Neural Collaborative Filtering. *arXiv:1708.05031*.

16.   Xiangnan He and Tat-Seng Chua. 2017. Neural Factorization Machines for Sparse Predictive Analytics. In *Proceedings of the 40th International ACM Conference on Research and Development in Information Retrieval (SIGIR)*, 355–364.

17.   Huifeng Guo, Ruiming Tang, Yunming Ye, Zhenguo Li, and Xiuqiang He. 2017. DeepFM: A Factorization-Machine Based Neural Network for CTR Prediction. In *Proceedings of the 26th International Joint Conference on Artificial Intelligence(IJCAI)*, 1725–1731.

18.   R. Salakhutdinov and A. Mnih. 2008. Probabilistic Matrix Factorization. In *NIPS*, 1–8.

19.   H. Zhang, Y. Yang, H. Luan, S. Yang, and T.-S. Chua. 2014. Start from Scratch: Towards Automatically Identifying, Modeling, and Naming Visual Attributes. In *MM*, 187–196.

20.   N. Srivastava and R. R. Salakhutdinov. 2012. Multimodal Learning with Deep Boltzmann Machines. In *NIPS*, 2222–2230.

21.   Ashish Vaswani, Noam Shazeer, Niki Parmar, Jakob Uszkoreit, Llion Jones, Aidan N. Gomez, Łukasz Kaiser, and Illia Polosukhin. 2017. Attention is All You Need. In *Advances in Neural Information Processing Systems*, 5998–6008.

22.   A. K. Menon and C. Elkan. 2011. Link Prediction via Matrix Factorization. In *ECML PKDD*, 437–452.

23.   Yujia Li, Daniel Tarlow, Marc Brockschmidt, and Richard Zemel. 2015. Gated Graph Sequence Neural Networks. *arXiv preprint arXiv:1511.05493*.

24.   Ying Shan, T. Ryan Hoens, Jian Jiao, Haijing Wang, Dong Yu, and J. C. Mao. 2016. Deep Crossing: Web-scale Modeling Without Manually Crafted Combinatorial Features. In *Proceedings of the 22nd ACM SIGKDD International Conference on Knowledge Discovery and Data Mining*. ACM, 255–262.

25.   Weiping Song, Chence Shi, Zhiping Xiao, Zhijian Duan, Yewen Xu, Ming Zhang, and Jian Tang. 2019. AutoInt: Automatic Feature Interaction Learning via Self-Attentive Neural Networks. In *The 28th ACM International Conference on Information and Knowledge Management (CIKM '19), November 3–7, 2019, Beijing, China*. ACM, New York, NY, 10 pages.

26.   Alexander Miller, Adam Fisch, Jesse Dodge, Amir-Hossein Karimi, Antoine Bordes, and Jason Weston. 2016. Key-Value Memory Networks for Directly Reading Documents. In *Proceedings of the 2016 Conference on Empirical Methods in Natural Language Processing. Association for Computational Linguistics*, 1400–1409.

27.   Steffen Rendle, Walid Krichene, Li Zhang, and John Anderson. 2020. Neural Collaborative Filtering vs. Matrix Factorization Revisited. *arXiv:2005.09683v2*.

28.   Heng-Tze Cheng, Levent Koc, Jeremiah Harmsen, Tal Shaked, Tushar Chandra, Hrishi Aradhye, Glen Anderson, Greg Corrado, Wei Chai, Mustafa Ispir, et al. 2016. Wide & Deep Learning for Recommender Systems. In *Proceedings of the 1st Workshop on Deep Learning for Recommender Systems*. ACM, 7–10.

4 Recommendation System and Big Data
Its Types and Applications

Shweta Mongia, Tapas Kumar, and Supreet Kaur

CONTENTS

DOI: 10.1201/9781003319122-4

4.1   INTRODUCTION

There are many different factors on which the recommendation system is designed
to recommend things to the users. This system mainly processes a large volume
of existing information by filtering the most important information based on user-
supplied data and other factors while taking into account the user's preferences and
interests.[1] A typical recommender system cannot work without enough data. Big
data provides a large amount of user data to provide relevant and effective recommendations, such as past purchases, browsing history, and feedback to recommender
systems.[2] The main advantages of this system are it engages customers, transforms
shoppers into clients, increases average order value, boosts the number of items per
order, lowers work and overhead, and many more. Figure 4.1 shows the types of recommender systems. In this chapter, the authors discusses 10 recommender systems
such as content based, collaborative filtering, hybrid recommender system, content
aware recommender system, social network-based recommender system, group recommender system, genetic algorithm-based recommender system, fuzzy logic-based
recommender system, deep learning-based recommender system, and interactive
recommender system.[3]

4.2   TYPES OF RECOMMENDER SYSTEMS

4.2.1   CONTENT BASED

Content-based systems use the records that we take from a person via way of means
of a distinctive approach, which includes the rating (explicitly) or clicking on the link
(implicitly). In order to generate tips for the usage of this technique, capacity objects
are compared with the objects that had been rated by the person, and the matching
of the objects is determined. This gadget has the downside of restricted scope as it is
able to suggest objects that are just like the listed object, and cannot cope along with
the changing preferences of a person.[4][5]

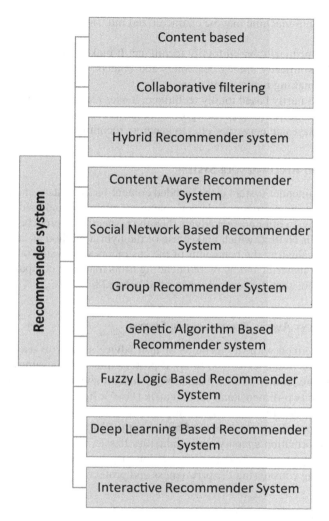

FIGURE 4.1 Types of recommender systems.

4.2.2 COLLABORATIVE FILTERING

The logic used here is that if two customers shared equal hobbies in the past, then, they may have a comparable flavour with each other in the future also. For example, say if customers P and Q have overlapping buy records then if person P has bought an object that person Q has now no longer visible then, the concept is to suggest this bought object to person Q as well. It calls for a massive quantity of facts about the person's interests, behaviours, and sports in order to offer correct recommendations.[6]

This method of machine may be characterized into two types:

4. Memory primarily based totally technique: It makes use of scores to compute the similarity among customers and objects, which may be similarly used for making recommendations.
2. Model primarily based totally technique: It uses records mining and gadget studying algorithms (consisting of associative rule mining, matrix factorization, Bayesian networks, etc.) to generate recommendations.[7]

4.2.3 Hybrid Recommender System

A hybrid recommender system is the blended content-based system and collaborative filtering method in an attempt to lessen sparsity, scalability, and cold-begin trouble and, additionally, to offer correct advice then the respective approaches. An example of this method is Netflix, which makes use of the hybrid method as advice listing is generated by evaluating the behaviour of the customers who watch or look for comparable content material and by recommending films that have comparable capabilities with the films that the consumer has rated before.[8]

4.2.4 Context Aware Recommender System

This may be defined with the instance of film advice similar to user-score matrix associate records (kids, teenagers, aged), if protected it could be supplementary and assist to generate greater correct results. With context aware recommender systems, in preference to two-dimensional score matrix (User × Item), tensor of order 3 (User × Item × Contextual records) come into play where contextual records refer to any records that approximate the state of affairs or entity. With the creation of every other dimension, information sparsity, and scalability hassle, in addition, get intensified. This huge information garage and computation may be laboured upon the usage of cloud computing considering the privateness and protection of users.[9]

4.2.5 Social Network-Based Recommender System

With this recommender system, the consumer has two profiles that indicate that it contains the consumer's personal information and social connection information. Leveraging social records such as social tagging, bookmarking, co-authoring, and trust offers opportunities for machines with very little information and unable to find comparable customers. Collaborative filtering, which is primarily based on social recommendation systems, falls primarily into the basic categories. Matrix factorization, primarily based on the complete recommendation engine, and matrix factorization, primarily based on the complete recommendation system, further divide the closest neighbours.[10]

4.2.6 Group Recommender System

The group recommender system is a statistics filtering device that aids a collection of customers when face-to-face interplay isn't viable in making decisions, for instance, for deciding to make plans for a dinner or a vacation. Despite many kinds of research, group recommender systems suffer from all demanding situations such as cold-start, sparsity, and privateness and extra superior demanding situations such as evolving character choices with time and situation, person profile shortage, and locating extra appropriate elicitation and aggregation methods. The future of group recommender systems lie in having a device where there is a facilitator to assist a collection to attain to a choice, and a mediator, with the aid of which, it will suggest gadgets which are popular with the aid of using the complete organization, but at the same time, keeping a person's privateness.[11]

4.2.7 Genetic Algorithm-Based Recommender System

Genetic algorithms are evolutionary techniques implemented to optimize the characteristics of a target. In the genetic algorithm, a question encoded as a string is called a chromosome, a set of answer candidates is called a population, and a selection method is implemented on it to select an evolving answer. A genetic algorithm-based recommender system, however, ultimately is stochastic in nature where optimality is not guaranteed. Genetic algorithms are used in recommender systems for specific purposes of optimization of similarity functions and clustering in their work.[12]

4.2.8 Fuzzy Logic-Based Recommender System

Fuzzy logic-based recommender systems have recorded filtering software that handles and optimizes the impact of noise, which includes impreciseness, uncertainty in consumer preferences, vagueness in object capabilities, and consumer behaviour and therefore proves to be a step forward in the world. For example, elements or consumer profiles that often contain complex tree systems in enterprise software have been modeled more flexibly by the shape of the fuzzy tree. Complemented by collaborative filtering and tender computing, the fuzzy judgment has received top-notch attention. Studies of fuzzy logic recommender systems have shown the largest increase, but there is a lack of de facto units suitable for that evaluation.[13]

4.2.9 Deep Learning-Based Recommender System

Deep learning in recommender systems has garnered considerable interest in recent years owing to various techniques like deep characteristic mastering, inherent characteristic extraction, and abstraction inside facts in addition to its awesome overall performance in phrases of accuracy. Capturing non-linear, non-trivial user or item relationship or any intrinsic relation that exists within data sources, such as contextual and visual information, justifies the capability and great use of deep learning in a recommendation engine. Various deep learning techniques for generating recommendations exist and are applied depending upon the system's requirement. The multilayer perceptron is one such technique where nonlinear transformation can be added to generate recommendations and interpret it into neural extension.[14]

4.2.10 Interactive Recommender System (IRS)

The interactive recommender system is one such gadget that breaks the "black-hole" nature of RSs and permits the consumer to engage with the gadget, which ensures accelerated transparency. IRS similarly presents an explanatory interface and additionally triumphs over the hassle of faux and redundant profiles as customers can pick out neighbours in step with their choice. The hybridization of deep mastering strategies with IRS marks an exciting region that desires the researcher's attention.[15]

4.3 RECOMMENDER SYSTEMS APPLICATIONS AND BIG DATA

In this section, the authors mention diverse packages of recommender structures and their courting with big data; the instructional sector, tourism, bioinformatics, and healthcare will be mentioned.

4.3.1 EDUCATIONAL SECTOR

Diverse recommender structures were studied and what follows is the precise steps concerned in advice structures for instructional sectors as illustrated in Figure 4.2. [16, 17]

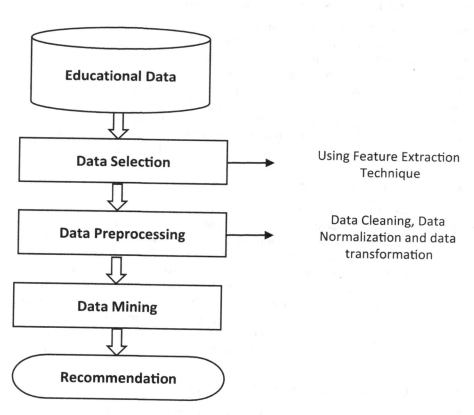

FIGURE 4.2 Recommendation system steps for the education sector.

Step 1: Acquire the information from instructional assets in which information and characteristic redundancy is taken care at this stage.

Step 2: Required attributes of information are decided on the use of diverse characteristic choice and extraction strategies. At this step, it reduces the extent of information such that analytical effects aren't affected.

Step 3: Data is processed by the following tasks:

Data cleaning: Data is wiped clean at this stage.

• Missing values are treated by filling in the ones values.
• Data that aren't conveying significant facts are treated with the use of smoothing strategies.
• Smoothing strategies create a feature to extract significant facts from information and forget about the noise.

Transformation of information: Data discretization or hierarchy era may be used for information transformation.

• Data discretization is to transform expression information into finite value.
• Hierarchy era reduces the information by changing a low degree idea, for instance, age, into better degree idea, for instance, youth.

Figure 4.3 shows the various types of recommendation systems for the education sector.

Various suitable statistics mining methods are used to achieve the preferred result. At this degree, statistics mining method are diagnosed that are used to generate the advice for users. Content primarily based totally advice machines, collaborative filtering primarily based totally advice machines, knowledge primarily based totally advice machines, and hybrid advice machines are the advice structures used for the schooling sector.[17]

4.3.2 Tourism Sector

Recommender systems can be a great help when one is planning a trip as it recommends the most suitable offers to customers.[18] A lot of surveys have been done, and

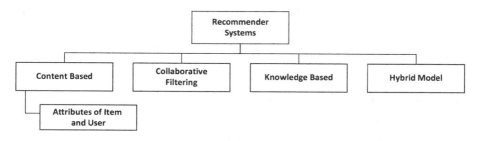

FIGURE 4.3 Types of recommendation systems for the education sector.

it is found that in the tourism sector the following recommender systems are used. In the following sections, the general architecture is also explained.

4.3.3   COLLABORATIVE FILTERING

The concept of collaborative filtering is to collect the interests of a user. There are numerous approaches used to evaluate the degree of appreciation. It recommends to the user the items that have been preferred by the users in the past.[19]

4.3.4   SOCIAL RECOMMENDER SYSTEM

With the assistance of social networks, studies have used data in calculating the similarities among a user's social area and the goal person to a particular metric. Recommender devices have additionally brought the contextual data. The principal intention is to make a contribution to the layout of tourism recommender structures with the aid of using featuring systems that screen how the hybrid advice technique works and supplying information for every step. It enables enhancements the visitor enjoys with the aid of using recommending the maximum applicable articles and permitting visitors to customize their itinerary. Current tourism advice strategies have numerous superior factors, and those may be labeled in lots of ways. The collaborative filtering technique affords site visitors with locations they have not visited yet, however it may additionally need some information based totally on their evaluated history. This technique is tough to fulfill the wishes of vacationers if it no longer suits the person's tourism history.[19]

4.3.5   CONTENT-BASED FILTERING

The maximum famous and extensively used approach is to carry out a similarity evaluation of content material formerly consulted through ability visitors. It additionally defines a background approach in which sources are primarily based totally on consumer options and object metadata, rank objects primarily based totally on multi-standards consumer feedback, and improve a fixed of guidelines via semantic relationships among objects. The main predicament of this kind of technique is that similar to the overall and wealthy illustration of the element's content material, it could be afflicted by the hassle of over-specialization. This kind of recommender machine is referred to as context-based while customers use the context of their calculations to expect what they're probably interested in. Connected objects (internet-linked cellular telephones) are extensively used to seize and offer a wealth of statistics that can improve the present-day context and its variations.[19]

4.3.6   HYBRID RECOMMENDER MACHINE

A hybrid recommender machine is a technique to triumph over the shortcomings and strengths of every era I used, but is the concern of few researchers. The machine is a hybrid of three approaches: content material primarily based totally, social, and context primarily based totally. Almost 90% of the answers are aware of objects in the unmarried category, so they are handiest to offer statistics on tourism offerings to make the tours more enjoyable; however, most of those works use a single technique and the context primarily based totally technique is actually predominant. Therefore, for conceptual frameworks, we want to gather advocated approaches, but we also want to offer one-of-a-kind tourism sources in a single architecture.[20]

4.3.7 Architecture for Tourism Recommender System

This structure is primarily based totally on a hybrid advice approach. The principal reason for this version is to enhance users' ability to enter tourism assets in statistics retrieval systems, including tourism portals and provider documentary extranets. In phrases of innovation, the proposed device is going past a listing of advocated visitor sites and may be taken into consideration as a multi-day planning tool. Thus, the customers could be furnished with a branched listing of visitor assets that meet precisely their possibilities and needs.

The architecture model can be decomposed into five main modules.

1. **Visitor profile:** This will contain in particular information about the user that can be used to determine user preferences in terms of items.
2. **Services repository:** This contains information about tourism services and related multimedia content.
3. **Contextual meta-model:** In order to make these recommendations, many factors will be involved, including time, location, place, distance between two places, routes, and the travel history of tourists.
4. **The hybrid filtering process:** This will return a list of items that include the level of gratitude that the target user will give to each item.
5. **Trip planner:** This selects items that are likely to be relevant to the user and uses operations research techniques to correlate these decisions in the form of a journey.

4.3.8 Conceptual Framework of the Proposed Architecture

This conceptual framework includes three subprocesses, which might be a consumer profiling system, a content material selection/filtering system that fine fits consumer profiles, and an experience-making plans system. These procedures arise on the intersection of various fields of laptop technological know-how research, which include synthetic intelligence and operational research. The cause of the filtering system is to discover ways to classify new records primarily based totally on formerly displayed records that have been implicitly or explicitly flagged by the consumer as inspiring or uninteresting.

4.3.8.1 User Profiling Process

This is a process of four scenarios, and it is a very important step in the proposed framework. The four scenarios are registration, social login, "no login" advice, and context. Upon registration, the user expresses their interest in the system through the registration form. Social login allows users to log in to social networks such as

Google, Twitter, and Facebook using their existing login details, rather than creating a new system-specific login account. In social advice, this behaviour is called "trace of use". This basically relies on observational analysis of user behaviour and is implicitly performed by the application. In a recommender system, everything runs "in the background" without asking the user.

The covered strains are signs that describe operations including copying/pastings textual content from the web page, attempting to find textual content at the web page, including or eliminating objects from the purchasing cart, ordering objects (for e-trade applications), and more. They include and consist of save or print a web page, etc. Navigation signs include surfing frequency and duration, web page or hyperlink clicks and mouse pointers, scrolling, etc. Finally, the context is dynamic and personalized go-to routes.

The filtering technique takes and enters all of the modules that make up the goal consumer's profile. The consumer profile consists of three modules: the collaboration module, the content primarily based totally module, and the demographic module. The collaborative module consists of score statistics for the referenced articles.

Content primarily based modules describe the traits of traveller destinations/sports that customers have regarded beyond the key-word vectors generated after the indexing phase. It is to be noted that those key phrases are commonly robotically extracted on the time of session or manually assigned on the time of registration. The demographic module consists of the demographic attributes of the consumer. These attributes may be entered with the aid of using the consumer with the aid of using filling out the registration shape or extracted from social login. This method returns a listing of gadgets at the extent of gratitude that the goal consumer can deliver to every item.

For the travel planning process, after assessing the degree of gratitude, the system considers its context, selects items that are considered relevant to the user, and uses operations research techniques in the form of a journey to correlate these recommendations.

4.3.9 INTEGRATION OF AI AND BIG DATA FOR THE PROPOSED ARCHITECTURE

The intention is to apply machines and deep mastering strategies to construct massive facts answers primarily based totally on hybrid recommendations, sentiment analysis, and opinion analysis. It additionally presents a clever device for deciding on and recommending to the traveller corresponding with the consumer's profile and monitoring and analyzing their reviews to enhance the client's demands. To acquire this, a four-tier technique is offered that describes a method that integrates massive facts and AI into the proposed system.[21]

These layers are as follows:

4. **Tourist facts aggregation layer:** This layer presents quite a few virtual gear to decorate the visibility and attraction of tourism services. Various gear offers a huge quantity of beneficial content. The device presents the tourist with a real immersive feeling on the destination. Tourism facts are regularly

great and non-uniform, so massive facts are wanted to shop this huge form of facts. It employs a huge variety of revolutionary generation answers, such as NoSQL database control structures and allotted report structures.

2. **Recommendation layer:** The goal is to pick out the consumer profiles on the basis of choice, with the aid of using the modules that make up the consumer profile and picking the proper endorsed method to apply and layout the proper algorithms to run to in order to take gain of huge datasets. Big facts generation implements quite a few gadget mastering and deep mastering strategies on a huge scale, such as classification, clustering, correlation rules, regression, collaborative filtering, and recurrent neural networks. Based on those strategies, one-of-a-kind vacationers may be processed in actual time and the records may be analyzed; and the outcomes acquired may be used to expect the traveller's subsequent pastimes and propose suitable guides and journey routes.

3. **Results visualization layer:** This layer accompanies vacationers at each degree of their "before/middle/after" trip from guidance to online sharing.

4. **Layer for validating the proposed solution:** This layer includes tracking and analyzing tourist reviews and feelings offered with the aid of using tourism agencies on blogs and social media, know-how adjustments of their desires, and sharing records that impacts their decisions.

4.4   BIOINFORMATICS SECTOR

Bioinformatics is an interdisciplinary area that develops one-of-a-kind techniques and software program gear for the higher knowledge of the organic information, specially whilst the information units are huge and complicated to understand.[22]

Bioinformatics is, in particular, used to extract know-how from organic information via the improvement of algorithms and software program. Bioinformatics is broadly implemented withinside the exam of genomics, proteomics, 3D systems modelling of proteins, image analysis, drug designing, and loads more. A widespread utility of bioinformatics may be located withinside the fields of precision and preventive medicines this is particularly targeted on growing measures to prevent, manipulate, and treat dreadful infectious diseases.[23]

4.4.1   RECOMMENDER SYSTEMS USED IN THE BIOINFORMATICS SECTOR

This singular price decomposition (SPD) is a collaborative filtering method. SPD is primarily based totally on a matrix factorization approach that tries to reduce the mistake of the ratings via stochastic gradient descent (SGD). Each score is predicted using following equation.

$$\hat{r}_{ij} = \mu + p_i + p_j + q_i^T P_j \qquad\qquad 3.1$$

μ is the average score of all datasets across all learners; p_i is the estimated bias for algorithm i, initially zero; p_j is the estimated bias for dataset j, initially zero; q_i is a vector of factors associated with algorithm i, and P_j is the vector of factors associated with dataset j, both initialized from normal distributions centred at zero.[24]

4.4.2 HEALTHCARE SECTOR

As the data generated by the healthcare business grows day by day, leveraging big data analytics (BDA) is essential to raising the bar for healthcare. The BDA system helps perform predictive analytics on patient data. This helps to make patients aware of their health risks early on. It also helps physicians provide effective, real-time treatment for the patient's health risks. Diagnosis can be improved by using expert recommendations from medical forums.[25] Following are use cases of recommender systems in healthcare.

4.4.2.1 Healthcare Big Data Use Cases

Spark processes large amounts of complex healthcare knowledge very quickly. It provides the ability to perform in-memory calculations. This helps process knowledge 100 times faster than saving an old card. With Sparks Net for Lambda Design, you can run any batch and real-time process.[26]

> **Case 1:** Integration of knowledge from multiple sources. Gather healthcare-related knowledge from a variety of sources, including filter conversions using Spark.
> **Case 2:** High performance execution calculation and retry process.
> **Case 3:** Predictive analytics abuse Spark streaming in this Mlib helps perform predictive analytics in machine learning programs for healthcare abuse algorithms. These libraries make it easy to perform real-time analysis of the knowledge generated by wearable healthcare devices.

4.4.3 DESIGNING HEALTHCARE RECOMMENDATION SYSTEM

This recommender arrangement supports information and patient central facts smartly perforated and given at acceptable occasions to boost attention duties. Also, healthcare recommender system ways have a really universal feature of giving written records from different beginnings for clinical sickness scheme application and verifying acceptable approvals within the list of sickness, drug interaction alerts, safeguard care alerts, suggesting patient with medical insurance plans, necessary shipping alerts from the hospital, shipping alerts to inmates concerning add-ups, diet approvals, replacement cures, etc.[27]

Depending on the data of a healthcare recommender system shopper, two separate use cases are used.

4.4.3.1 Case A: Healthcare Provider as Final User

In this case, a healthcare practitioner uses a healthcare recommendation system (HRS) to record sufficient facts, such as existing sickness or the clinical road or analysis from fitness forums, which is computed definitively. This method of case-related facts advancement capability assists a medical practitioner in the method of sickness as current analysis findings can be used for the conclusion and support of the situation.

4.4.3.2 Case B: Patient as Final User

In this case, a patient interacts with an HRS, which is compatible with patient health record s(PHR). HRS generates helpful content based on the patient's medical history. The relevant articles are recommended to the user. PHRs are integrated with the HRS. The PHR is a digital platform allowing patients to access and share their health information securely. This method is beneficial for patients who want to achieve specific health goals. PHR supports users in achieving their desired health outcomes by providing relevant recommendations. A health recommender system can assist patients at different stages of the healthcare process, from preventative care to diagnosis and treatment. HRS is commonly used to ensure accurate diagnosis, prevent avoidable illness, recommend appropriate insurance plans and treatments, provide drug dosage recommendations, and detect adverse drug reactions.

4.4.4 HEALTHCARE RECOMMENDER SYSTEM FRAMEWORK

We will constitute care recommender machine by prediction and recommendation.[28] It relies upon on a set of education of the affected person's case history, expert regulations, and social media data to train and construct a version that's capable of expecting and proposing illness dangers, designations, and one-of-a-kind medicines. Predictions and recommendations rectangular degree accredited by physicians. HRS machine wishes enter information to provide you with predictions and recommendations. For the duration of this paintings polygenic disease data is hired as case study.[25]

4.4.4.1 Training Information

Piles of ancient clinical facts of diabetic patients (935 facts) have been amassed from hospitals. The amassed data facts rectangular degree delineates by type of attributes, values, and doctors' designations for each case. Designation scale degrees from 1 to 10 supported the severity of the illness; 5 represents critical situation, 4 represents intense wishes for instant treatment, 3 represents slight wishes for extra investigation, 2 represents traditional, and 1 represents amongst management.

4.4.4.2 Demographic Data of an Energetic Affected Person

It refers back to the user's data, such as name, age, location, schooling level, wearable device, lifestyle, meals conduct, and any sort of belongings. Medical chronicle of polygenic disease Patient: It consists of domestic test info like glucose, pressure in step with unit area, and weight. Designation data consists of medication notes, paintings result, and medications. A polygenic disease data set is amassed from a area of expertise hospital and conjointly downloaded from University of California Irvine machine learning repository. The output of the machine is prediction and recommendation: prediction is expressed as a numerical really well worth that represents the illness danger designation for destiny instances supported energetic patients. Recommendations are expressed based on the proposal wished for by the users. For instance, non-healthcare professionals could require one-of-a-kind treatments for treating polygenic disease. Care experts could also be looking for illness designation techniques supporting similarly affected people.

4.4.5   BUILDING THE PREDICTIVE VERSION

4.4.5.1   Step 1: Processing

Data filtering is crucial to avoid the introduction of ambiguous or irrelevant fashions and enhance the instructional version performance. In our machine, the polygenic disorder dataset is filtered by figuring out the applicable alternatives through the information gain attribute eval attribute desire technique; moreover, the data is made over to a kind of perfect to the classification.

4.4.5.2   Step 2: Classification of Victimization Bayesian Network

Bayesian approaches have become an increasing preferred withinside the clinical evaluation because of their effectiveness in developing better predictions. The polygenic disorder may be a continual situation that occurs as soon as the frame can't flip out sufficient or can't efficaciously use hormones. The Bayesian classifier is hired to expect polygenic disorder correctly in spite of fewer quantities of training knowledge. Bayesian facts permit one to create companion diploma estimates regarding the opportunity of a declare after which replace those estimates as new evidence will become at the market. In Bayes' Theorem the probability of a speculation is received by multiplying the preceding probability with the power of the brand new knowledge. The new, up-to-date probability is called the "posterior probability", or simply "the posterior". This will be the aggregation of opportunities of all doubtlessly applicable hypotheses.[29]

4.5   TOOLS AND TECHNIQUES TO SET UP A RECOMMENDATION SYSTEM FOR BIG DATA

The tools that guide large-scale facts are as follows:[30]

4.5.1   HADOOP

The Hadoop framework uses low-level programming scripts to distribute methods assigned from widely used datasets across computer clusters. Designed to scale from one server to hundreds of machines, each provides local computing and storage capacity. The main components of Hadoop are Hadoop Common, which supports alternative Hadoop modules, and Hadoop Distributed Gadgets (HDFS), which provide access to software data and high throughput. Hadoop Yet Another Resource Negotiator (YARN) can be a framework for programming useful Hadoop cluster resource controls. Hadoop MapReduce relies on the YARN gadget. It provides a huge amount of factual information processing.

4.5.2 Mahout

Apache Motivkraft is an open supply partner diploma library for promoting gadget mastering in the Apache Bundle Foundation, which implements many gadget mastering algorithms with many instructions such as collaborative filtering, clustering, typing, and dimensionality reduction. Motivkraft co-uses Hadoop for BigFacts methods.

4.5.3 Crab Recommender Framework in Python

Crab scikits.recommender could be Python's recommender engine. Crab could be a Python framework for building recommended engines included in medical Python applications (NumPy, SciPy, matplotlib). This helps with recommended algorithms such as full user-based filtering and fully collaborative object-based filtering.

4.5.4 MLlib by Spark

The cclib is being developed as part of the Apache Spark project. Spark is a partner diploma engine for large-scale processing. The two applications are spark.mllib and spark.ml.MLlib, and they are gadget mastering (ML) libraries that include algorithms such as type, regression, clustering, collaborative filtering, and spatial reduction. It is new compared to different information mining information method and processing tools. The facts method victimization MLlib is fantastically short due to the fact that the method takes region in memory.

4.6 CONCLUSION

This chapter discussed about the various recommender systems such as content based, collaborative filtering, hybrid, context-aware, social network, interactive, genetic algorithm-based, fuzzy logic-based, and artificial intelligence-based recommender systems. The authors also discussed the various recommender systems and their methodology used for various applications in areas such as the education sector, tourism sector, bioinformatics, and healthcare sector. In conclusion, the authors discussed various tools and techniques to set up a recommendation system for big data.

REFERENCES

1. Resnick, P., & Varian, H. R. (1997). Recommender systems. *Communications of the ACM, 40*(3), 56–58.
2. Bansal, S., & Baliyan, N. (2019). A study of recent recommender system techniques. *IJKSS, 10*(2), 13–41.
3. Alhijawi, B., & Kilani, Y. (2020). The recommender system: A survey. *International Journal of Advanced Intelligence Paradigms, 15*(3), 229–251.
4. Lops, P., Gemmis, M. D., & Semeraro, G. (2011). Content-based recommender systems: State of the art and trends. In *Recommender systems handbook* (pp. 73–105). DOI: 10.1007/978-0-387-85820-3_3
5. Aggarwal, C. C. (2016). Content-based recommender systems. In *Recommender systems* (pp. 139–166). Springer, Cham.

6.   Sharma, R., Gopalani, D., & Meena, Y. (2017, February). Collaborative filtering-based recommender system: Approaches and research challenges. In *2017 3rd international conference on computational intelligence & communication technology (CICT)* (pp. 1–6). IEEE.

7.   Aditya, P. H., Budi, I., & Munajat, Q. (2016, October). A comparative analysis of memory-based and model-based collaborative filtering on the implementation of recommender system for E-commerce in Indonesia: A case study PT X. In *2016 international conference on advanced computer science and information systems (ICACSIS)* (pp. 303–308). IEEE.

8.   Li, Q., & Kim, B. M. (2003, October). Clustering approach for hybrid recommender system. In *Proceedings IEEE/WIC international conference on web intelligence (WI 2003)* (pp. 33–38). IEEE.

9.   Haruna, K., Akmar Ismail, M., Suhendroyono, S., Damiasih, D., Pierewan, A. C., Chiroma, H., & Herawan, T. (2017). Context-aware recommender system: A review of recent developmental process and future research direction. *Applied Sciences, 7*(12), 1211.

10. He, J., & Chu, W. W. (2010). A social network-based recommender system (SNRS). In *Data mining for social network data* (pp. 47–74). Springer, Boston, MA.

11. Guo, Z., Zeng, W., Wang, H., & Shen, Y. (2019). An enhanced group recommender system by exploiting preference relation. *IEEE Access, 7,* 24852–24864.

12. Gupta, A., Shivhare, H., & Sharma, S. (2015, September). Recommender system using fuzzy c-means clustering and genetic algorithm based weighted similarity measure. In *2015 international conference on computer, communication and control (IC4)* (pp. 1–8). IEEE.

13. Jain, A., & Gupta, C. (2018). Fuzzy logic in recommender systems. In *Fuzzy logic augmentation of neural and optimization algorithms: Theoretical aspects and real applications* (pp. 255–273). Springer, Cham.

14. Zhang, S., Yao, L., Sun, A., & Tay, Y. (2019). Deep learning based recommender system: A survey and new perspectives. *ACM Computing Surveys (CSUR), 52*(1), 1–38.

15. Steck, H., van Zwol, R., & Johnson, C. (2015, September). Interactive recommender systems: Tutorial. In *Proceedings of the 9th ACM conference on recommender systems* (pp. 359–360). DOI: 10.1145/2792838.2792840

16. Xin, X., Shi, T., & Sohail, M. (2022). Knowledge-based intelligent education recommendation system with IoT networks. *Security and Communication Networks, 2022.*

17. Singh, P. K., Pramanik, P. K. D., Dey, A. K., & Choudhury, P. (2021). Recommender systems: An overview, research trends, and future directions. *International Journal of Business and Systems Research, 15*(1), 14–52.

18. Hamid, R. A., Albahri, A. S., Alwan, J. K., Al-Qaysi, Z. T., Albahri, O. S., Zaidan, A. A., . . . & Zaidan, B. B. (2021). How smart is e-tourism? A systematic review of smart tourism recommendation system applying data management. *Computer Science Review, 39,* 100337.

19. Garipelly, V., Adusumalli, P. T., & Singh, P. (2021, July). Travel recommendation system using content and collaborative filtering-a hybrid approach. In *2021 12th international conference on computing communication and networking technologies (ICCCNT)* (pp. 1–4). IEEE.

20. Al Fararni, K., Nafis, F., Aghoutane, B., Yahyaouy, A., Riffi, J., & Sabri, A. (2021). Hybrid recommender system for tourism based on big data and AI: A conceptual framework. *Big Data Mining and Analytics, 4*(1), 47–55.

21. Hajli, N., Shirazi, F., Tajvidi, M., & Huda, N. (2021). Towards an understanding of privacy management architecture in big data: An experimental research. *British Journal of Management, 32*(2), 548–565.

22. Rehman Khan, H. U., Lim, C. K., Ahmed, M. F., Tan, K. L., & Bin Mokhtar, M. (2021). Systematic review of contextual suggestion and recommendation systems for sustainable e-tourism. *Sustainability, 13*(15), 8141.

23. Ebrahimi, F., Asemi, A., Nezarat, A., & Ko, A. (2021). Developing a mathematical model of the co-author recommender system using graph mining techniques and big data applications. *Journal of Big Data, 8*(1), 1–15.

24. La Cava, W., Williams, H., Fu, W., Vitale, S., Srivatsan, D., & Moore, J. H. (2021). Evaluating recommender systems for AI-driven biomedical informatics. *Bioinformatics, 37*(2), 250–256.

25. Chicaiza, J., & Valdiviezo-Diaz, P. (2021). A comprehensive survey of knowledge graph-based recommender systems: Technologies, development, and contributions. *Information, 12*(6), 232.

26. Tran, T. N. T., Felfernig, A., Trattner, C., & Holzinger, A. (2021). Recommender systems in the healthcare domain: State-of-the-art and research issues. *Journal of Intelligent Information Systems, 57*(1), 171–201.

27. Li, W., Chai, Y., Khan, F., Jan, S. R. U., Verma, S., Menon, V. G., & Li, X. (2021). A comprehensive survey on machine learning-based big data analytics for IoT-enabled smart healthcare system. *Mobile Networks and Applications, 26*(1), 234–252.

28. De Croon, R., Van Houdt, L., Htun, N. N., Štiglic, G., Abeele, V. V., & Verbert, K. (2021). Health recommender systems: Systematic review. *Journal of Medical Internet Research, 23*(6), e18035.

29. Himeur, Y., Alsalemi, A., Al-Kababji, A., Bensaali, F., Amira, A., Sardianos, C., ... & Varlamis, I. (2021). A survey of recommender systems for energy efficiency in buildings: Principles, challenges and prospects. *Information Fusion, 72*, 1–21.

30. Tripathi, A. K., Mittal, H., Saxena, P., & Gupta, S. (2021). A new recommendation system using map-reduce-based tournament empowered whale optimization algorithm. *Complex & Intelligent Systems, 7*(1), 297–309.

5 The Role of Machine Learning/AI in Recommender Systems

N R Saturday, K T Igulu, T P Singh, and F E Onuodu

CONTENTS

5.1 INTRODUCTION

An online user is always faced with options that pop up on any landing page especially when the user is on the page for the first time. The user requires an advisor on what content to browse and take decision. The recommender system (RS) serves as an advisor to an online user regardless of the specific content the user is interested in. These systems offer a wide range of options when the user is indecisive on decisions like 'listen to a music genre', 'hire an expert', 'buy from a brand shop', etc. A recommender system is an intelligent computerized technique used to ameliorate the indecision of an online user over a large option of online information depending on the online behaviour of the user. These systems are used by most corporate organization that have an online presence. For example, eBay recommends products to buy; Facebook recommends friends to connect with; TripAdvisor recommends vacation

DOI: 10.1201/9781003319122-5

destinations; YouTube recommends videos to view; Goodreads recommends books to read; Glassdoor recommends appropriate jobs; Amazon recommends good products to buy; MathWorks recommends good certifications and trainings to enroll in; Netflix recommends movies to see, etc. In order to efficiently deploy recommender systems, there have been various contributions from specialists in the field of artificial intelligence (AI), data mining, business and marketing, approximate theory, information security and privacy, information retrieval, information security, etc. [1]; thus Figure 5.1 shows the flow of a recommender system that is implemented with an algorithm. Algorithms are necessary in recommender system to ensure actualization of desired results as well as to take into account the Internet of Things (IoT) shown in Figure 5.2. The ubiquitous wide range of smart devices that

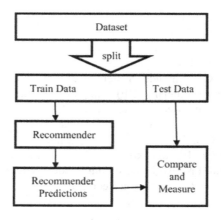

FIGURE 5.1   The structure and flow of an algorithmic recommender system [3].

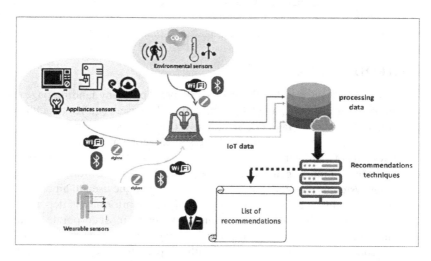

FIGURE 5.2   The flow of a recommender system with IoT devices [2].

are connected online poses the need to apply recommender systems due to services these smart devices provide in various application domain like agriculture, telemedicine, smart offices, education, smart homes, etc. [2].

5.2 MACHINE LEARNING/AI ALGORITHMS

Machine learning has gotten a high attraction in the aspect of solving problem that deals with prediction and classification by making assumptions on trained models. Thus, there a wide range of machine learning algorithm that can be used for recommender systems [4]. These algorithms are subdivided in three types: supervised learning, unsupervised learning, and semi-supervised learning. However, the choice of which algorithm to apply for different recommender systems is usually difficult since each algorithm has its unique problem and open-ended questions that requires some measure of evaluation [4]. AI's concept or purpose is to embed various types of intelligence in computer systems. AI allows for a higher quality of recommendation than is possible with traditional methods. This has ushered in a new era for recommender systems, which has allowed for more advanced insights into user-item relationships, the presentation of more complex data representations, and the discovery of comprehensive information in demographical, textual, virtual, and contextual data [5]. Some AI tools and techniques are fuzzy logic, neural and deep neural networks, evolutionary techniques, machine learning, etc. that can effectively model recommender systems.

5.3 CLASSIFICATION OF RECOMMENDER SYSTEMS

Recommender systems are fundamentally categorized into three, as follows.

5.3.1 COLLABORATIVE FILTERING (CF)

This technique used in recommender systems has been in application over 20 years [4]. A collaborative filtering recommender is built on the history of users' ratings and ranks top on the most used recommender systems [2], [4]. The CF simply infer from the similar preferences of users to recommend products and services to this category of users; and this is achieved via three stages: 1. selection of users that aim on the same preferences, 2. analysis on the similarities between users, and 3. recommend based on group ratings. This technique is further classified in two types: memory-based collaborative filtering and model-based collaborative filtering. Memory-based CF is based on comparing user-to-user rating as well item-to-item thereby making an inference on the future rating on a product or service. The memory-based CF technique uses the heuristic algorithms such as the nearest neighbour algorithm. This algorithm is evidently efficient, simple, and able to yield accurate result. However, this technique cannot handle the entry of a new user or item in the system, and this is a disadvantage. Also, it cannot handle the factor of an unpopular item in the system since such an item will seldom have ratings as well as not able to perform real-time recommendations. It performs its heuristic process over a long duration as a result of large dimensional user-item matrix. This technique cannot scale up to practical applications in real life. Model-based CF simply builds a model adopting machine learning algorithm to make prediction on user rating on an item; data mining methods can also be used for predictions. In order to remedy the pitfalls of memory-based CF, additional information such as tags, location, and reviews are considered in building this model. This model produces good result when combined with matrix factorization. Matrix factorization is the most popular algorithm amongst other algorithm in this area of specialization. It captures both user space and item space onto the same latent factor space so that they are compared. Matrix factorization possess three advantages that helps project its popularity. Firstly, the dimension of the user-item rating matrix can be significantly reduced, so the scalability of the system using matrix factorization is secured. Secondly, the process of factorization makes a dense rating matrix so that the sparsity problem can be handled [5]. Users who have a few ratings can get relatively more accurate recommendation through matrix factorization, which is a significant advantage over memory-based methods. Thirdly, matrix factorization is very suitable for integrating a variety of additional information [6]. This aids in profiling user preferences and improves the overall performance of recommender systems. However, in cases where the model is built on a training set, the model is less accurate than the memory-based method [2].

5.3.2 Content-Based Methods

This method borders on recommendation of items primarily on previous targets by the user. Content-based method recommendations are made based on the user's track record of preferences and profile where the features of the items are factored into consideration [6]. For example, a user who liked or purchased a particular item with certain features and a certain price range is more likely to show interest in another item with the same features. The profile usually is a combination of information about what the user has liked or disliked previously. Thus, the process of profiling can be seen as a typical problem of binary classification, which has been well studied in the field of machine learning and data mining [2]. Algorithms usually adopted here are naïve Bayes, nearest neighbour algorithms, and decision trees. In other words, recommendation in a content-based recommender system is a process of filtering and matching between the item representation and the profiled user based on the features acquired during the analysis, thereby forwarding the matched items and removing the items the user usually dislike. So the relevance evaluation of the recommendation is clearly dependent on the accuracy of the represented item and the profile of the user. This method has advantages, such as user independence because content-based recommendation is based on item representation and is thus user independent; as such, this recommender system does not suffer from the problem of data sparsity. These recommender systems have the ability to recommend new items to users, which solve the problem of new item cold-start. Content-based recommender systems (Figure 5.3) can provide a clear explanation of the recommendation result. This recommender system is transparent and is a huge advantage compared to other techniques in real-world applications. Nevertheless, there are

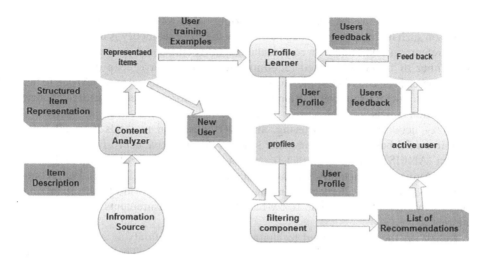

FIGURE 5.3 Content-based recommender system [6].

several limitations to content-based recommender systems. It still suffering from the new user problem because the lack of user profile information affects the accuracy of the result.

5.3.3 HYBRID RECOMMENDER SYSTEM

Frequently, hybrid recommendation algorithms are employed to compensate for or enhance the performance of one of the fundamental types of recommendation strategies. Intuitively, hybrid recommender systems combine the characteristics of the based types to compensate for the shortcomings of individual RS algorithms.

5.4 AI/ML TECHNIQUES IN RS

In this section, we explore the various applications of AI/ML techniques in RSs.

5.4.1 FUZZY LOGIC (FL) AND RS

According to [7–9], fuzzy logic is a type of soft computing that is capable of dealing with imprecision, vagueness, and uncertainty. FL is widely used in a variety of aspects of intelligent systems. In the context of RSs, item characteristics and user behaviours are frequently imprecise, subjective, and ambiguous [10]. Fuzzy set and fuzzy relation theories are powerful tools for dealing with problems of information uncertainty and can also be used in recommender systems [5].

Fuzzy approaches are used in two stages of content-based recommender systems: profiling and matching of acceptable items. To convey uncertainty in item features, especially ambiguous and partial item descriptions, as well as subjective user comments on such items, fuzzy sets can be employed. Fuzzy set theory is used to uncover user preferences and build item representations in recommendation systems [10], [11]. A number of fuzzy tree-based recommender systems have been developed for e-commerce [12], B2B electronic services [13], and e-learning systems [13] due to the fact that product information is often presented in the form of tree-structured content information and user preferences are vague and fuzzy [22].

Fuzzy network, fuzzy clustering, and fuzzy Bayesian methods have all been used in model-based CF recommender systems [5]. Adaptive neuro-fuzzy inference system (ANFIS) is used to extract fuzzy rules from sparse CF data and anticipate user preferences, particularly for multi-criteria CF (Nilashi et al., 2014). For recommender systems, [15] adopted a combined ANFIS with a hybrid of self-organizing map (SOM) based on multiple fuzzy-based distance measurements and similarity metrics.

Fuzzy set theory is utilized to characterize the uncertainty in consumer preferences in memory-based CF recommender systems [15]. These strategies can increase accuracy in specific areas by matching users interests with the service supplied and reducing the natural noise of uncertainty [16]. Fuzzy relationships were used to describe user preferences and similarities in order to recommend one-and-only items for personalized e-government by [17]. Fuzzy intuitionistic recommender systems were utilized by [18] to improve clinical medicine diagnoses. A strategy developed by [19] to handle dynamic user preferences in rapidly changing huge data, employing fuzzy relationships to gauge user interest consistency, has been described.

As a result, fuzzy approaches are well-suited to handling ambiguous user preference descriptions, knowledge representation, and gradual accumulation of user preference profiles. Fuzzy neural networks, as well as fuzzy profiling and fuzzy relationships, will be used to improve the performance of recommender systems in the future [5].

5.4.2 Deep Neural Networks in Recommender Systems

Because the purpose of recommendation is to rate rather than classify items, neural networks are rarely used in recommender systems. On the contrary, deep learning in the disciplines of natural language processing, speech recognition, and computer vision has achieved considerable progress [20]. There has been an increase in the amount of data available (e.g., user-generated comments or visual photographs of things), which necessitated the creation of deep learning-based recommender systems [21].

Factorization machines use a multi-layer perceptron to aid with feature engineering. Non-linear and linear models can be combined into a single recommendation framework. For non-linear relationships between users and items, He et al. (2017) developed neural collaborative filtering (NCF) in conjunction with matrix factorization. Recommendation systems frequently use NCF, which is based on multi-layer perceptrons, as a general model for user interactions. Other variants of deep neural

[19] Q. Zhang, D. Wu, G. Zhang, and J. Lu, "Fuzzy user-interest drift detection based recommender systems," in *2016 IEEE International Conference on Fuzzy Systems (FUZZ-IEEE)*, 2016, pp. 1274–1281. doi: 10.1109/FUZZ-IEEE.2016.7737835.

[20] N. G. Polson and V. O. Sokolov, "Deep Learning - Nature Review," *Nature*, vol. 521, no. 7553, 2018.

[21] S. Zhang, L. Yao, A. Sun, and Y. Tay, "Deep learning based recommender system: A survey and new perspectives," *ACM Computing Surveys*, vol. 52, no. 1, 2019, doi: 10.1145/3285029.

[22] H. Tahmasebi, R. Ravanmehr, and R. Mohamadrezaei, "Social movie recommender system based on deep autoencoder network using Twitter data," *Neural Computing and Applications*, vol. 33, no. 5, 2021, doi: 10.1007/s00521-020-05085-1.

[23] M. He, Q. Meng, and S. Zhang, "Collaborative Additional Variational Autoencoder for Top-N Recommender Systems," *IEEE Access*, vol. 7, 2019, doi: 10.1109/ACCESS.2018.2890293.

[24] M. F. Aljunid and M. D. Huchaiah, "An efficient hybrid recommendation model based on collaborative filtering recommender systems," *CAAI Transactions on Intelligence Technology*, vol. 6, no. 4, 2021, doi: 10.1049/cit2.12048.

[25] S. Sedhain, A. K. Menony, S. Sannery, and L. Xie, "AutoRec: Autoencoders meet collaborative filtering," in *WWW 2015 Companion - Proceedings of the 24th International Conference on World Wide Web*, 2015. doi: 10.1145/2740908.2742726.

[26] D. Kim, C. Park, J. Oh, S. Lee, and H. Yu, "Convolutional matrix factorization for document context-aware recommendation," in *RecSys 2016 - Proceedings of the 10th ACM Conference on Recommender Systems*, 2016. doi: 10.1145/2959100.2959165.

[27] Q. Diao, M. Qiu, C. Y. Wu, A. J. Smola, J. Jiang, and C. Wang, "Jointly modeling aspects, ratings and sentiments for movie recommendation (JMARS)," in *Proceedings of the ACM SIGKDD International Conference on Knowledge Discovery and Data Mining*, 2014. doi: 10.1145/2623330.2623758.

[28] D. Kim, C. Park, J. Oh, S. Lee, and H. Yu, "Convolutional Matrix Factorization for Document Context-Aware Recommendation," in *Proceedings of the 10th ACM Conference on Recommender Systems*, in RecSys '16. New York, NY, USA: Association for Computing Machinery, 2016, pp. 233–240. doi: 10.1145/2959100.2959165.

[29] Q. Diao, M. Qiu, C.-Y. Wu, A. J. Smola, J. Jiang, and C. Wang, "Jointly Modeling Aspects, Ratings and Sentiments for Movie Recommendation (JMARS)," in *Proceedings of the 20th ACM SIGKDD International Conference on Knowledge Discovery and Data Mining*, in KDD '14. New York, NY, USA: Association for Computing Machinery, 2014, pp. 193–202. doi: 10.1145/2623330.2623758.

[30] C. Y. Wu, A. Ahmed, A. Beutel, A. J. Smola, and H. Jing, "Recurrent recommender networks," in *WSDM 2017 - Proceedings of the 10th ACM International Conference on Web Search and Data Mining*, 2017. doi: 10.1145/3018661.3018689.

[31] H. Dai, Y. Wang, R. Trivedi, and L. Song, "Recurrent Coevolutionary Feature Embedding Processes for Recommendation," *arXiv preprint arXiv*, 2016.

[32] X. He, Z. He, X. Du, and T. S. Chua, "Adversarial personalized ranking for recommendation," in *41st International ACM SIGIR Conference on Research and Development in Information Retrieval, SIGIR 2018*, NY, 2018, pp. 355–364. doi: 10.1145/3209978.3209981.

[33] J. Wang *et al.*, "IRGAN: A minimax game for unifying generative and discriminative information retrieval models," in *SIGIR 2017 - Proceedings of the 40th International ACM SIGIR Conference on Research and Development in Information Retrieval*, 2017. doi: 10.1145/3077136.3080786.

[34]   J. Wang *et al.*, "IRGAN: A Minimax Game for Unifying Generative and Discriminative Information Retrieval Models," in *Proceedings of the 40th International ACM SIGIR Conference on Research and Development in Information Retrieval*, in SIGIR '17. New York, NY, USA: Association for Computing Machinery, 2017, pp. 515–524. doi: 10.1145/3077136.3080786.

[35]   R. Yin, K. Li, G. Zhang, and J. Lu, "A deeper graph neural network for recommender systems," *Knowl Based Syst*, vol. 185, 2019, doi: 10.1016/j.knosys.2019.105020.

[36]   R. Ying, R. He, K. Chen, P. Eksombatchai, W. L. Hamilton, and J. Leskovec, "Graph convolutional neural networks for web-scale recommender systems," in *Proceedings of the ACM SIGKDD International Conference on Knowledge Discovery and Data Mining*, 2018. doi: 10.1145/3219819.3219890.

[37]   Y. Zhang, B. Cao, and D. Y. Yeung, "Multi-domain collaborative filtering," in *Proceedings of the 26th Conference on Uncertainty in Artificial Intelligence, UAI 2010*, 2010. Accessed: Apr. 04, 2023. [Online]. Available: https://doi.org/10.48550/arXiv.1203.3535

[38]   N. E. I. Karabadji, S. Beldjoudi, H. Seridi, S. Aridhi, and W. Dhifli, "Improving memory-based user collaborative filtering with evolutionary multi-objective optimization," *Expert Syst Appl*, vol. 98, 2018, doi: 10.1016/j.eswa.2018.01.015.

[39]   Y. Chen, X. Sun, D. Gong, Y. Zhang, J. Choi, and S. Klasky, "Personalized Search Inspired Fast Interactive Estimation of Distribution Algorithm and Its Application," *IEEE Transactions on Evolutionary Computation*, vol. 21, no. 4, 2017, doi: 10.1109/TEVC.2017.2657787.

[40]   C. Rana and S. K. Jain, "A study of the dynamic features of recommender systems," *Artif Intell Rev*, vol. 43, no. 1, 2015, doi: 10.1007/s10462-012-9359-6.

[41]   G. Adomavicius and Y. Kwon, "Multi-criteria recommender systems," in *Recommender Systems Handbook, Second Edition*, 2015, pp. 847–880. doi: 10.1007/978-1-4899-7637-6_25.

[42]   G. Adomavicius and A. Tuzhilin, "Toward the next generation of recommender systems: A survey of the state-of-the-art and possible extensions," *IEEE Transactions on Knowledge and Data Engineering*, vol. 17, no. 6. 2005. doi: 10.1109/TKDE.2005.99.

[43]   G. Adomavicius and A. Tuzhilin, "Toward the next generation of recommender systems: a survey of the state-of-the-art and possible extensions," *IEEE Trans Knowl Data Eng*, vol. 17, no. 6, pp. 734–749, 2005, doi: 10.1109/TKDE.2005.99.

[44]   H. Steck, L. Baltrunas, E. Elahi, D. Liang, Y. Raimond, and J. Basilico, "Deep Learning for Recommender Systems: A Netflix Case Study," *AI Mag*, vol. 42, no. 3, 2021, doi: 10.1609/aimag.v42i3.18140.

[45]   C. A. Gomez-Uribe and N. Hunt, "The netflix recommender system: Algorithms, business value, and innovation," *ACM Trans Manag Inf Syst*, vol. 6, no. 4, 2015, doi: 10.1145/2843948.

[46]   C. Alvino and J. Basilico, " Learning a Personalized Homepage.," 2015. In Netflix Tech Blog. http://techblog.netflix.com/2015/04/ learning-personalized-homepage.html (accessed May 03, 2022).

[47]   S. Lamkhede and S. Das, "Challenges in search on streaming services: Netflix case study," in *SIGIR 2019 - Proceedings of the 42nd International ACM SIGIR Conference on Research and Development in Information Retrieval*, 2019. doi: 10.1145/3331184.3331440.

[48]   K. Cho *et al.*, "Learning Phrase Representations using RNN Encoder–Decoder for Statistical Machine Translation," in *Proceedings of the 2014 Conference on Empirical Methods in Natural Language Processing (EMNLP)*, Doha, Qatar: Association for Computational Linguistics, Oct. 2014, pp. 1724–1734. doi: 10.3115/v1/D14-1179.

[49]   S. Hochreiter and J. Schmidhuber, "Long Short-Term Memory," *Neural Comput*, vol. 9, no. 8, pp. 1735–1780, 1997, doi: 10.1162/neco.1997.9.8.1735.

6 A Recommender System Based on TensorFlow Framework

Hukam Singh Rana and T P Singh

CONTENTS

6.1 INTRODUCTION

Recommender systems are a type of artificial intelligence algorithms used to predict what a user might want to buy or watch. They are used to recommend items based on the user's past behaviour. Netflix, Amazon, and Spotify use recommender systems to suggest new content for their users.

The development of the online recommender system is booming with the growth of data through online transactions. The massive increase in data availability has led to a higher demand for developing better recommendation systems. These systems

DOI: 10.1201/9781003319122-6

aim to predict what users might want or need given their past behaviour and preferences. It could be anything from products on e-commerce websites to recommended articles or videos on social media platforms.

One reason for this increased demand is that traditional methods used by businesses, such as focus groups and surveys, are no longer feasible when it comes to big data sets. A recommender system can help businesses use all the data they have acquired to identify patterns and trends that would otherwise be missed.(1, 2) In addition, personalization has become an essential factor in today's digital age, with users expecting a more tailored experience when using websites or apps. A well-functioning recommender system can provide this customized experience by predicting what each user might want or need based on their past behaviour and preferences. Netflix is the most well-known example of a recommender system. The company uses algorithms to predict which movies and TV shows its users might like based on their past watching habits.(3) If a user has watched many action movies, for example, Netflix may suggest that the user watch the latest Marvel movie.

Recommender systems can also be used to recommend products for online stores. Amazon uses them to suggest products that its customers might be interested in buying. It also uses them to recommend similar products when someone is looking at something they want to buy on the website.(4) It helps users find other things they may want while shopping on Amazon. There are many different recommendation models, but they can generally be categorized into three types: collaborative filtering, content-based recommender systems, and hybrid recommender systems. Each type of system has its advantages and disadvantages.

Collaborative filtering is the most common type of recommendation model.(5) It relies on users' past behaviours to recommend items they may be interested in. This method effectively recommends items that a user may not have known about or considered before. However, it can be less accurate if a user's past behaviour does not reflect their current interests accurately.

Content-based recommender systems use information about the recommended items to determine which other items a user might like.(6) This approach is more accurate than collaborative filtering, but it can be less efficient because it requires detailed knowledge about all the items in the system. Hybrid recommender systems combine aspects of both collaborative filtering and content-based recommenders to create a more effective system overall.(7)

Deep learning is a subset of machine learning concerned with algorithms that learn to represent data in multiple layers of abstraction, called deep nets.(8, 9) Deep nets are composed of many interconnected processing nodes or neurons that can learn to recognize patterns in data by adjusting the strengths of their connections. Deep learning networks have been successful in object recognition, natural language processing, and speech recognition because they can learn features at different levels of abstraction. Recently, deep learning is also applied to the recommender system. A deep learning-based recommender system (DLR) is a model that uses a neural network to learn the relationships between items in a dataset and user preferences.

Compared with traditional methods, DLR has several advantages:

1) It can learn complex patterns automatically by using large-scale data.
2) It can handle both positive and negative feedback data effectively.
3) It performs well even when the number of items or users is enormous.
4) It is more accurate than traditional models for cold-start recommendations (i.e., recommendations for new users or items).

However, some challenges are associated with implementing deep learning-based recommender systems. One challenge is the scale of data. For a deep learning-based recommendation system to learn user preferences effectively, it must have access to lots of data on which to train its algorithms. The data set can be huge and needs to be processed quickly to return results in real-time. Another challenge is configuring the network architecture correctly; getting it wrong can lead to inaccurate recommendations or even incorrect predictions. Finally, debugging deep learning models can be tricky and time-consuming; any errors must be tracked down and corrected before the system will produce accurate results.

TensorFlow Recommenders (TFRS) is an open-source library that uses deep learning for recommendations. Google developed it, and it is based on the TensorFlow machine learning platform.(10) TFRS provides an easy-to-use solution for creating scalable deep learning-based recommendation systems quickly and easily. It includes all of the tools necessary for training models and making predictions using real-world data sets. TensorFlow Recommenders also makes it easy to incorporate feedback data into your models so that you can get the best possible recommendations for your users.

In this chapter, you will learn to build a recommender system based on deep learning. This chapter aims to provide all the nitty-gritty details to implement a recommender system. Section 6.3 discusses the advantages of TensorFlow and TFRS in building a recommender system. A detailed description of the data selection, loading, model implementation, and training is provided in Section 6.4. Finally, the chapter concludes with Section 6.5.

If you want to be able to follow the code examples given in this chapter, you will need to have a basic understanding of the Python programming language. Python is a versatile language used for scripting, data analysis, web development, and more. If you are not familiar with Python yet, I recommend checking out some of the books on the Python programming language.(11, 12)

6.2 RECOMMENDER SYSTEM

A recommendation system is a great way to filter through a corpus of items or documents to find the best candidates for your needs. By giving it a query (context) and filter, it can quickly narrow down the options to a shortlist of perfect candidates for what you need. The first example will use books as the item being recommended. If someone wants to read a mystery novel, they might go to their local library and search for "mystery novels" in the card catalogue or on the computer. However, if they only know what genre they want but not any specific titles, it becomes more difficult to find something that matches their interests. A recommendation system could help by giving them several options based on their interests within the mystery genre instead of just one title that might not be exactly what they are looking for.

Another scenario where using a recommendation system can come in handy is when someone needs suggestions for new music to listen to. They might have heard about some new artists or bands but do not know any of their songs yet. Using a music recommendation program, they could get introduced to new songs and bands without spending hours browsing different websites or streaming services trying to find something that catches their attention.

In both cases, using a well-designed recommender system provides users with relevant items without wasting time searching through everything themselves which can be especially helpful when there are many items in question or when there is not enough time available. In big data, it is more important than ever to have efficient ways of filtering through large amounts of information to find what a user needs. Researchers believe that practical recommender systems have two phases: retrieval and ranking.(13, 14) However, a third phase, re-ranking or optimization, is often necessary to get the most accurate results. A diagram explaining the phases of recommender system development is shown in Figure 6.1.

The retrieval phase involves generating a list of all potential candidates for the recommended item. This can be done in many different ways, but typically it involves querying massive data for relevant information based on the user history and context. The ranking phase then takes this giant list and ranks each candidate according to some criterion—such as how similar they are to the recommended item or how popular they are or on the user context. The re-ranking or optimization phase then looks at this ranked list and tries to find the best possible match for the recommended item based on whatever criteria were used in Phase 2. This process may involve tweaking specific parameters or running multiple iterations until an optimal result is found.

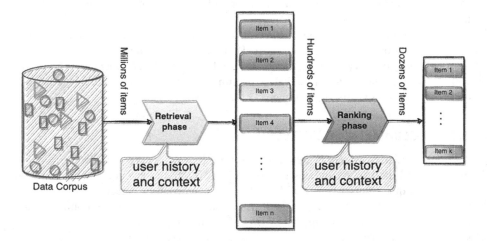

FIGURE 6.1   Phases of recommender systems.

While this three-phase approach may seem like it takes more time and effort upfront, it often leads to much better recommendations than if only one phase was used.

6.3 WHY TO USE TENSORFLOW AND TFRS

TensorFlow is an open-source software library for data analysis and machine learning. The Google Brain Team developed it in 2015. TensorFlow has many advantages over other machine learning libraries. It is very flexible and can be used on various devices from smartphones to supercomputers. TensorFlow is a powerful open-source software library for data analysis and machine learning. It has become increasingly popular due to its ease of use and flexibility. TensorFlow offers many features that are useful for creating recommender systems, including the ability to train models on large amounts of data and export models for deployment in production environments.

TFRS is an open-source TensorFlow package that makes building, evaluating, and serving sophisticated recommender models easy. TFRS was created by Google engineers as a way to make it easier for developers to build recommender systems using TensorFlow. TFRS is based on TensorFlow 2.x and Keras, which makes it instantly familiar and user-friendly. One advantage of using TFRS for building recommender systems is that users can quickly scale up their system by adding more hardware resources. This is vital because most real-world datasets are large enough that they cannot fit into memory on a single machine. TensorFlow allows users to distribute their workload across multiple machines (or even clusters) so that you can continue training your model even if your dataset exceeds the capacity of a single machine. Another advantage of using TensorFlow is its support for exporting models into production environments. Once a user has trained a model with TensorFlow, the user can deploy it in any environment where Python is supported (including web applications). It means that once a user model has been trained, it can be used by anyone who has access to the user's application without requiring any additional installation steps or configuration changes.

6.4 IMPLEMENTATION OF RECOMMENDER SYSTEM

The implementation of a recommender system in TFRS usually has the following steps:

1) Steps to install TensorFlow and TFRS
2) Dataset selection for recommender systems
3) Load and explore data in TFRS
4) Data pre-processing
5) Features embedding
6) Recommender model implementation

   (a) Implementation and training of the retrieval model
   (b) Implementation, training, and evaluation of the ranking model

6.4.1 INSTALL TFRS

TFRS can be installed on any system that has Python 3.4+ installed using the pip command in Figure 6.2.

```
1  pip install -q tensorflow-recommenders
2  pip install -q --upgrade tensorflow-datasets
```

FIGURE 6.2   TFRS installation; code snippet.

6.4.2 DATASET SELECTION FOR RECOMMENDER SYSTEMS

Dataset is a critical component of a recommender system. The quality and size of the dataset will affect the accuracy of the recommendations produced by the system. There are several factors to consider when selecting a dataset for use in a recommender system.

The first consideration is the type of data that is being used. The dataset should be representative of what is being recommended. Another consideration is how recent the data is. Datasets that are updated frequently will produce more accurate recommendations than those not updated often.

The size of the dataset also impacts its usefulness in building a recommender system. A large enough dataset will allow more sophisticated algorithms to be employed, which results in better recommendations. However, too large a set can also lead to overfitting, which results in inaccurate predictions. It is essential to strike a balance between these two extremes.

Finally, another important factor when selecting datasets for recommendation systems is how clean and well-organized it is. A messy or incomplete dataset could lead to inaccurate results or crashes during training or testing phases.

TensorFlow provides several public datasets available online that can be used for training and testing recommender systems (e.g., MovieLens, Netflix Prize).

6.4.3 LOAD AND EXPLORE DATA IN **TFRS**

The MovieLens dataset is a collection of user ratings for movies from movielens.org. (15) The dataset contains over 18,000 ratings for over 1,300 movies. It can train and evaluate machine learning models for predicting movie ratings.

The MovieLens dataset has developed several machine learning models for predicting movie ratings. One such model is the linear regression model, which uses a set of input features to predict the rating given to a movie by a user. This model's most crucial input feature is the user's age; older users are more likely to give higher ratings than younger users. Other essential features include whether or not the user has rated that particular movie before and how many times they have rated it (the "frequency"). The MovieLens dataset can also evaluate machine learning models by comparing their predictions against actual data from movielens.org. It can help a user determine which models are best at predicting movie ratings and how accurate they are relative to each other.

TensorFlow provides five versions of the MovieLens dataset: "25M", "latest-small", "100K", "1M", and "20M". The 25M, latest-small, and 20M datasets contain only movie and rating data. The 1M and 100K datasets include demographic data in addition to movie and rating information. In order to view only the movies data in each type of dataset, users must add a suffix that contains "-movies" (e.g., "25M-movies") or they may also view the ratings data for the 1M and 100K datasets by including a suffix that contains "-ratings" (e.g., "25M-ratings"). The features of MovieLens are as follows.

The -movie suffix dataset features are *movie_id, movie_title*, and *movie_genres*. The *movie_id* column is a unique identifier for each movie. The *movie_title* column contains the title of the movie. The *movie_genres* column contains a list of genres that the movie belongs to. The rating suffix dataset is an excellent resource for anyone looking to study movie ratings. It includes the following features:

- *movie_id:* This is the unique identifier for each movie.
- *movie_title:* The title of the movie.
- *movie_genres:* The genres of the movie.
- *user_id:* The unique identifier for each user who rated the movie.
- *user_rating:* The rating given by the user, on a scale from 1 to 5 stars.
- *timestamp:* The timestamp at which the rating was given

Now that TensorFlow and TFRS are installed, it is time to load the MovieLens dataset using the code snippet in Figure 6.3. However, before that, you need to load all necessary Python libraries.

It is important to remember that not everything needs to be loaded into memory at once when working with large datasets! There are several ways to reduce the size of a dataset while still allowing for meaningful analysis. Using the *take()* function, you can avoid loading the entire data set into memory at once, which can be costly in terms of time and resources. The *take()* function allows you to load only a portion of the data set into memory, which can help to improve performance and reduce resource usage (Figures 6.4 and 6.5).

```
1  import os
2  import pprint
3  import tempfile
4  import pandas as pd
5  from typing import Dict, Textimport numpy as np
6  import tensorflow as tf
7  import tensorflow_datasets as tfds
```

FIGURE 6.3 Loading all necessary Python library; code snippet.

```
1  # Ratings data.
2  ratings = tfds.load("movie_lens/100k-ratings", split="train")
3  # Features of all the available movies.
4  movies = tfds.load("movie_lens/100k-movies", split="train")##
      Print Total number of ratings
5  print("Total number of ratings are: ",len(ratings))
6  ## Print total number of rated movies
7  print("Total number of rated movies are: ",len(movies))
```

FIGURE 6.4 Load the dataset using tensorflow_datasets tfdf.load wraps the user rating data as dictionary in rating and movies objects; code snippet.

```
1  ## Import the Pandas library to create dataframe
2  import pandas as pd
3  ## Create dataframe to hold the rating data and movie data
4  ratingdf=pd.DataFrame()
5  moviedf=pd.DataFrame()
6  ##Loading the entire data in memory is a costly operation so ##
      load it with the help of the take() function
7  for rating in ratings.take(100).as_numpy_iterator():
8    ratingdf=ratingdf.append(rating,ignore_index=True)
9  for movie in movies.take(100).as_numpy_iterator():
10   moviedf=moviedf.append(movie,ignore_index=True)
11 ##Display Rating Data
12 display(ratingdf.head())
13 ##Display Movie Data
14 display(moviedf.head())
```

FIGURE 6.5 The first few rows of the data, code snippet.

6.4.4 DATA PREPROCESSING

Data preprocessing is an essential step in the development of a recommender system. It is used to clean and prepare the data to be used effectively to generate recommendations. There are several steps in data preprocessing.

6.4.4.1 Data Cleaning

This involves removing any inaccurate or incomplete data from the dataset. It ensures that only accurate and complete information is used to generate recommendations.

TensorFlow stores the data in *tensorflow_dataset* after cleaning. So the MovieLens dataset is already clean and ready to use.

6.4.4.2 Feature Extraction

To generate meaningful recommendations, the dataset must be analyzed, and features (characteristics) must be extracted (Figure 6.6). These features can then be used as input for recommendation algorithms. This process can be done manually by human experts. However, it is often more efficient and accurate to automatically use machine learning algorithms to identify which features are most predictive of user preferences. *user_id*, *movie_id*, *movie_title*, *user_rating*, and *timestamp* are the important features for movie recommendations.(16)

6.4.4.3 Split the Data

Once the data cleaning and feature extraction steps are completed on the entire dataset, it is time to split it into training and validation (Figure 6.7). The purpose of splitting up the dataset like this is to ensure that the model is not overfitted on the training set.

```
1  ## Feature selection
2  # Ratings data.
3  ratings = tfds.load("movielens/100k-ratings", split="train")
4  # Features of all the available movies.
5  movies = tfds.load("movielens/100k-movies", split="train")
6  ratings = ratings.map(lambda x: {
7      "movie_title": x["movie_title"],
8      "user_id": x["user_id"],
9      "timestamp": x["timestamp"],
10 })
11 movies = movies.map(lambda x: x["movie_title"])
```

FIGURE 6.6 Feature selection; code snippet.

```
1  #Split dataset randomly (80% for train and 20% for test) is a #
       popular technique in machine learning.
2  tf.random.set_seed(42)
3  ratings_shuffled = ratings.shuffle(100_000, seed=42,
       reshuffle_each_iteration=False)ratings_train = ratings_shuffled
       .take(80_000)
4  rating_test = ratings_shuffled.skip(80_000).take(20_000)
```

FIGURE 6.7 Splitting data in train and test datasets; code snippet.

Overfitting occurs when a model becomes too specialized on one particular dataset and does not generalize well to other datasets. Using a validation set, you can catch overfitting before it causes problems with your final model. Data split would most likely be done by time in an industrial recommender system. The data up to time T would be used to predict interactions after T. This is because the past can better predict the future in many cases than the present can. For example, if someone has always ordered a specific type of coffee in the past, they will likely continue to do so in the future. Shuffling the dataset elements before splitting them into training and validation sets can help prevent overfitting. When the dataset is split randomly, different parts of the data are used to train and evaluate the model, which helps avoid bias favouring specific data points.

Additionally, shuffling ensures that each data point is used for both training and validation equally, which further prevents overfitting.

6.4.5 FEATURES EMBEDDING

Looking at the first few rows of the training data, we can see that our dataset contains *movie_id, user_id, ratingData* as categorical features, *movie_title* as text feature, and *timestamp* as a numerical feature (Figure 6.1).

These features are different types and in different formats. Recommender system algorithms can process only numerical features on the same scale to give the good recommendation, so there is a requirement for a process that can transform the raw features into standard numerical features. This process is called feature engineering.(17, 18)

Feature engineering is a method for transforming raw data into a more suitable form for machine learning algorithms. In many cases, this involves creating new features that were not present in the original data set. Feature engineering is a critical step in many machine learning workflows. It also helps remove any bias or variability in the dataset due to factors such as sampling bias or measurement error. Several feature engineering techniques can be applied to the different features like numerical, categorical, and text features.

6.4.5.1 Numerical Features

One common preprocessing step for numerical features is standardizing them. In feature standardization, subtract the minimum and divide by the (maximum value-minimum) value for each feature. This helps ensure that all features are on a similar scale to be more easily compared and combined later in the modelling process. Another common preprocessing step is discretization. Discretization is the process of

TABLE 6.1
Features of the training dataset

movie_id	ratingData movie_title	timestamp	user_id	user_rating
b'357'	b'One Flew Over the Cuckoo's Nest (1975)'	879024327	b'138'	4
b'709'	b'Strictly Ballroom (1992)'	875654590	b'92'	2
b'412'	b'Very Brady Sequel, A (1996)'	882075110	b'301'	4
b'56'	b'Pulp Fiction (1994)'	883326919	b'60'	4
b'895'	b'Scream 2 (1997)'	891409199	b'197'	3

dividing a continuous feature into a series of discrete values. It can improve performance when working with large data sets or to simplify calculations. In many cases, discretization can also improve the accuracy of results. There are several different methods for discretizing data, each with advantages and disadvantages. Choosing the appropriate method for the dataset is critical for obtaining accurate results.

6.4.5.2 Categorical Features

Another common feature is categorical data, which consists of discrete values rather than continuous ones like numerical data. TCategorical data is a type of data that is represented as sparse tensors. Sparse tensors are a particular array type with more zero entries than non-zero ones.

Traditional methods for representing and manipulating sparse vectors can be inefficient when applied to large datasets. MovieLens 100K dataset contains 1,000 unique *movies_id*. In order to train a recommender system, each *movie_id* can be represented as a 1,000 dimensional sparse vector. Unfortunately, this model is very computationally expensive.

Recently, embeddings have emerged as an effective solution to translate large sparse vectors into a lower-dimensional space that preserves semantic relationships.

Embeddings are generated by training a neural network on a large dataset (Figure 6.8). The input vector x can be represented as $y = f(x)$, where y is the low-dimensional representation of x and f is some nonlinear function. The advantage of using embeddings is that much smaller representations can be used to encode the same information as the original vector x. Embeddings can be implemented in a neural network in several ways. One common approach is to use an embedding layer, which inputs an arbitrary number of feature vectors and outputs a smaller number of feature vectors (Figure 6.9). These output vectors

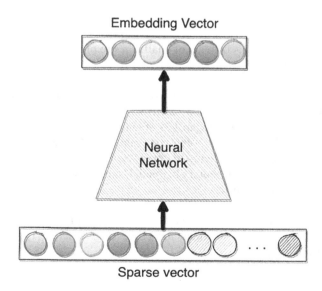

FIGURE 6.8 Embedding of a sparse vector.

```
1  timestamps = np.concatenate(list(ratings.map(lambda x: x["
       timestamp"]).batch(100)))
2  ## To Normalize the time stamp
3  max_timestamp = timestamps.max()
4  min_timestamp = timestamps.min()
5  ## Buckets bounderies for for bucketization
6  timestamp_buckets = np.linspace(
7      min_timestamp, max_timestamp, num=1000,
8  )##Total categories of the movie_title
9  unique_movie_titles = np.unique(np.concatenate(list(movies.batch
       (1000))))
10 ##Total categories of the movie_title
11 unique_user_ids = np.unique(np.concatenate(list(ratings.batch(1
       _000).map(
12     lambda x: x["user_id"]))))
```

FIGURE 6.9   Prerequisite for features engineering; code snippet.

are usually much closer together than the input vectors were, meaning that they have been compressed into a lower-dimensional space.

6.4.5.3   Text Features

Textual information poses its own set of challenges in preprocessing because words have different lengths and frequencies, which affects how they are treated during modelling. A popular technique for dealing with text inputs is tokenization, which splits text strings into individual tokens (words). After tokenization has been performed, another functional operation called stemming can be applied. Stemming reduces words to their root form, regardless of tense or plurality. So "running" would become "run" after being applied—the last primary task when working with text inputs is lemmatization. After lemmatization, each token needs to be assigned a number with the help of the vocabulary learned. Using a neural network, embeddings for specific words can be learned.

The Keras processing layer is a high-level neural networks application programming interface (API) written in Python and capable of running on top of TensorFlow. (19) It provides end-to-end solutions for processing different types of features (Figures 6.10 and 6.11).

```
1
2   class UserFeaturesEmbedding(tf.keras.Model):  def __init__(self):
3       super().__init__()
4       ## Categorical Feature user_id processing
5       self.userid_embedding = tf.keras.Sequential([
6           ## Finds a unique number for every user_id
7           tf.keras.layers.StringLookup(
8               vocabulary=unique_user_ids, mask_token=None),
9           ##Change the number to an embeded vector of dimention 32
10          tf.keras.layers.Embedding(len(unique_user_ids) + 1, 32),
11      ])
12      self.timestamp_embedding = tf.keras.Sequential([
13          ##Divide the numarical feature into buckets
14          tf.keras.layers.Discretization(timestamp_buckets.tolist())
            ,
15          ##Change the number to an embeddeding vector
16          tf.keras.layers.Embedding(len(timestamp_buckets) + 1, 32),
17      ])
18      ## time stamp normalization
19      self.normalized_timestamp = tf.keras.layers.Normalization(
20          axis=None
21      )
22      self.normalized_timestamp.adapt(timestamps)  def call(self,
            inputs):
23      ## Concatenate the embedding of all user features
24      return tf.concat([
25          self.userid_embedding(inputs["user_id"]),
26          self.timestamp_embedding(inputs["timestamp"]),
27          tf.reshape(self.normalized_timestamp(inputs["timestamp"]),
                (-1, 1)),
28      ], axis=1)
```

FIGURE 6.10 User's ratings data has two features: *user_id* (categorical feature) and *time-stamp* (numerical feature); code snippet.

```
1   class MovieFeaturesEmbedding(tf.keras.Model):
2   ## Finds two different embeddings of movie_title and
3   ##concatenate both of them into a single vector
4     def __init__(self):
5       super().__init__()     max_tokens = 15_000
6       ## movie_title is considered as categorical feature
7       self.movie_title_embedding = tf.keras.Sequential([
8         ## Finds a unique number for every user_id
9         tf.keras.layers.StringLookup(
10            vocabulary=unique_movie_titles,mask_token=None),
11            ##Change the number to an embeddeding vector
12          tf.keras.layers.Embedding(len(unique_movie_titles) + 1, 32)
13        ])
14      ## movie_title is considered as text feature
15      ## For learning text embedding it apply following
            transformations
16      ##1. divide the movie title into the tokens and learn the
            vocabulary
17      ## Change each token into a number with the help of the
            vocabulary
18      self.movie_title_vectorizer = tf.keras.layers.
            TextVectorization(
19          max_tokens=max_tokens)     self.movie_title_text_embedding
                = tf.keras.Sequential([
20          self.movie_title_vectorizer,
21          tf.keras.layers.Embedding(max_tokens, 32, mask_zero=True),
22          tf.keras.layers.GlobalAveragePooling1D(),
23        ])     self.movie_title_vectorizer.adapt(movies)     def call(self
            , titles):
24      return tf.concat([
25          self.movie_title_embedding(titles),
26          self.movie_title_text_embedding(titles),
27        ], axis=1)
```

FIGURE 6.11 *movie_title* is only feature of movies dataset; code snippet.

6.4.6   Recommender Model Implementation

The most common approach to designing a recommender system is the two-phase model, which consists of:

Phase 1: Retrieval—This phase involves extracting information about items from various data sources such as databases or documents.

Phase 2: Ranking—This phase takes the retrieved information about items and ranks them according to how well they match the needs expressed by the user.

6.4.6.1   Implementation and Training of the Retrieval Model

A popular approach to building a retrieval system is a two-tower system. This approach uses two towers: a movies tower and a user's tower.(20) The movies tower learns the embedding of all movies that are being recommended. In contrast, the user tower learns the embedding of all the users who have been recommended items from the movie tower. This two-phase approach allows for more personalized recommendations by considering what users have watched in the past and what others have watched about those same movies. When a user is looking for something to watch, the two-tower model calculates the retrieval score by comparing a user embedding with every movie embedding and retrieving the k number of movies corresponding to the top k retrieval score.

The architecture of the two-tower retrieval system is illustrated in Figures 6.12–6.16.

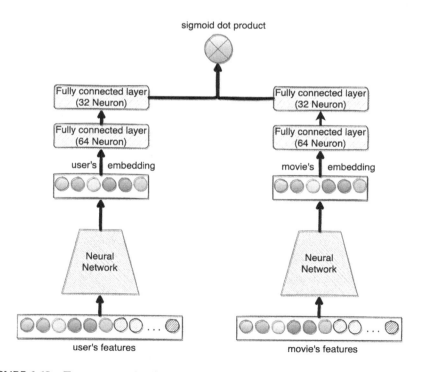

FIGURE 6.12   Two tower retrieval model.

```
1  class UserModel(tf.keras.Model):
2    """Model for encoding user """  def __init__(self, layer_sizes):
3
4      super().__init__()    # Generate the users embedding from
          UserFeatures model
5      self.embedding_model = UserFeaturesEmbedding()    # To
          construct deep model add some fully Connected layes
6      self.dense_layers = tf.keras.Sequential()
7      for layer_size in layer_sizes[:-1]:
8        self.dense_layers.add(tf.keras.layers.Dense(layer_size,
            activation="relu"))    # No activation function in the
            last layer.
9      for layer_size in layer_sizes[-1:]:
10        self.dense_layers.add(tf.keras.layers.Dense(layer_size))
          def call(self, inputs):
11      feature_embedding = self.embedding_model(inputs)
12      return self.dense_layers(feature_embedding)
```

FIGURE 6.13   User tower model implementation; code snippet.

```
1  class MovieModel(tf.keras.Model):
2    """Model to find the  movies encodeing.""" def __init__(self,
        layer_sizes):
3
4      super().__init__()    # Generate the users embedding from
          UserFeatures model
5      self.embedding_model = MovieFeaturesEmbedding()    # To
          construct deep model add some fully Connected layes
6      self.dense_layers = tf.keras.Sequential()
7      for layer_size in layer_sizes[:-1]:
8        self.dense_layers.add(tf.keras.layers.Dense(layer_size,
            activation="relu"))    # No activation function in the
            last layer.
9      for layer_size in layer_sizes[-1:]:
10        self.dense_layers.add(tf.keras.layers.Dense(layer_size))
          def call(self, inputs):
11      feature_embedding = self.embedding_model(inputs)
12      return self.dense_layers(feature_embedding)
```

FIGURE 6.14   Movie tower implementation; code snippet.

```
1  class Recommender_RetrivalModel(tfrs.models.Model): def __init__(
       self, layer_sizes):
2      super().__init__()
3      ## User Tower model
4      self.query_model = UserModel(layer_sizes)
5      ##Movie Tower model
6      self.candidate_model = MovieModel(layer_sizes)
7      ## Metric for the retrieval task
8      self.task = tfrs.tasks.Retrieval(
9          metrics=tfrs.metrics.FactorizedTopK(
10             candidates=movies.batch(128).map(self.candidate_model)
                   ,
11         ),
12     )  def compute_loss(self, features, training=False):
13     # We only pass the user id and timestamp features into the
           user model to compute the loss
14     query_embeddings = self.query_model({
15         "user_id": features["user_id"],
16         "timestamp": features["timestamp"],
17     })
18     movie_embeddings = self.candidate_model(features["movie_title
           "])
19 ## Retrieval task to calculate the score
20 ## by compairing a user embedding with every movie embedding
21     return self.task(
22         query_embeddings, movie_embeddings, compute_metrics=not
               training)
```

FIGURE 6.15 Recommender retrieval model. We can train the model once it has been implemented; code snippet.

6.4.6.2 Implementation, Training, and Evaluation of the Ranking Model

The ranking stage is an essential part of the recommendation process. It fine-tunes the retrieved recommendations based on the output of the retrieval model. Its task is

```
 1   ##make the batches of the data and cache its elements for ##better
         performance
 2   ratings_cached_train = ratings_train.shuffle(100_000).batch(2048)
 3   ratings_cached_test = rating_test.batch(4096).cache()
 4   num_epochs=100
 5   ##Make the model
 6   model = Recommender_RetrivalModel([64, 32])
 7   model.compile(optimizer=tf.keras.optimizers.Adagrad(0.1))
 8   ##Train the model
 9   history = model.fit(
10       ratings_cached_train,
11       validation_data=ratings_cached_test,
12       validation_freq=5,
13       epochs=num_epochs,
14       verbose=0)
15   ##Print the model accuracy
16   accuracy = history.history["val_factorized_top_k/
         top_100_categorical_accuracy"][-1]
17   print(f"Top-100 accuracy: {accuracy:.2f}.")
```

FIGURE 6.16   Model training; code snippet.

to narrow down the set of items the user may be interested in into a shortlist of likely candidates.

Many factors go into determining which items are included in this shortlist. The ranking stage considers things like how often each item has been recommended, how recently it was recommended, and how popular it is among other users. The ranking model has a simple architecture compared to the retrieval model. The ranking model takes the *user_id* and *movie_title* as input. First, it learns the embeddings of *user_id* and *movie_title*. In order to rank, these embeddings are fed into a multi-layer perceptron that minimizes the difference between predicted and actual rankings. the architecture of the ranking model is illustrated in Figure 6.17.

The implementation of ranking model is shown in Figure 6.18.

The implementation of ranking model using TFRS is shown in Figure 6.19.(21)

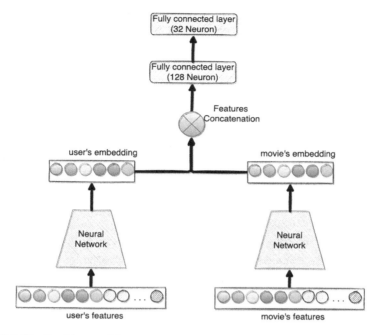

FIGURE 6.17 Ranking model.

```
1  ratings = ratings.map(lambda x: {
2      "movie_title": x["movie_title"],
3      "user_id": x["user_id"],
4      "user_rating": x["user_rating"]
5  })
6  tf.random.set_seed(42)
7  rating_shuffled = ratings.shuffle(100_000, seed=42,
       reshuffle_each_iteration=False)ranking_train = rating_shuffled.
       take(80_000)
8  ranking_test = rating_shuffled.skip(80_000).take(20_000)
9  ##Find the unique movie title and unique users to learn the
       embedding.
10 movie_titles = ratings.batch(1_000_000).map(lambda x: x["
       movie_title"])
11 user_ids = ratings.batch(1_000_000).map(lambda x: x["user_id"])
       unique_movie_titles = np.unique(np.concatenate(list(
       movie_titles)))
12 unique_user_ids = np.unique(np.concatenate(list(user_ids)))
```

FIGURE 6.18 Data preparation; code snippet.

```
1   class Recommender_RankingModel(tf.keras.Model):  def __init__(self
    ):
2     super().__init__()
3     embedding_dimension = 32    # embeddings for users.
4     self.user_embeddings = tf.keras.Sequential([
5       # Assign a unique number to each user
6       tf.keras.layers.StringLookup(
7         vocabulary=unique_user_ids, mask_token=None),
8         #Convert the number to an embedding
9       tf.keras.layers.Embedding(len(unique_user_ids) + 1,
          embedding_dimension)
10    ])    # find the embeddings for movies.
11    self.movie_embeddings = tf.keras.Sequential([
12      # Assign a unique number to each movie
13      tf.keras.layers.StringLookup(
14        vocabulary=unique_movie_titles, mask_token=None),
15        #Convert the number to an embedding
16      tf.keras.layers.Embedding(len(unique_movie_titles) + 1,
          embedding_dimension)
17    ])    # multi layer perceptron model regression model
18    # To predict the rank of a movies    self.ratings = tf.keras.
        Sequential([
19
20      tf.keras.layers.Dense(256, activation="relu"),
21      tf.keras.layers.Dense(64, activation="relu"),
22
23      tf.keras.layers.Dense(1)
24    ])   def call(self, inputs):    user_id, movie_title = inputs
        user_embedding = self.user_embeddings(user_id)
25    movie_embedding = self.movie_embeddings(movie_title)    return
          self.ratings(tf.concat([user_embedding, movie_embedding],
          axis=1))
```

FIGURE 6.19 Ranking model for recommender; code snippet.

```
1  class MovielensModel_Ranking(tfrs.models.Model):  def __init__(
      self):
2     super().__init__()
3     self.ranking_model: tf.keras.Model = Recommender_RankingModel
          ()      #Define the metric to learn the rank for the
          regression model
4     self.task: tf.keras.layers.Layer = tfrs.tasks.Ranking(
5        loss = tf.keras.losses.MeanSquaredError(),
6        metrics=[tf.keras.metrics.RootMeanSquaredError()]
7     )  def call(self, features):
8     return self.ranking_model(
9        (features["user_id"], features["movie_title"]))  def
             compute_loss(self, features, training=False):
10    labels = features.pop("user_rating")    rating_predictions =
          self(features)      return self.task(labels=labels,
          predictions=rating_predictions)
```

FIGURE 6.20 Ranking model; code snippet.

```
1  # Divide the data into the batches and
2  # cache the elements for better performance
3  cached_train = ranking_train.shuffle(100_000).batch(8192).cache()
4  cached_test = ranking_test.batch(4096).cache()
5  #Create Model
6  model = MovielensModel_Ranking()
7  model.compile(optimizer=tf.keras.optimizers.Adagrad(learning_rate
      =0.1))
8  # Divide the data into the batches and
9  # cache the elements for better performance
10 cached_train = ranking_train.shuffle(100_000).batch(8192).cache()
11 cached_test = ranking_test.batch(4096).cache()#Model training
12 model.fit(cached_train, epochs=r)#Model Evaluation
13 model.evaluate(cached_test, return_dict=True)
```

FIGURE 6.21 Model training and evaluation; code snippet.

6.5 CONCLUSION

This chapter has focused on implementing a deep learning network-based recommender system using TensorFlow and TFRS.

TFRS is an excellent library built on top of TensorFlow and makes it easy to build recommender systems. TFRS provides all the functionality you need to train and deploy your recommenders, including preprocessing utilities, data loading mechanisms, model implementation options, evaluation metrics, training algorithms, and more.

In Section 6.4, we provided details on building a recommender system using TFRS. We explored the details of selecting the dataset recommender system. We also provided a detailed exploration of the MovieLens dataset and versions and the features of each version. Section 6.4.3 explored how to load and analyze data in TFRS. We discussed different preprocessing techniques like data cleaning and feature extraction in Section 6.4.4. There are many methods for feature engineering, but the most crucial part is choosing the suitable method for the problem at hand. In Section 6.4.5, we looked at some of the most popular methods, but many more options are out there. The two-phase recommender system implementations details are outlined in Section 6.4.6. It is a reliable and efficient way to recommend items to users.

Choosing the right recommended model is a complex task limited by problem-specific constraints. However, we hope that by taking advantage of these techniques discussed in this chapter, the reader will be able to implement much more complex recommender systems with ease.

REFERENCES

[1]   Dietmar Jannach, Markus Zanker, Alexander Felfernig, and Gerhard Friedrich. *Recommender systems: An introduction*. Cambridge University Press, 2010.

[2]   Francesco Ricci, Lior Rokach, and Bracha Shapira. Recommender systems: Introduction and challenges. In *Recommender systems handbook*, 2015.

[3]   Xavier Amatriain and Justin Basilico. Recommender systems in industry: A Netflix case study. In *Recommender systems handbook*, 2015.

[4]   Brent Smith and Greg Linden. Two decades of recommender systems at Amazon. com. *IEEE Internet Computing*, 21(3):12–18, 2017.

[5]   Gediminas Adomavicius and Alexander Tuzhilin. Toward the next generation of recommender systems: A survey of the state-of-the-art and possible extensions. *IEEE Transactions on Knowledge and Data Engineering*, 17(6):734–749, 2005.

[6]   Pasquale Lops, Marco de Gemmis, and Giovanni Semeraro. Content-based recommender systems: State of the art and trends. In *Recommender systems handbook*, pages 73–105, Springer, 2011. DOI:10.1007/978-0-387-85820-3_3

[7]   Robin Burke. Hybrid recommender systems: Survey and experiments. *User Modeling and User-Adapted Interaction*, 12(4):331–370, 2002.

[8]   Yann LeCun, Yoshua Bengio, and Geoffrey Hinton. Deep learning. *Nature*, 521(7553):436–444, 2015.

[9]   Ian Goodfellow, Yoshua Bengio, and Aaron Courville. *Deep learning*. MIT Press, 2016.

[10] Martín Abadi, Ashish Agarwal, Paul Barham, Eugene Brevdo, Zhifeng Chen, Craig Citro, Greg S. Corrado, Andy Davis, Jeffrey Dean, and Matthieu Devin. Tensorflow: Large-scale machine learning on heterogeneous distributed systems. *arXiv preprint arXiv:1603.04467*, 2016.

[11]   Jake VanderPlas. *Python data science handbook: Essential tools for working with data.* SPD OReilly.

[12]   Wes McKinney. *Python for data analysis: Data wrangling with Pandas, NumPy, and IPython.* SPD OReilly.

[13]   Paul Covington, Jay Adams, and Emre Sargin. Deep neural networks for youtube recommendations. In *Proceedings of the 10th ACM conference on recommender systems,* pages 191–198, 2016.

[14]   Jiaqi Ma, Zhe Zhao, Xinyang Yi, Ji Yang, Minmin Chen, Jiaxi Tang, Lichan Hong, and Ed Chi. Off-policy learning in two-stage recommender systems. In *WWW '20: The Web conference 2020,* pages 463–473, 04 2020. https://doi.org/10.1145/3366423.3380130

[15]   F. Maxwell Harper and Joseph A. Konstan. The MovieLens datasets: History and context. *ACM Transactions on Interactive Intelligent Systems,* 5(4), December 2015. https://doi.org/10.1145/2827872

[16]   Mahesh Goyani and Neha Chaurasiya. A review of movie recommendation system. *ELCVIA: Electronic Letters on Computer Vision and Image Analysis,* 19(3):18–37, 2020.

[17]   Alice Zheng and Amanda Casari. *Feature engineering for machine learning: Principles and techniques for data scientists.* O Reilly Media.

[18]   Max Kuhn and Kjell Johnson. *Feature engineering and selection: A practical approach for predictive models.* CRC Press, 2019.

[19]   François Chollet. *Keras.* The Keras Blog, 2015.

[20]   Xinyang Yi, Ji Yang, Lichan Hong, Derek Zhiyuan Cheng, Lukasz Heldt, Aditee Kumthekar, Zhe Zhao, Li Wei, and Ed Chi. Sampling-bias-corrected neural modeling for large corpus item recommendations. In *Proceedings of the 13th ACM conference on recommender systems,* pages 269–277, 2019.

[21]   TensorFlow Recommenders. https://www.tensorflow.org/recommenders/examples/basic_ranking?hl=en

7 A Marketing Approach to Recommender Systems

K T Igulu, T P Singh, F E Onuodu, and N S Agbeb

CONTENTS

7.1 INTRODUCTION

An abundance of statistics exists regarding the new normal for businesses—namely, businesses conducted over the internet. According to the Content Marketing Institute, [1] 61 percent of online consumers in the United States have made a purchase as a result of reading a blog's suggestions. In addition, 59 percent of Millennials will go to Amazon first when it comes to online shopping, according to another interesting statistic [2]. Approximately 95 percent of all purchases are expected to be made online by the year 2040, according to [3]. Therefore, the world is transitioning away from traditional sales methods such as physical and personal sales to sales conducted online. In a nutshell, the Web enables consumers to access services 24 hours a day and to search for and compare products, prices, catalogues, descriptions, and technical specifications. Apart from searching for and comparing characteristics of goods and services on the Web, consumers can comment on and learn about the purchases and comments of other consumers. Consumption on the Web becomes more connected [4].

To keep pace with the growing volume and complexity of information available on the Web, an automated and assistive tool is required. This tool will enable users to make informed choices about the products or services they sincerely desire while surfing the Web. Users are exposed to the most interesting items, and recommender

DOI: 10.1201/9781003319122-7

systems (RSs) provide novelty, surprise, and relevance, thereby assisting in overcoming the problem of information overload [5]. An important goal of RS research is to increase the precision and accuracy of recommendations, which is seen as a key sign of an effective RS [6–7].

According to [8], marketing is the activity, set of institutions, and processes for creating, communicating, delivering, and exchanging offerings that have value for customers, clients, partners, and society at large. Marketing is a function of a business. It encompasses all activities undertaken by a business to sell products or services to other businesses (wholesalers, retailers) or directly to end consumers. Marketing is fundamentally an interaction between marketers and consumers of goods and services, and it necessitates management making the decision to create valuable products and services and then sell them at reasonable prices based on market segment characteristics [9]. Furthermore, management is in charge of ensuring meaningful access to goods and services, as well as the use of appropriate media to communicate product and/or service messages [10].

It is clear that marketing is all about attracting customers, converting them into sales, and retaining them. Traditional marketing approaches such as the segmentation, targeting, and positioning (STP) strategy create specific customer engagement and subsequent sales based on preferences. The STP strategy is technically a divide-and-conquer strategy. Marketers will need to gain a deep understanding of their customers and segment them based on various marketing elements, such as products, pricing, utility, etc. Market segmentation is an approach to determine, from a target-population, distinct groups of consumers according to the utility that they expect from a product [11]. Management's job is to assess and select a specific market segment and to adopt appropriate positioning tactics. Advertising could be a part of positioning.

In today's era of big data and Web collaborations, recommender systems are essential components that act as a complement to search engine algorithms in the process of finding and retrieving information. A "virtual sales rep" is now a common feature of many online businesses, and this is because of the use of information filtering techniques that allow them to make product recommendations based on the information available to them. Sure, recommendation systems filter information based on the demographics and preferences of users (such as what they look at or buy, for example) to come up with suggestions or forecast future user behaviour. Individual or group preferences are frequently used to generate recommendations on the Web, which are displayed as hierarchical lists or schemes (collaborative filtering). [12–15] are recent surveys on the technical aspects of implementing and analyzing recommendation systems.

It suffices to state that recommender systems are marketing assistive tool, and as such, this chapter examines it from a marketing perspective.

7.2 RECOMMENDER SYSTEMS (RS)

We frequently come into contact with recommender systems when we use digital services and apps like Amazon, Netflix, and news aggregators. Recommender systems are basically computer programs that forecast what a specific user will enjoy, such as a particular social media post. Predictions about a user's preferences (e.g., movies/products) are functions that take this information and output a prediction about the rating that a user would assign to a collection of items under evaluation (e.g., new products available) and how they would rank the collection of items individually or as a bundle [12]. Recommender systems, in their most basic form, help consumers make informed decisions about products and services based on their own prior digital activities or other consumers' that share similar features (demographics) or preferences (Quah, 2003).

A typical RS assumes that there are N distinct users with n distinct features, each of whom may request recommendations for M Web goods (WGs) with m distinct features. All possible user-WG pairings are described in a n + m dimensional space. Users and WGs can only be identified by a single feature, creating a two-dimensional space. Users' ratings of Web goods are summarized in the N x M matrix. Ratings can be made explicitly or implicitly according to a predefined scale.

The function that follows represents the recommendation function (R_{gen}) in its simplest form:

$$R_{gen}: User_{feat} \times Web\ Good_{feat} \text{ à rating} \tag{1}$$

Specific recommender systems' functions are modifications of this function.

7.2.1 CLASSIFICATION OF RECOMMENDER SYSTEMS

Content-based recommender systems (CRS), collaborative filtering recommender systems (CFRS), and hybrid recommender systems are three main types of recommender systems [16], [11] made further classification of recommender system based on the techniques used for rating estimation—heuristic-based or model-based. They adopted an orthogonal dimension to classify the recommender systems research in the 2 × 3 matrix presented in Table 7.1. The categorizations

---

TABLE 7.1
List of Symbolic Representations of the Main Variables in Recommendations Systems' Frameworks [4]

U	$1, 2, \ldots, N$ Users with n distinct features
I	$1, 2, \ldots, M$ Web goods with m distinct features
$User_{feat}$	the user features (e.g., age, location, income)
$User_{id}$	a unique identifier of the users
$Web\ Good_{feat}$	Web good features (e.g., ID, price, availability)
$Web\ Good_{id}$	a unique identifier of the Web goods
$Rating$	the ratings given by the users to the Web goods
R_{gen}	the general recommendation function

are not mutually exclusive. Content-based recommendation systems make recommendations based on the content of items that are ready to be recommended and those that have previously been marked as favourites by the user. But CFRS make recommendations for the user based on the opinions of others who share the user's interests. Hybrid recommender systems are basically a functional combination of content-based and collaborative filtering RSs.

We adopt the symbols in [4] for illustrations as seen in Table 7.1.

By far the most popular RSs on the web are CFRSs. Similar user preferences collaborate to filter items from a large set of alternatives in this type of RS. If two users previously shared interests, they may share them again in the future. Alternatively, if user1 recently purchased a Samsung mobile phone that user2 has not seen or purchased previously, the idea is to recommend this previously unseen new item to user2. Correlation between items or users is the foundation of collaborative filtering (CF) techniques [17]. As a result, CF techniques can be classified into two categories:

- The technique is referred to as the neighbourhood-based technique or the memory-based technique. The recommendation is based on the user or item of information's neighbourhoods in this technique. These neighbourhoods are determined by the degree to which the active user or selected item is similar to other users or unseen pieces of information.
- A technique that is based on models and employs data mining and machine learning techniques. Additionally, they are referred to as predictive models. Random forest (RF), Bayesian model, latent semantic analysis, and rule-based models are all examples of model-based methods.

TABLE 7.2
Classification of Recommender Systems

Recommendation Approach	Recommendation Technique	
	Heuristic-Based	Model-Based
Content-based	• TF-IDF (Term Frequency - Inverse Document Frequency) (information retrieval) • Clustering [18]–[20]	• Bayesian classifier • Clustering • Decision trees • Artificial neural networks (ANN) [21]–[24]
Collaborative	• Nearest neighbor • Clustering • Graph theory [25]–[33]	• Bayesian classifier • Clustering • Artificial neural networks (ANN) [33]–[51]

Recommendation Approach	Recommendation Technique	
	Heuristic-Based	Model-Based
Hybrid (Combines content-based and collaborative components)	• Various voting schemes • Linear combination of predicted ratings • Incorporating one component as part of the heuristic for the other [20], [52]–[56]	• Incorporating one component as part of the model for the other • Building one unifying model [57]–[64]

When it comes to making predictions, CRSs and CFRSs differ in that CRSs use both item and user characteristics, whereas CFRSs rely solely on item rating data [17]. Information retrieval is the source of the CRSs. In order to recommend products to users, CRSs and information retrieval are focused on analyzing the data content.

7.3 RECOMMENDER SYSTEMS—MARKETING PERSPECTIVE

Recommender systems' objectives go far beyond the simple retrieval of information [16]. Data from several studies indicate that recommender systems enhance sales, enhance cross-selling, reduce customer churn, help new visitors, build credibility through community, encourage customers to return, and build long-term relationships [65–67]. Numerous studies have attempted to incorporate firm-specific measures into the item selection process in recent years and to situate the issue of recommender design within a profit-maximizing context [16], [67]. Consequently, while recommender systems were initially developed to aid consumers in their Web surfing, they quickly evolved into a tool for improving the efficacy of corporate marketing campaigns.

Bodapati (2008) examined the relevance-profitability trade-off in recommender system design. Recommendations were modelled as marketing actions capable of influencing customers' purchasing decisions in ways other than what they would have done in the absence of the intervention. He contended that if a recommender system only recommends the most relevant items, it would be ineffective if customers didn't purchase those items in the first place. Rather than recommending the most likely product to be purchased, the system should recommend items with the highest probability of being influenced by the recommendation.

A conventional recommender system was combined with the profitability factor and compared to four alternative systems (personalized/non-personalized and including/excluding profitability). Including profitability in a recommendation does not, according to their findings, reduce its accuracy in any way [68].

In addition, [69] investigated how to recommend products that help companies increase profits instead of recommending products that are most likely to be purchased by customers. If you want to maximize profits, you need to choose products with the highest margins and those that are most relevant.

A model that uses the output of a traditional recommender system and adjusts it based on item profitability was developed by [70]. An analysis of consumer response behaviour was used by the authors to demonstrate the profitability of their new design.

According to [4], recommendation systems particularly contribute in the fulfilment of marketing objectives by:

- Identifying customer requirements
  - facilitating massive, more detailed, and cheaper data acquisition
  - extending one-to-one marketing analysis
- Anticipating customer requirements
  - enriching statistical modelling of customer's behaviour
  - extending market basket analysis
- Satisfying customer requirements
  - providing more informed, personalized, and adaptive recommendations
  - implementing one-to-one marketing analysis
  - facilitating better merchandising and atmospherics

7.3.1 WEB GOODS (WGS) AND USERS

On a technical level, recommender systems are most useful on the internet and in relation to Web-based products and services. Because of this, it is necessary to introduce the concept of Web goods (also referred to as "items" or "products"). Web goods are essentially sequencing of binary digits that are uniquely identified by their assigned uniform resource identifier (URI) and hypertext format and have an effect on the utility or payoff of some individual in the economy [71]. Their market value is derived from the digital information they contain and a particular component of it, hyperlinks, which connect resources and facilitate navigation across a network of Web goods. The following categories can be used to further define Web goods. Pure Web goods are the primary focus of Web science research [72], as they are defined as goods that are primarily exchanged and consumed on the Web and are not inextricably linked to an ordinary good or service (pre-)existing in the physical world. For example, a blog entry discussing the used car market is a pure Web good, whereas a car sales advertisement is not. Web goods are classified into commercial (e.g., sponsored search results) and non-commercial categories based on production incentives (e.g., Wikipedia entries). In comparison to commercial Web goods, non-commercial Web goods are produced outside of traditional market mechanisms such as price and property, and they are based on openness, peer production, and qualitative ex post reward schemes.

The Web goods are definitely not isolated entities. They are meant for consumptions. The Web users are the producers and consumers of Web goods.

Navigators and editors are the two most basic categories of Web users, according to a simple classification [71]. Navigators consume information by navigating (browsing, surfing, or accessing) the Web network. Editors are producers of WGs. Editors are responsible for creating, updating, and deleting digital content and links on the World Wide Web. Editors are divided into two categories—amateur and professional—based on the financial spurs they receive for production. In comparison to amateur editors (e.g., Wikipedia editors), professional editors are profit-maximizing and produce WGs with an eye toward direct financial compensation (e.g., Facebook). Amateur editors in not-for-profit community settings (e.g., open source software) are motivated by personal acclaim and reputation building, which, in addition to moral reward and self-confidence, increases their prospects for high-paying employment. This temporal disconnection between effort and reward explains why editors may freely provide knowledge, effort, and time [71]. In social networking, amateur editors may be motivated by a desire to achieve a higher relative contribution status in comparison to their peers and future consumption utility from the connected goods provided by their peers [71]. Amateur editors are the primary producers of WGs that are then packaged and commercialized by a professional editor acting as a platform. This massive function in Web necessitates an economically viable distinction between editors based on function. Editors can be further classified into simple and aggregators based on their aggregation capability. Aggregators are classified into search engines, platforms, and reconstructors based on their automated mechanisms for selecting and presenting WGs (Figure 7.1). Their primary function is to generate content by linking to existing WGs.

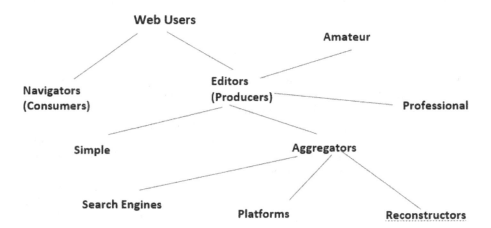

FIGURE 7.1 Web users' categorization [71].

7.3.2   ONE-TO-ONE MARKETING, PERSONALIZATION, AND ADAPTATION IN THE WEB

In contrast to traditional marketing, which aims to reach a large number of people, one-to-one marketing (also known as personalized marketing) focuses on a single customer and tailors its offerings to meet his or her specific needs [4], [73], [74]. As a result, one-to-one marketing serves two purposes:

- know the specific requirements of each and every one customer
- advise customers on the best products to meet their needs.

According to [73], there are four main principles that define one-to-one marketing namely (i) customer identification, (ii) customer differentiation, (iii) customer interaction, and (iv) product customization for each customer.

Because of the widespread use of recommendation systems on the Web, one-to-one marketing can now be implemented for all users, not just "the most profitable customers," as [75] suggest. This type of marketing relies heavily on content-based and hybrid recommendations.

Personalization and adaptation, long studied in computer science and related fields, are at the heart of Web-based one-to-one marketing. Web personalization can be defined as the dynamic alteration of a website's content, layout, and functionality based on a user's characteristics in order to provide personalized recommendations [74], [76].

There are two types of personalization: information on the internet and one-on-one marketing, according to [74]. However, recommendation and feedback mechanisms integrated into participatory Web commerce can unify these aspects. In practice, Web merchants are attempting to combine personalized and adaptive information in order to produce successful marketing mixtures. System-driven personalization is another way to look at online content adaption (not to be confused to adaptability which is user-driven personalization) [4].

7.3.3   WEB MERCHANDISING AND ATMOSPHERICS

Merchandising and store ambience are critical components of meeting customer requirements, which fall under the third axe of marketing objectives.

These fields are responsible for the efficient placement of products on the "shelf" and the creation of an appropriate store atmosphere to attract and retain new customers in traditional marketing of physical stores. With the advent of click-and-mortar commerce, significant changes and transformations occurred in the business functions of merchandising and store atmosphere.

Merchandising "consists of the activities involved in acquiring particular products and making them available at the places, times, prices and in the quantity to enable a retailer to reach its goals" [77]. There is no physical shelf, retailer, or merchandiser on the Web; instead, products are presented and disposed of via websites. These items are stored in warehouses, homes, and databases (in the case of pure Web goods). Web merchandising is concerned with the process of making products available on the

Web. Online merchandisers are in charge of product collection and display, as well as promotional activities such as cross-selling and up-selling [78]. According to Lee et al. (2000), Web merchandising research has been classified into four categories (i) product assortment, (ii) merchandising cues, (iii) shopping metaphor, and (vi) Web design features.

The use of merchandising cues in online stores is a method of presenting and/or grouping products in order to encourage customers to make a purchase. Aside from traditional promotional methods, recommendation systems are a great example of merchandising cues that should be considered [79]. Functionality and analysis of Web design features have a lot in common with Web atmospherics, which is a field of study in its own right.

Designing Web environments to elicit positive user reactions is known as Web atmospherics. Customers' perceptions and experiences in an online store can be influenced by the atmosphere, just as brick-and-mortar retailers' atmospherics do in brick-and-mortar stores [80].

Not only can recommendation systems be used to optimize product placement, promotion, and related functions, but they can also be used to enhance the online environment and atmosphere through dynamic and adaptive features that adapt to the user's and product's characteristics. On the Web, mass merchants (e.g., Amazon) rely heavily on various forms of recommendation (both content-based and collaborative) to construct the majority of their store's architecture, functionality, and adaptability [4].

7.3.4 MARKET BASKET ANALYSIS

Market basket analysis (MBA) examines the contents of shopping baskets in order to ascertain the purchasing behaviour of customers [81]. Additionally, it is referred to as association rule mining, which is a technique for identifying customer purchasing patterns through the extraction of associations from transactional databases of retailers [82]. According to [81], Market basket refers to the collection of items purchased by a customer during a single shopping session [81].

The mathematical definition of MBA is given by [82]:

Given two non—overlapping subsets of product items, X and Y, an association rule in form of X|Y indicates a purchase pattern that if a customer purchases X then he or she also purchases Y. Two measures, support and confidence, are commonly used to select the association rules. Support is a measure of how often the transactional records in the database contain both X and Y, and confidence is a measure of the accuracy of the rule, defined as the ratio of the number of transactional records with both X and Y to the number of transactional records with X only.

Despite the fact that both MBA and Web commerce recommendation systems use the same transaction data as an input, their methods and results are tailored to different types of end users. By extracting associations from the data, MBA helps marketing managers make informed decisions, while recommendation systems provide relevant information to Web users [4].

Physical store purchasing data is the exclusive property of the store owner and contains less information about the customer's purchasing habits than in online stores. If you're looking for an example of this, look no further than online shopping. Each transaction is recorded with a unique time stamp, and users' feedback is often incorporated into the purchasing process. In addition to providing an advantage to online merchants, these features of commerce data analysis on the Web raise concerns about excessive market power and the abuse of private information by selling it to third parties or profiling people without their knowledge or consent to do so [4].

What is new in Web commerce is that parties other than the store owner/administrator can begin (partial) MBA by gathering online recommendations. For instance, Amazon, the world's largest online retailer, is built on a successful collaborative filtering system based on items that provides a broad range of general and personalized recommendations. More precisely, the list of "most customers who bought this item also bought" (BLB) recommended products displays items that were frequently purchased in conjunction with the product in question [4]. BLB recommendations are derived from the store's network of co-purchases and can be visualized as a directed graph with nodes representing products and directed links connecting each product to its recommended products [83].

7.3.5 Ad Targeting

Advertisement (ad) targeting, or more broadly offer targeting, is a method of determining which consumers should receive an offer based on their prior behaviour. Traditional marketers monitor for a particular "event" in a customer's life and then target the consumer with specific advertisements or offers. When a consumer applies for his first credit card, he begins receiving offers for the card from numerous banks. He begins receiving offers for loan consolidation, second mortgages, life insurance, and aluminium siding after purchasing a home. When he becomes a parent, he is inundated with advertisements for everything from diapers and formula to book clubs and, of course, life insurance. Consumers are treated as both individuals and members of a market group when it comes to offer targeting. Typically, offers are made to all consumers whose names appear on a list (e.g., the list of "newly acquired mortgages"). Individual customers, on the other hand, are added and removed from these lists based on their unique behaviour. Achieving a "life event" automatically adds a customer to a list. Consumers who continue to disregard the offers will be dropped from the list.

To put it another way, ad targeting or offer targeting is the process of determining which customers should be contacted with a promotional offer based on their previous purchasing habits [66]. When a specific "event" in a customer's life occurs, traditional marketers wait for an opportunity to target them with specific ads or offers. Rather than focusing on a single customer, offer targeting focuses on a group of customers and treats them as such. All customers whose names appear on a list (i.e., the "just acquired a mortgage" list) are typically offered promotions. Each customer's behaviour is taken into consideration when adding or removing them from these lists. When a customer accomplishes a "life event," they are added to the customer database. In the long run, customers who continue to reject the company's offers will be removed from its database.

7.4 CONCLUSION

Consumers' private preferences and expectations are made public in Web, allowing other customers to benefit from this information. Connected consumption takes place on the internet. This necessitates the development of new methods for studying internet phenomena. Consumers and WGs producers will both benefit from the change. As the amount of data and information grows, so does the difficulty of analyzing it and making decisions at both ends of the purchasing process. Natural remedies for the overabundance of information are recommender systems. In this chapter, we explored recommender systems from a marketing standpoint. It is, however, expedient to note that future recommendations systems challenges will not be purely technical or business-oriented. They shall deal with things like semantic and ubiquitous Web environments, market competition, and regulation—all of which raise privacy, trust, and provenance concerns.

REFERENCES

[1] Julia McCoy, "9 Stats that will make you want to invest in content marketing," 2017. https://contentmarketinginstitute.com/articles/stats-invest-content-marketing/ (accessed Apr. 04, 2023).

[2] Jamie Inviqa, "Millennial retail trends: online retail in the Amazon Era," 2018. https://inviqa.com/blog/millennial-retail-trends-online-retail-amazon-era (accessed Apr. 04, 2023).

[3] GuruFocus, "UK Online Shopping and E-Commerce Statistics for 2017," 2017. https://www.nasdaq.com/articles/uk-online-shopping-and-e-commerce-statistics-2017-2017-03-14 (accessed Apr. 04, 2023).

[4] V. Michalis and O. Michael, "Recommendation systems: a joint analysis of technical aspects with marketing implications," *CoRR*, vol. 11, no. 1, 2010.

[5] F. Ricci, B. Shapira, and L. Rokach, "Recommender systems: Introduction and challenges," in *Recommender Systems Handbook, Second Edition*, 2015. doi: 10.1007/978-1-4899-7637-6_1.

[6] B. Alhijawi and Y. Kilani, "A collaborative filtering recommender system using genetic algorithm," *Inf Process Manag*, vol. 57, no. 6, 2020, doi: 10.1016/j.ipm.2020.102310.

[7] Q. Li, S. H. Myaeng, and B. M. Kim, "A probabilistic music recommender considering user opinions and audio features," *Inf Process Manag*, vol. 43, no. 2, 2007, doi: 10.1016/j.ipm.2006.07.005.

[8] AMA, "What is Marketing? — The Definition of Marketing — AMA," *American Marketing Association*. 2013.

[9] Chux Gervase, "What is Marketing?," 2014. http://customerthink.com/209180/ (accessed Apr. 11, 2022).

[10] S. Jørgensen, "Marketing," in *Handbook of Dynamic Game Theory*, G. Başar Tamer and Zaccour, Ed., Cham: Springer International Publishing, 2018, pp. 865–905. doi: 10.1007/978-3-319-44374-4_22.

[11] G. Adomavicius and A. Tuzhilin, "Toward the next generation of recommender systems: A survey of the state-of-the-art and possible extensions," *IEEE Transactions on Knowledge and Data Engineering*, vol. 17, no. 6. 2005. doi: 10.1109/TKDE.2005.99.

[12] N. Hazrati and F. Ricci, "Recommender systems effect on the evolution of users' choices distribution," *Inf Process Manag*, vol. 59, no. 1, 2022, doi: 10.1016/j.ipm.2021.102766.

[13] R. Sabitha, S. Vaishnavi, S. Karthik, and R. M. Bhavadharini, "User interaction based recommender system using machine learning," *Intelligent Automation and Soft Computing*, vol. 31, no. 2, 2022, doi: 10.32604/iasc.2022.018985.

[14] S. Wang, L. Cao, Y. Wang, Q. Z. Sheng, M. A. Orgun, and D. Lian, "A Survey on Session-based Recommender Systems," *ACM Comput Surv*, vol. 54, no. 7, 2022, doi: 10.1145/3465401.

[15] H. Khojamli and J. Razmara, "Survey of similarity functions on neighborhood-based collaborative filtering," *Expert Syst Appl*, vol. 185, 2021, doi: 10.1016/j.eswa.2021.115482.

[16] U. Panniello, "How to use recommender systems in e-business domains," *Webology*, vol. 11, no. 2, 2014.

[17] O. Ibrahim and E. Younis, "Recommender Systems and Their Fairness for User Preferences: A Literature Study." Apr. 2018. doi: 10.13140/RG.2.2.35330.12487.

[18] K. Lang, "NewsWeeder: Learning to Filter Netnews," in *Machine Learning Proceedings 1995*, 1995. doi: 10.1016/b978-1-55860-377-6.50048-7.

[19] M. Pazzani and D. Billsus, "Learning and Revising User Profiles: The Identification of Interesting Web Sites," *Mach Learn*, vol. 27, no. 3, 1997, doi: 10.1023/A:1007369909943.

[20] Y. Shoham and M. Balabanović, "Fab: Content-Based, Collaborative Recommendation," *Commun ACM*, vol. 40, no. 3, 1997.

[21] R. J. Mooney and L. Roy, "Content-based book recommending using learning for text categorization," *Proceedings of the ACM International Conference on Digital Libraries*, 2000, doi: 10.1145/336597.336662.

[22] R. J. Mooney, P. N. Bennett, and L. Roy, "Book Recommending using Text Categorization with Extracted Information," in *IN RECOMMENDER SYSTEMS. PAPERS FROM 1998 WORKSHOP*, 1998.

[23] Y. Lin, F. Lin, L. Yang, W. Zeng, Y. Liu, and P. Wu, "Context-aware reinforcement learning for course recommendation," *Appl Soft Comput*, vol. 125, 2022, doi: 10.1016/j.asoc.2022.109189.

[24] C. Ma, Y. Sun, Z. Yang, H. Huang, D. Zhan, and J. Qu, "Content Feature Extraction-based Hybrid Recommendation for Mobile Application Services," *Computers, Materials and Continua*, vol. 71, no. 2, 2022, doi: 10.32604/cmc.2022.022717.

[25] F. Zhang, Y. Qu, Y. Xu, and S. Wang, "Graph embedding-based approach for detecting group shilling attacks in collaborative recommender systems," *Knowl Based Syst*, vol. 199, 2020, doi: 10.1016/j.knosys.2020.105984.

[26] H. Cai and F. Zhang, "BS-SC: An Unsupervised Approach for Detecting Shilling Profiles in Collaborative Recommender Systems," *IEEE Trans Knowl Data Eng*, vol. 33, no. 4, 2021, doi: 10.1109/TKDE.2019.2946247.

[27] P. Resnick, N. Iacovou, M. Suchak, P. Bergstrom, and J. Riedl, "GroupLens: An open architecture for collaborative filtering of netnews," in *Proceedings of the 1994 ACM Conference on Computer Supported Cooperative Work, CSCW 1994*, 1994. doi: 10.1145/192844.192905.

[28] J. A. Konstan, B. N. Miller, D. Maltz, J. L. Herlocker, L. R. Gordon, and J. Riedl, "GroupLens," *Commun ACM*, vol. 40, no. 3, 1997, doi: 10.1145/245108.245126.

[29] B. Sarwar, G. Karypis, J. Konstan, and J. Riedl, "Item-based collaborative filtering recommendation algorithms," in *Proceedings of the 10th International Conference on World Wide Web, WWW 2001*, 2001. doi: 10.1145/371920.372071.

[30] C. Li and K. He, "CBMR: An optimized MapReduce for item-based collaborative filtering recommendation algorithm with empirical analysis," *Concurr Comput*, vol. 29, no. 10, 2017, doi: 10.1002/cpe.4092.

[31] S. Wang, Y. Xie, and M. Fang, "A collaborative filtering recommendation algorithm based on item and cloud model," *Wuhan University Journal of Natural Sciences*, vol. 16, no. 1, 2011, doi: 10.1007/s11859-011-0704-4.

[32] Y. Chen, Y. Wang, X. Zhao, H. Yin, I. Markov, and M. De Rijke, "Local Variational Feature-Based Similarity Models for Recommending Top-N New Items," *ACM Trans Inf Syst*, vol. 38, no. 2, 2020, doi: 10.1145/3372154.

[33] A. Gupta and P. Srinath, "A recommender system based on collaborative filtering, graph theory using HMM based similarity measures," *International Journal of System Assurance Engineering and Management*, vol. 13, 2022, doi: 10.1007/s13198-021-01537-6.

[34] J. Jiang, J. Lu, G. Zhang, and G. Long, "Scaling-up item-based collaborative filtering recommendation algorithm based on Hadoop," in *Proceedings - 2011 IEEE World Congress on Services, SERVICES 2011*, 2011. doi: 10.1109/SERVICES.2011.66.

[35] J. Chen, C. Zhao, Uliji, and L. Chen, "Collaborative filtering recommendation algorithm based on user correlation and evolutionary clustering," *Complex and Intelligent Systems*, vol. 6, no. 1, 2020, doi: 10.1007/s40747-019-00123-5.

[36] P. Tian, "Collaborative filtering recommendation algorithm in cloud computing environment," *Computer Science and Information Systems*, vol. 18, no. 2, 2021, doi: 10.2298/CSIS200119008T.

[37] C. Li *et al.*, "The multimedia recommendation algorithm based on probability graphical model," *Multimed Tools Appl*, vol. 81, no. 14, 2022, doi: 10.1007/s11042-020-10129-8.

[38] H. Wang, Y. Sun, X. Li, Y. Xie, and Y. Qi, "A Stock Secommendation System Using with Distributed Graph Computation and Trust Model-Collaborative Filtering Algorithm," in *Proceedings of 2018 2nd IEEE Advanced Information Management, Communicates, Electronic and Automation Control Conference, IMCEC 2018*, 2018. doi: 10.1109/IMCEC.2018.8469762.

[39] J. Xiao, L. Yuan, C. Huang, and B. Wu, "Parallel collaborative filtering recommender algorithm based on learning to rank," *Huazhong Keji Daxue Xuebao (Ziran Kexue Ban)/Journal of Huazhong University of Science and Technology (Natural Science Edition)*, vol. 46, no. 3, 2018, doi: 10.13245/j.hust.180307.

[40] D. Billsus, D. Billsus, M. J. Pazzani, and M. J. Pazzani, "Learning collaborative information filters," *Proceedings of the Fifteenth International Conference on Machine Learning*, vol. 54, 1998.

[41] A. Kontogianni, E. Alepis, and C. Patsakis, "Promoting smart tourism personalised services via a combination of deep learning techniques," *Expert Syst Appl*, vol. 187, 2022, doi: 10.1016/j.eswa.2021.115964.

[42] C. Troussas, F. Giannakas, C. Sgouropoulou, and I. Voyiatzis, "Collaborative activities recommendation based on students' collaborative learning styles using ANN and WSM," *Interactive Learning Environments*, vol. 31, no. 1, 2023, doi: 10.1080/10494820.2020.1761835.

[43] R. Fuji and K. Okamoto, "Model-based collaborative filtering with transparency using linear regression," *Transactions of the Japanese Society for Artificial Intelligence*, vol. 35, no. 1, 2020, doi: 10.1527/tjsai.D-J61.

[44] A. Paterek, "Improving regularized singular value decomposition for collaborative filtering," *KDD Cup and Workshop*, 2007.

[45] K. Hughes-Lartey, Z. Qin, F. E. Botchey, and S. Dsane-Nsor, "An Assessment of data location vulnerability for human factors using linear regression and collaborative filtering," *Information (Switzerland)*, vol. 11, no. 9, 2020, doi: 10.3390/INFO11090449.

[46] R. Fuji and K. Okamoto, "Model-based collaborative filtering with transparency using linear regression," *Transactions of the Japanese Society for Artificial Intelligence*, vol. 35, no. 1, 2020, doi: 10.1527/tjsai.D-J61.

[47] L. Getoor and M. Sahami, "Using probabilistic relational models for collaborative filtering," *Workshop on Web Usage Analysis and User Profiling*, 1999.

[48] D. Liang, R. G. Krishnan, M. D. Hoffman, and T. Jebara, "Variational autoencoders for collaborative filtering," in *The Web Conference 2018 - Proceedings of the World Wide Web Conference, WWW 2018*, 2018. doi: 10.1145/3178876.3186150.

[49] H. Langseth and T. D. Nielsen, "A latent model for collaborative filtering," *International Journal of Approximate Reasoning*, vol. 53, no. 4, 2012, doi: 10.1016/j.ijar.2011.11.002.

[50] A. Das, "Google News Personalization : Scalable Online," *Practice*, 2007.

[51] Y. Chen, X. Sun, D. Gong, and X. Yao, "DPM-IEDA: Dual probabilistic model assisted interactive estimation of distribution algorithm for personalized search," *IEEE Access*, vol. 7, 2019, doi: 10.1109/ACCESS.2019.2904140.

[52] J. Parthasarathy and R. B. Kalivaradhan, "An effective content boosted collaborative filtering for movie recommendation systems using density based clustering with artificial flora optimization algorithm," *International Journal of Systems Assurance Engineering and Management*, 2021, doi: 10.1007/s13198-021-01101-2.

[53] P. Melville, R. J. Mooney, and R. Nagarajan, "Content-boosted collaborative filtering for improved recommendations," in *Proceedings of the National Conference on Artificial Intelligence*, 2002.

[54] M. Claypool, A. Gokhale, T. Miranda, P. Murnikov, D. Netes, and M. Sartin, "Combining content-based and collaborative filters in an online newspaper," in *Proceedings of the ACM SIGIR '99 Workshop on Recommender Systems: Algorithms and Evaluation*, 1999.

[55] D. Billsus and M. J. Pazzani, "Adaptive news access," in *Lecture Notes in Computer Science (including subseries Lecture Notes in Artificial Intelligence and Lecture Notes in Bioinformatics)*, 2007. doi: 10.1007/978-3-540-72079-9_18.

[56] D. Billsus and M. J. Pazzani, "User modeling for adaptive news access," *User Modelling and User-Adapted Interaction*, vol. 10, no. 2–3, 2000, doi: 10.1023/A:1026501525781.

[57] A. Popescul, D. M. Pennock, and S. Lawrence, "Departmental Papers (CIS) Probabilistic Models for Unified Collaborative and Content-Based Recommendation in Sparse-Data Environments," *Artif Intell*, vol. 2001, no. Uai, 2001.

[58] A. Gunawardana and C. Meek, "A unified approach to building hybrid recommender systems," in *RecSys'09 - Proceedings of the 3rd ACM Conference on Recommender Systems*, 2009. doi: 10.1145/1639714.1639735.

[59] Z. Huang, D. D. Zeng, and H. Chen, "A Unified Recommendation Framework Based on Probabilistic Relational Models," *SSRN Electronic Journal*, 2011, doi: 10.2139/ssrn.906513.

[60] L. Yao, Q. Z. Sheng, A. H. H. Ngu, J. Yu, and A. Segev, "Unified collaborative and content-based web service recommendation," *IEEE Trans Serv Comput*, vol. 8, no. 3, 2015, doi: 10.1109/TSC.2014.2355842.

[61] T. T. Truyen, D. Q. Phung, and S. Venkatesh, "Preference networks: Probabilistic models for recommendation systems," *Conferences in Research and Practice in Information Technology Series*, vol. 70, 2007.

[62] N. Zhou, W. K. Cheung, G. Qiu, and X. Xue, "A hybrid probabilistic model for unified collaborative and content-based image tagging," *IEEE Trans Pattern Anal Mach Intell*, vol. 33, no. 7, 2011, doi: 10.1109/TPAMI.2010.204.

[63] C. Basu, H. Hirsh, and W. Cohen, "Recommendation as classification: Using social and content-based information in recommendation," in *Proceedings of the National Conference on Artificial Intelligence*, 1998.

[64] A. I. Schein, A. Popescul, L. H. Ungar, and D. M. Pennock, "Methods and metrics for cold-start recommendations," in *SIGIR Forum (ACM Special Interest Group on Information Retrieval)*, 2002. doi: 10.1145/564418.564421.

[65] D. Fleder and K. Hosanagar, "Blockbuster culture's next rise or fall: The impact of recommender systems on sales diversity," *Manage Sci*, vol. 55, no. 5, 2009, doi: 10.1287/mnsc.1080.0974.

[66] J. ben Schafer, J. A. Konstan, and J. Riedl, "E-commerce recommendation applications," *Data Min Knowl Discov*, vol. 5, no. 1–2, 2001, doi: 10.1007/978-1-4615-1627-9_6.

[67] Y. F. Wang, D. A. Chiang, M. H. Hsu, C. J. Lin, and I. L. Lin, "A recommender system to avoid customer churn: A case study," *Expert Syst Appl*, vol. 36, no. 4, 2009, doi: 10.1016/j.eswa.2008.10.089.

[68] L. S. Chen, F. H. Hsu, M. C. Chen, and Y. C. Hsu, "Developing recommender systems with the consideration of product profitability for sellers," *Inf Sci (N Y)*, vol. 178, no. 4, 2008, doi: 10.1016/j.ins.2007.09.027.

[69] K. Hosanagar, R. Krishnan, and L. Ma, "Recomended for you: The impact of profit incentives on the relevance of online recommendations," in *Proceedings of International Conference on Information Systems*, 2008.

[70] A. Das, C. Mathieu, and D. Ricketts, "Maximizing profit using recommender systems," *arXiv preprint arXiv:0908.3633*, 2009.

[71] M. Vafopoulos, "Modeling the Web Economy: Web Users and Goods," Apr. 2011.

[72] J. Hendler, N. Shadbolt, W. Hall, T. Berners-Lee, and D. Weitzner, "Web science: An interdisciplinary approach to understanding the web," *Commun ACM*, vol. 51, no. 7, 2008, doi: 10.1145/1364782.1364798.

[73] D. A. Pitta, "Marketing one-to-one and its dependence on knowledge discovery in databases," *Journal of Consumer Marketing*, vol. 15, no. 5, 1998, doi: 10.1108/EUM0000000004535.

[74] W. Kim, "Personalization: Definition, status, and challenges ahead," *Journal of Object Technology*, vol. 1, no. 1, 2002, doi: 10.5381/jot.2002.1.1.c3.

[75] M. L. Gillenson, D. L. Sherrell, and L. Chen, "Information Technology as the Enabler of One-to-One Marketing," *Communications of the Association for Information Systems*, vol. 2, 1999, doi: 10.17705/1cais.00218.

[76] J. Blom, "Personalization - A taxonomy," in *Conference on Human Factors in Computing Systems - Proceedings*, 2000. doi: 10.1145/633292.633483.

[77] B. Berman and J. R. Evans, *Retail management : A Strategic Approach*. 2018.

[78] J. Lee, M. Podlaseck, E. Schonberg, R. Hoch, and S. Gomory, "Analysis and visualization of metrics for online merchandising," in *Lecture Notes in Computer Science (including subseries Lecture Notes in Artificial Intelligence and Lecture Notes in Bioinformatics)*, 2000. doi: 10.1007/3-540-44934-5_8.

[79] J. Lee, M. Podlaseck, E. Schonberg, and R. Hoch, "Visualization and analysis of clickstream data of online stores for understanding web merchandising," *Data Min Knowl Discov*, vol. 5, no. 1–2, 2001, doi: 10.1023/A:1009843912662.

[80] S. Eroglu, K. Machleit, and L. Davis, "Empirical Testing of a Model of Online Store Atmospherics and Shopper Responses," *Psychol Mark*, vol. 20, pp. 139–150, Apr. 2003, doi: 10.1002/mar.10064.

[81] A. Mild and T. Reutterer, "An improved collaborative filtering approach for predicting cross-category purchases based on binary market basket data," *Journal of Retailing and Consumer Services*, vol. 10, no. 3, 2003, doi: 10.1016/S0969-6989(03)00003-1.

[82] Y. L. Chen, K. Tang, R. J. Shen, and Y. H. Hu, "Market basket analysis in a multiple store environment," *Decis Support Syst*, vol. 40, no. 2, 2005, doi: 10.1016/j.dss.2004.04.009.

[83] G. Oestreicher-Singer and A. Sundararajan, "Recommendation networks and the long tail of electronic commerce," *MIS Q*, vol. 36, no. 1, 2012, doi: 10.2307/41410406.

8 Applied Statistical Analysis in Recommendation Systems

Bikram Pratim Bhuyan and T P Singh

CONTENTS

8.1 INTRODUCTION

The expansion of internet services such as YouTube, Amazon, Netflix, and a myriad of others has led to recommender systems (RSs) becoming increasingly pervasive in our lives over the last few decades.[1] Recommender systems are becoming an integral part of our online lives, whether they're used in e-commerce (by proposing things to consumers based on their interests) or online advertising (by recommending appropriate information based on a user's preferences).[2] Briefly stated, recommender systems are algorithms developed to assist customers in locating appropriate goods and services (movies to watch, text to read, products to buy, or anything else depending on the industry).[3]

In the field of recommender systems, there exist software tools and methodologies that may provide suggestions for things that a user may find beneficial.[3] In order to aid users in making various selections, such as what items to buy or listen to on the radio or television, the suggestions are presented in a logical and understandable manner. Users of the Internet have discovered that recommender systems are a great tool for coping with the avalanche of information available on the Internet.[4] Because of this, numerous approaches for generating suggestions

DOI: 10.1201/9781003319122-8

have been created and tested in commercial contexts over the course of the last decade. It has become one of the most widely used and successful tools for doing business on the Internet.[5]

Techniques for proposing goods and services that are content-based, collaborative-based, or hybrid in nature are the most often used. A person's recent actions, such as what he or she has recently bought or seen, are taken into consideration when the content-based (CB) technique selects the most appropriate recommendations for that user to view.[6] Cooperative filtering (CF) is a technique for making suggestions to users based on the preferences and interests of other users who have previously shown an interest in the same topic. And last, combining two or more separate recommendation components or algorithms into a single recommendation system is known as the hybrid approach.[7] Nonetheless, these traditional RSs rely on the recommendation process being based on a single-criteria rating in order to function well and effectively (overall rating). Since overall ratings do not represent the fine-grained analysis that goes into understanding a user's behaviour, it is impossible to appropriately score a proposal based on a single criterion alone. It resulted in a large number of new research searching for practical methods to enhance the RS's performance as a consequence of this broadening of the scope of the RS study area.[8]

Social media platforms such as Facebook and Twitter are becoming popular venues for consumers to voice their frustrations and express their appreciation for one another. Many customers base their purchase decisions on what other people have to say about a product or service they are considering.[9] As a result, the number of online points of view has increased significantly (i.e., user reviews). The opinions stated in each review are those of the consumer, whether it is about a purchase, a movie, or a reservation for a lodging facility. Customers and businesses alike find these testimonials to be a valuable source of information. Despite the many benefits of these evaluations, their huge size and distinct characteristics make it difficult to extract important information from them in a timely manner. Written natural language, in contrast to other structured data sources, is more difficult for robots to grasp for the purposes of review, and as a result, most recommendation systems do not use it to make suggestions. Natural language processing, text mining, and opinion mining are just a few of the fields that are engaged in analysing reviews and extracting useful information from the data they include (or sentiment analysis).[10] Positive and negative polarity are determined by using sentiment analysis to assess whether or not a specific entity is positive or negative in nature.

In this chapter, we begin with the definitions behind a recommendation system and its sub-types. We define the formal statistics behind the evaluation of the system and, finally, the data modelling approaches using statistics in the domain. We conclude with a note of importance of statistics towards recommendation systems.

8.2 RECOMMENDATION SYSTEMS

A recommendation system must foresee that an item is worthy of recommendation as part of its main task.[1] This is possible if the system can predict the usefulness of some of them or, at the very least, compare the utility of some of them and then choose which things to propose depending on the results of the comparison. Even if the prediction phase is not explicitly included in the recommendation process, we may still use this unifying model to describe the overall function of a RS. Rather than providing a full discussion of all of the different recommendation techniques, our goal in this section is to provide the reader with a broad overview of the topic.

Think about a simple, non-personalised recommendation system that just proposes the most popular songs as an example of the prediction stage of a RS. This is an example of the prediction stage of a RS. Anything that is enjoyed (has high utility) by a large number of users will be liked by a generic user as well or, at the very least, more than another randomly selected song will be liked by a generic user. A good example of this is the argument for using this method, and, as a consequence, it is projected that these popular songs would be of moderate to high use to this user.

The formal definitions can be designed for the problem statement as:

Definition 1: It is necessary for a song to have at least one instance in order for it to be considered a class of objects (users).

Definition 2: A user is any person who has the opportunity to express their own likeness via an item or song rating. The Likeness matrix is thus represented as:

$$L = U \times S \tag{1}$$

where 'U' is total number of users with 'S' as the total number of songs to choose from.

Definition 3: The Fitness function for the Likeness matrix 'L' is defined as:

$$\rho = U_i \rightarrow S_i \tag{2}$$

for each user U_i and each song S_i.

The first problem to solve is figuring out how to assess a system in the first place. It has a practical as well as a theoretical component to it. A strategy that takes into account the characteristics that are most essential to the user is one that makes sense. The pursuit of maximum profit and the endeavour to be as close as possible to the real preferences of consumers are both reasonable aims, but they do not necessarily go together in practise. What we are talking to here is a mathematical definition of measure that is consistent and easy to manipulate, such as square distance instead of absolute value, as opposed to absolute value.

In content-based challenges, it is necessary to access object properties. Because we just have a metric to deal with in the case of electronics like mobile phones and laptops, this approach is straightforward. Annotating music and movies, on the other hand, becomes considerably more difficult, and abstract visuals, for example, become almost impossible to annotate. The types of recommendation system are shown in Figure 8.1.

8.2.1 Content Based

Content-based filtering is often used in recommendation or recommender systems. In this case, the term "content" refers to the traits or characteristics of the products you are interested in.[11] The system suggests things that you may enjoy based on your

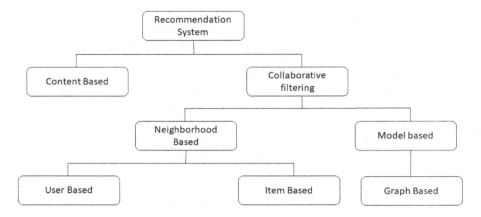

FIGURE 8.1 Recommendation system and its sub-types.

preferences and traits. There is a great deal of information available about you and your preferences, and it makes recommendations based on that information. Content-based filtering tries to provide similar goods to consumers by categorising things according to certain keywords and analysing what those customers want.[12]

When creating database objects, it is vital to provide attributes that allow an algorithm to learn anything about each particular object. These considerations should be taken into consideration when providing recommendations for products or services or for any other kind of material. User profiles are yet another important component of content-based recommender systems to consider. User profiles include information about the database objects with which a user has engaged, such as those that were bought, browsed, read, watched, or listened to, as well as information about their related qualities.[13]

An attribute that occurs often in a large number of items is given more weight than an attribute that appears in a small number of objects. Given that not all of an object's characteristics are equal to the user, this helps to demonstrate the object's worth. It is critical for customers to provide feedback when it comes to assessing a product's weight, which is why many recommendation websites require users to rate products, services, and content.[14]

In order to provide personalised recommendations, the recommender system builds a unique model of each user's preferences based on attribute weightings and histories. Based on the user's previous behaviours, the model incorporates characteristics that the user is likely to appreciate or dislike depending on their preferences. All database items are compared to user models, and a score is assigned based on how closely they reflect the user profile. The database items are compared to the user models.[15]

8.2.2 COLLABORATIVE FILTERING

In the context of recommender systems, "collaborative filtering" refers to techniques that depend extensively on earlier interactions between users and the things being suggested.[16]

Consequently, a collaborative filtering system will include all of the user's prior interactions with target objects into its computation of filtering criteria. Most of the time, this information is stored in the form of a matrix, with the rows representing people and the columns representing goods. In order to create an accurate prediction, the algorithm assumes that a user's previous data is sufficient.[17] To put it another way, we don't need any further information beyond what has already been gathered, including user comments, current trends, or anything else that may have been gathered.

Collective filtering techniques are subdivided into two sub-groups: memory-based collaborative filtering and model-based collaborative filtering.[18] A collection of things that are based on past choices by the user is required for collaborative filtering to work well. This system does not need a big number of product features in order to perform well. An embedding or feature vector is created for each item and user, which characterises them and sinks them both into a corresponding embedding location. It creates its own enclosures for both objects and people.

A product's response from other consumers is taken into consideration when suggesting it to the primary user. Before recommending the most popular item, it examines the overall behaviour of all of the users. In addition, a resemblance in liking and behaviour toward the main customer's favourite product may be utilised to link comparable consumers to the primary customer.[19]

Two alternative ways are used to record the interaction of a product user with the product. In the first place, the user's behaviours, such as clicking, listening to music tracks, searching, buying records, visiting web pages, and so on, are utilised to record and notice their preferences, which are then saved. In the case of a product rating on a scale of 1–5, a consumer conveys his or her dissatisfaction or delight by offering specific feedback. A mechanism for consumers to voice their opinions about a product directly to the maker is provided by this feature. This document includes both favourable and negative comments.[20]

People who liked a product will continue to like it in the future, owing to a recommendation engine known as collaborative filtering, which is used to make recommendations. This kind of algorithm is referred to as a product-based collaborative shift in another context. In this filtering, rather than objects, each user is attached to a filter through which information is sent. The behaviours of the users are the only ones taken into consideration by this system. It is not enough to just glance at their posts and profiles on social media. Positive product ratings will be connected to the actions of other users who have provided comparable ratings in order to determine their validity.[21]

This method is centred on proposing new items to customers based on their resemblance in behaviour to previous customers. Let's take a look at one more scenario for the purpose of completeness. If we are interested in watching a new film, you'll almost certainly ask around to find out what your friends think of it before attending. It is assumed that people trust their friends since they feel they know their friends' preferences in films and television shows. As a consequence, we are more likely to take the advise of friends who have similar interests to our own.

As a consequence, while deciding how similar two items are, the link between the object and its users is taken into consideration in collaborative filtering.[22]

8.2.3 HYBRID FILTERING

A hybrid method takes into consideration the film's background as well as the suggestions it makes when providing recommendations. When providing suggestions, it is also crucial to take into account the connections that exist between users and things, as well as between users themselves. Through usage of this framework, movie recommendations are created based on the user's existing knowledge, resulting in more customised choices for each individual consumer and better meeting their requirements. The website collects information about a user's profile, and the context of a film takes into consideration the user's watching of the film as well as the movie's score information.[23]

The data is composed of a collection of similar calculations. In a hybrid method, both tactics are used to achieve the desired outcomes, which is referred to as the hybrid approach. If we compare our strategy to other ways, we can see that it delivers more accurate suggestions. The primary reason for this is a lack of understanding of the domain dependencies of the filters as well as a lack of interest on the part of the general public in a content-based system.[24]

When used in conjunction with one another, they give a better knowledge of the underlying content as well as new collaborative filtering processes based on buyer behaviour data, which results in improved outcomes. It implements both systems and eliminates the bulk of the limitations of each system's algorithms while also boosting the overall performance of the system. Classification and grouping methods are used to improve the quality of the recommendations that are provided.[25]

8.3 STATISTICS IN EVALUATION OF RECOMMENDATION SYSTEM

The selection of the most appropriate algorithm for evaluation is given main consideration. While comparing algorithms in pairs rather than ranking algorithms based on a single statistic is sometimes useful, in most cases it is not necessary. When dealing with this circumstance, statistical significance tests and other traditional statistical approaches may be used.

In the case of continuous random variables, the probability density function (PDF) defines the probability function characterising the density of the range of values within which the variable might be observed. To put it another way, the probability density function determines the likelihood that a random variable will have a certain set of values. Alternatively, a probability distribution function, or simply a probability function, may be used to refer to it. Although this function is described as having a large range of values in many publications, it really has a narrow range of values in many publications. In many cases, it is used as a cumulative distribution function or as a probability mass function (PMF). In practise, however, the PDF defines continuous random variables, and the PMF defines discrete random variables.[26]

Definition 4: The probability of a random variable 'Z' in the interval (x, y) is defined as:

$$P\left(x \leq Z \leq y\right) = \int_{x}^{y} f\left(z\right) dz \qquad (3)$$

Definition 5: Some properties that is observed for the same random variable 'Z' are:

$$\int_{-\infty}^{\infty} f(z)\, dz = 1 \tag{4}$$

$$P(Z) = \frac{1}{\sigma\sqrt{2\pi}} e^{-\frac{1}{2}\left(\frac{z-\mu}{\sigma}\right)^2} \tag{5}$$

if Z follows Normal Distribution with a mean of μ and a variance of σ^2; denoted as $Z \sim N(\mu, \sigma^2)$.

$$P(Z = x) = \binom{n}{x} p^z (1-p)^n \tag{6}$$

if Z follows Binomial Distribution.

$$P(Z = x) = \frac{\lambda^z}{z!} e^{-\lambda} \tag{7}$$

if Z follows Poisson Distribution.

$$P(x \le Z \le y) = \int_x^y \frac{1}{y - x}\, dx \tag{8}$$

if Z follows Uniform Distribution.

$$P(Z = z) = \lambda e^{-\lambda z} \tag{9}$$

if Z follows Exponential Distribution.

First and foremost, algorithms were evaluated based on their ability to predict user preferences—the better the algorithm, the more accurate the prediction. The ability to make accurate predictions is not necessarily what people expect. Individuals are also interested in a variety of other things, such as learning about new topics, safeguarding their privacy, lowering the likelihood of being unsatisfied, and obtaining prompt service, among others. User joy is not the most important value for an e-commerce business; rather, utility (such as customer health for a pharmacy or profit for an e-commerce company) is the most important value.

To compute the rating accuracy, we use the error functions used in statistics and try to minimize the same. Some of the error functions listed in statistics are defined as follows.

Definition 6: The Root mean squared function (RMS) is used to find the mean distance from the original value to the predicted value and finding the root of the same.

$$RMS = \sqrt{\frac{1}{n} \sum_{i \in n} \left(L_i - L_i'\right)^2} \tag{10}$$

The original and predicted likeness function for each user 'i' is defined as L_i and L_i' respectively.

Definition 7: The Absolute mean error function (MA) is used to find the absolute mean distance from the original value to the predicted value.

$$MA = \frac{1}{n}\sum_{i \in n} W_i \left(L_i - L_i' \right)^2 \tag{11}$$

Definition 8: The Weighted root mean squared function (wRMS) is used to find the weighted mean distance from the original value to the predicted value finding the root of the same.

$$wRMS = \sqrt{\frac{1}{n}\sum_{i \in n} W_i \left(L_i - L_i' \right)^2} \tag{12}$$

where W_i is the weight or priority of each user likeness.

Apart from using an optimization algorithm to minimize the error in order to find the best fit of likeness function, we can also use statistics in order to compute the accuracy of usage of each user. Some of the functions are defined as:

Definition 9: True positive '++' is defined as the number of items which were recommended and were actually used.

Definition 10: False negative '−' is defined as the number of items which were not recommended and were not used.

Definition 11: True negative '+ −' is defined as the number of items which were recommended and were not used.

Definition 12: False positive '− +' is defined as the number of items which were not recommended and were actually used anyway.

Based on the previous functions, we can compute some statistics as:

Definition 13: Precision (PE) of a recommendation system is defined as:

$$PE = \frac{|++|}{|++| + |-+|} \tag{13}$$

Definition 14: Recall (R) of a recommendation system is defined as:

$$R = \frac{|++|}{|++| + |--|} \tag{14}$$

Definition 15: Specificity (S) of a recommendation system is defined as:

$$R = \frac{|--|}{|-+| + |--|} \tag{15}$$

Definition 16: Accuracy (A) of a recommendation system is defined as:

$$A = \frac{|++|}{|++| + |--| + |-+| + |+-|} \tag{16}$$

A fixed recommendation list length allows for the comparison of the accuracy of different algorithms to be performed. The quality of predictions changes with the size of the list, but it is difficult to determine the optimal quantity. The trade-off between accuracy and memory, as well as the true positive rate and the false positive rate, is routinely computed and shown in clinical settings. Following the precision-recall curve (precision-recall), it is the receiver operating characteristic (REC) that is ranked first (ROC curve).[27]

Precision-recall, on the other hand, is restricted to a certain area of application. ROC curves are used in cases when the false positive rate is high in order to lower the cost of false positives. As an example, a company that gives out freebies to encourage new customers may be adversely impacted. For example, a DVD recommender in a video rental company may use ROC curves to improve the quality of predictions rather than to reduce the cost of incorrect forecasts, since the cost of incorrect forecasts is so low in this industry. A ranking function can be devised for ranking items for the users. It is being defined as:

Definition 17: A ranking function δ can be defined on the items recommended for each individual users as:

$$\delta = \frac{1}{n} \frac{\sum_i \left(L_i - \bar{L}\right)\left(\hat{L}_i - \bar{\hat{L}}\right)}{\sigma(L)\sigma(\hat{L})} \tag{17}$$

where L_i is the likeness of each user, $\bar{L}$ is the mean of the likeness factor, $\hat{L}_i$ is the likeness of each user computed by the system, $(\bar{\hat{L}})$ is the mean of the likeness of each user computed by the system, $\sigma(L)$ is the standard deviation of the likeness function of users and finally, $\sigma(\hat{L})$ is the standard deviation of the system computed likeness function.

In order to quantify the coverage of the recommendation system, we tend to use a function:

Definition 18: The coverage function can be computed by using a molded function from Gini Index 'G' defined as:

$$G = \frac{1}{n-1} \sum_i \left(2i - n - 1\right) P(i) \tag{18}$$

We can also use an entropy function for the same purpose.

$$G - \sum_i P(i) \log P(i) \tag{19}$$

8.4 STATISTICS IN DATA MODELLING OF RS

Before the start of modelling any system, we have to find the distribution of each sampling. The sampling distribution is a statistical probability distribution that is dependent on the number of samples obtained from a given population in a certain time period. The sampling distribution of a population is the range of potential outcomes for a certain statistic, which is stated as the frequency distribution of various alternative outcomes for the population.

An appropriate statistical sample is selected from the whole population in statistical analysis, as explained earlier. If you have a huge collection of items, events, people, or measurements in your population, you may use the phrase "population." As a result, a population is defined as an observation of a group of people who have been brought together in one place. Although, we can have a variety of distribution which the sample follows, we can use the central limit theorem for a common Gaussian or normal distribution.

To put it another way, regardless of how the data are dispersed, the mean of a sample's data will tend to be closer to the average of the population. Or to put it another way, the data is valid irrespective of how the data is distributed. It is common practise to use the central limit theorem in conjunction with the law of large numbers, which states that as sample size increases, the average of sample means and standard deviations will approach those of the population mean and standard deviation as a result of the law of large numbers.

Definition 19: If we have 'k' samples of size 'n', where $30 \leq n$; the mean of the samples will be Normally distributed.

Definition 20: The law of large numbers ensures that,

$$\mu = \frac{\overline{x_1} + \overline{x_2} + \ldots + \overline{x_k}}{|k|} \tag{20}$$

The ability of recommendation algorithms to cope with large volumes of data and sparseness is becoming more challenging to achieve. It raises concerns about the costs of computation as well as the low quality of the ideas that are generated as a consequence of them. For this topic, dimensionality reduction algorithms are used in order to minimise processing costs while simultaneously improving prediction. When high-dimensional input data is transformed into lower levels of latent data, the process is known as "data reduction," which is also known as "dimensionality reduction." The process of matrix factorization involves reducing a data matrix D to the product of many low-rank matrices, which is similar to the process of dimensionality reduction.[28]

Definition 21: The singular value decomposition (SVD) technique is a powerful dimensionality reduction method. The primary problem in using an SVD is to discover a smaller feature space with fewer dimensions. The SVD matrix factorization algorithm divides a $|U|$ x $|S|$ matrix L into three matrices as follows:

$$L = A \times B \times C' \tag{21}$$

where 'B' is a diagonal matrix with singular values of 'L', also 'A' and 'C' are orthogonal matrices.

SVD may be used in recommender systems for a variety of different applications. As a starting point, it is used to collect latent connections between consumers and goods, which allows us to predict whether or not a certain client would purchase a particular product. The use of this approach makes it feasible to create a two-dimensional representation of the original customer-product region and to do future calculations in that area. It is then used to provide them with a list of the top-N items available on the market.

In the context of Matrix Factorization MF, Principal Component Analysis (PCA) is a sophisticated approach for decreasing dimensionality that may be used. PCA employs an orthogonal transformation to obtain a collection of values known as principal components from a set of possibly correlated data. Principal components are variables that are linearly uncorrelated when compared to the other variables in the set of potentially correlated data (PC).

The number of computers used is less than or equal to the number of variables input into the computation at the outset. An orthogonal transform is constructed in such a way that all of its components are orthogonal to the components that came before them, and the first PC has the greatest variance feasible. They are orthogonal because they are eigenvectors of the covariance matrix, which makes them mutually exclusive. The relative scale of the original variables has an impact on the PCA.

Theorem 1: If 'E' is the eigen vector matrix of LL', in a non-ascending order of eigen values, the dimensionality reduction of L is given as $E'L$.

Another type of methodology for data prepossessing in RS is clustering methods. It is possible to group items based on their degree of resemblance to one another, as opposed to their degree of similarity to other objects in the same cluster. For detecting patterns in large datasets that might otherwise go undiscovered, clustering is a typical unsupervised machine-learning approach used in data mining. Because it is predicated on the notion that things within a dataset are more similar to one another than they are to items inside other datasets, it splits the dataset into several groups or clusters, which are then further divided. If a dataset has n features, then a clustering algorithm will regard each item as a distinct point in a wider n-dimensional space, rather than as a collection of points.

Historically, in recommendation systems, the neighbours of a target user have been determined by utilising similarity-based algorithms to determine who they are. In real-time recommender systems, it is not feasible for all users to assess, be interested in, or become familiar with all of the items that are available. It is likely that the user-item rating matrix will be sparse when there is a relationship or interaction between the two variables. "Sparsity" is the term used to describe this critical problem, which has an influence on the accuracy of rating forecasts made by the recommendation engine. Similarity-based models are useless for generating an effective list of similar users because of the increasing need to address the sparsity problem, but the inability to do so due to the lack of resources available. While similarity measures are computationally costly, they become progressively more difficult to apply as the amount of data in the dataset gets exponentially larger. Using clustering approaches, it is possible to divide people into various groups in order to handle issues such as selecting individuals in close proximity based on their commonalities. Clustering is often characterised as the process of bringing together a group of database users into a single unit while maintaining a high degree of similarity among them. As a result, items of interest to the members of the cluster are recommended to the user who has been recognised as having interests that are similar to the target user's interests. Clustering techniques in recommendation systems help to improve performance by finding groups of users who have similar interests. They are also more resistant to sparsity issues than other approaches. Clustering approaches such as fuzzy self-organizing maps (SOM) and k-means clustering are two of the most often employed.[29]

When it comes to making product recommendations, product similarity is the most effective strategy available. If a user is browsing or searching for a certain product, they may be offered with similar things. Users often expect to find what they're searching for quickly, and if they don't, they'll leave the site and go to a different one. Users who buy a product may be shown with related items when they click on one of those products, or they may be offered discounts and promotions for comparable products if they purchase a product from us. When we don't know much about the customer, but we do know what goods they're looking at, product similarities may be quite useful in identifying them.

The term "user similarity" refers to the ability to compare the similarities and differences between two individuals. Because they both like the same thing, we may deduce that the two persons have interests that are comparable to each other. Receiving a product suggestion from a reputable source is analogous. User similarity, on the other hand, has the disadvantage of requiring the user's whole data set in order to offer suggestions. Users must give past data in order to begin the recommendation process, which is why this issue is referred to as a "cold start difficulty." Websites that are just getting off the ground are particularly vulnerable to the "cold start" problem since they do not yet have a substantial number of visitors to their site.

Product similarity is not a problem since all that is required is product information as well as the preferences of the customer. This difficulty is solved by companies such as Netflix, which asks users what they prefer watching when they sign up for a new subscription.

When comparing two items, the distance measure is used to evaluate how similar they are.[30] As you get closer, the points become less significant; the closer you approach, the less significant the points become. Whether or whether there is any similarity is totally up to the person and varies tremendously depending on the subject matter and environment. Comparing two movies of the same genre, run time, or cast, for example, is a common practise. The use of caution should be used when calculating distances between unrelated dimensions and features. As a result, the distance computation may be biased by a single feature if the relative values between each element are not normalised.

Definition 22: In a numeric data format we can find the distance metric 'D(u,s)' as 'Minkowski Distance', defined as:

$$D(u,s) = \left(\sum_i \left(|U_i - S_i| \right)^q \right)^{\frac{1}{q}} \tag{22}$$

Definition 23: In a point between axis data format we can find the distance metric 'D(u,s)' as 'Manhattan Distance', defined as:

$$D(u,s) = \left(\sum_i \left(|U_i - S_i| \right)^q \right)^{\frac{1}{2}} \tag{23}$$

Definition 24: In an Euclidean space data format we can find the distance metric 'D(u,s)' as 'Euclidean Distance', defined as:

$$D(u,s) = \left(\sum_i \left(|U_i - S_i| \right)^2 \right)^{\frac{1}{2}} \tag{24}$$

Definition 25: In vector space data format we can find the similarity metric 'SIM(u,s)' as 'Cosine Similarity', defined as:

$$SIM(u,s) = \cos\theta = \frac{\vec{U_i} \cdot \vec{S_i}}{\vec{U_i} \cdot \vec{S_i}} \tag{25}$$

Definition 26: In object space data format we can find the similarity metric 'SIM(u,s)' as 'Jaccard Similarity', defined as:

$$SIM(u,s) = \frac{U_i \cap S_i}{U_i \cup S_i} \tag{26}$$

8.5 CONCLUSION

This chapter's goal was to provide a complete literature overview of the most extensively used statistical techniques to recommender systems; however, the emphasis was on the statistical underpinnings of those approaches rather than how they are implemented. This chapter extensively discussed clustering and elaborated on content-based, knowledge-based (and hybrid) collaborative filtering. As a consequence, probabilistic methods were presented. Each approach had formalised mathematical principles and methodologies. The assessment's main purpose was to find the most effective algorithm. There are several ways to compare algorithms, but for the most part, a basic pair comparison suffices.

REFERENCES

1. Kumar P, Thakur RS. Recommendation system techniques and related issues: a survey. *International Journal of Information Technology.* 2018 Dec;10(4):495–501.
2. Goyani M, Chaurasiya N. A review of movie recommendation system. *ELCVIA: Electronic Letters on Computer Vision and Image Analysis.* 2020 Aug 25;19(3):18–37.
3. Ali S, Hafeez Y, Humayun M, Jamail NS, Aqib M, Nawaz A. Enabling recommendation system architecture in virtualized environment for e-learning. *Egyptian Informatics Journal.* 2022 Mar 1;23(1):33–45.
4. Sharma L, Gera A. A survey of recommendation system: Research challenges. *International Journal of Engineering Trends and Technology (IJETT).* 2013 May;4(5):1989–1992.
5. Zhou R, Khemmarat S, Gao L. The impact of YouTube recommendation system on video views. In *Proceedings of the 10th ACM SIGCOMM conference on Internet measurement* (pp. 404–410). 2010 Nov 1. DOI: 10.1145/1879141.1879193
6. Patel K, Patel HB. A state-of-the-art survey on recommendation system and prospective extensions. *Computers and Electronics in Agriculture.* 2020 Nov 1;178:105779.

7. Hameed MA, Al Jadaan O, Ramachandram S. Collaborative filtering based recommendation system: A survey. *International Journal on Computer Science and Engineering.* 2012 May 1;4(5):859.

8. Bhatt B, Premal JP, Gaudani H. A Review Paper on Machine Learning Based Recommendation System. *International Journal of Engineering Development and Research.* 2014;2(4). https://www.researchgate.net/publication/283479282_A_Review_Paper_on_Machine_Learning_Based_Recommendation_System.

9. Moon J, Jang I, Choe YC, Kim JG, Bock G. Case study of big data-based agri-food recommendation system according to types of customers. *The Journal of Korean Institute of Communications and Information Sciences.* 2015;40(5):903–913.

10. Gigimol S, John S. A survey on different types of recommendation systems. *Engineering and Science.* 2016;1(4):111–113.

11. Pazzani MJ, Billsus D. Content-based recommendation systems. In *The adaptive web* (pp. 325–341). 2007. Springer, Berlin, Heidelberg.

12. Debnath S, Ganguly N, Mitra P. Feature weighting in content based recommendation system using social network analysis. In *Proceedings of the 17th international conference on world wide web* (pp. 1041–1042). 2008 Apr 21. DOI: 10.1145/1367497.1367646

13. Reddy SR, Nalluri S, Kunisetti S, Ashok S, Venkatesh B. Content-based movie recommendation system using genre correlation. In *Smart intelligent computing and applications* (pp. 391–397). 2019. Springer, Singapore.

14. Thorat PB, Goudar RM, Barve S. Survey on collaborative filtering, content-based filtering and hybrid recommendation system. *International Journal of Computer Applications.* 2015 Jan 1;110(4):31–36.

15. Rutkowski T, Romanowski J, Woldan P, Staszewski P, Nielek R, Rutkowski L. A content-based recommendation system using neuro-fuzzy approach. In *2018 IEEE international conference on fuzzy systems (FUZZ-IEEE)* (pp. 1–8). 2018 Jul 8. IEEE.

16. Schafer JB, Frankowski D, Herlocker J, Sen S. Collaborative filtering recommender systems. In *The adaptive web* (pp. 291–324). 2007. Springer, Berlin, Heidelberg.

17. Ekstrand MD, Riedl JT, Konstan JA. *Collaborative filtering recommender systems.* 2011. Now Publishers Inc. https://www.nowpublishers.com › HCI-009

18. Herlocker JL, Konstan JA, Terveen LG, Riedl JT. Evaluating collaborative filtering recommender systems. *ACM Transactions on Information Systems (TOIS).* 2004 Jan 1;22(1):5–3.

19. Elahi M, Ricci F, Rubens N. A survey of active learning in collaborative filtering recommender systems. *Computer Science Review.* 2016 May 1;20:29–50.

20. Suganeshwari G, Syed Ibrahim SP. A survey on collaborative filtering based recommendation system. In *Proceedings of the 3rd international symposium on big data and cloud computing challenges (ISBCC–16')* (pp. 503–518). 2016. Springer, Cham.

21. Hameed MA, Al Jadaan O, Ramachandram S. Collaborative filtering based recommendation system: A survey. *International Journal on Computer Science and Engineering.* 2012 May 1;4(5):859.

22. Wen Z. Recommendation system based on collaborative filtering. *CS229 Lecture Notes.* 2008 Dec 12. https://www.researchgate.net/publication/265656811_Recommendation_System_Based_on_Collaborative_Filtering

23. Geetha G, Safa M, Fancy C, Saranya D. A hybrid approach using collaborative filtering and content based filtering for recommender system. In *Journal of Physics: Conference Series* (Vol. 1000, No. 1, p. 012101). 2018 Apr 1. IOP Publishing. DOI: 10.1088/1742-6596/1000/1/012101

24. Jain KN, Kumar V, Kumar P, Choudhury T. Movie recommendation system: hybrid information filtering system. In *Intelligent Computing and Information and Communication* (pp. 677–686). 2018. Springer, Singapore.

25. Patel B, Desai P, Panchal U. Methods of recommender system: a review. In *2017 international conference on innovations in information, embedded and communication systems (ICIIECS)* (pp. 1–4). 2017 Mar 17. IEEE.

26. Ramberg JS, Dudewicz EJ, Tadikamalla PR, Mykytka EF. A probability distribution and its uses in fitting data. *Technometrics.* 1979 May 1;21(2):201–214.

27. Hoo ZH, Candlish J, Teare D. What is an ROC curve? *Emergency Medicine Journal.* 2017 Jun 1;34(6):357–359.

28. Hoecker A, Kartvelishvili V. SVD approach to data unfolding. *Nuclear Instruments and Methods in Physics Research Section A: Accelerators, Spectrometers, Detectors and Associated Equipment.* 1996 Apr 1;372(3):469–481.

29. Kohonen T. The self-organizing map. *Proceedings of the IEEE.* 1990 Sep;78(9): 1464–1480.

30. Guo G, Zhang J, Yorke-Smith N. A novel Bayesian similarity measure for recommender systems. In *IJCAI* (Vol. 13, pp. 2619–2625). 2013 Aug 3. https://doi.org/10.1145/2856037

9 An IoT-Enabled Innovative Smart Parking Recommender Approach

Ajanta Das and Soumya Sankar Basu

CONTENTS

9.1 INTRODUCTION

In this existing era of growing urbanisation and globalisation, almost every road is filled with smart cars and smart vehicles. So in this smart era and time-bound lifestyle, people get restless easily and face lot of difficulties when searching for a parking space nearby their chosen location. Even if some space suitable for parking is found, it is difficult to find the parking allocator in that space at that instant. So when the user releases the space, suddenly the parking allocator appears and, often, they charge very high. However, the person must pay the parking fees, no matter what is demanded. With high parking prices, people are parking their vehicles without any security. If the allocator is not around the vehicle is parked and the car is damaged, the driver cannot claim that from the parking allocator. To address these issues of traditional parking systems, smart parking provides lot of options and calmness for the driver while they are searching for a parking space on the road. Therefore, the application of a smart parking system enables drivers to solicit real time parking information and book parking slots.

DOI: 10.1201/9781003319122-9

In a smart parking system, an Internet of Things (IoT) device is installed in each parking spot to detect the availability of the spot and send status information to a service *allocator*. The service allocator allows drivers to check the available parking spaces and make online reservations. The important features of existing smart parking systems are to use unique identification ID and encryption algorithms for authentication and authorization and online secured payment using bitcoin to preserve privacy.

However, the already existing smart parking systems require drivers to disclose their sensitive information, such as their desired destinations. Moreover, existing schemes are centralized, which makes them vulnerable to failure problems and privacy breaches by service providers. So the aim of this chapter is to propose a similar-featured smart parking system with high privacy using blockchain and private information retrieval (Amiri et al., 2020).

The objective of the chapter is to propose the following functionalities with basic and general features of the smart parking application, RecoPark:

1. Prediction-based hourly basis parking space booking in crowded areas
2. User may reserve the parking space online for a specific location in advance
3. Reward-based smart parking facility
4. Recommendation of distance-based parking space and parking fees.

The organization of the chapter as follows. The chapter starts with literature review presented in Section 9.2, and the evolution of the smart parking system is briefly discussed in Section 9.3. In today's world, smart parking has become ubiquitous; therefore its necessity is explained in Section 9.4. An overview of the recommender system is illustrated in Section 9.5; while Section 9.6 presents the architecture of the proposed smart parking recommender system. Finally, the chapter concludes with Section 9.7.

9.2   RELATED WORK

This section briefly presents existing contributions towards smart parking solutions based on current research work.

Parking has been a pain area in cities. An INRIX report (Cookson, 2017) shows that, on average, an American driver spends 17 hours a year looking for a parking space. It is costing drivers in the United States and Germany dearly—at $96 billion and €45 billion respectively.

The idea of smart parking has been introduced to solve this problem. Smart parking has become part of smart city concepts. Advancements of sensors, radio-frequency identification (RFID), IoT, and faster networks contributed to the progress of smart parking solutions. Smart parking systems are broadly categorised into three categories based on usage patterns and scenarios.

First is a centralised-assisted smart parking system. This approach has a central server. It collects all necessary information and provide services. Parking guidance and information systems (Hui-ling et al., 2003), centralised assisted parking search (Kuran et al., 2015), and car park occupancy information systems (Bong et al., 2008) fall in this category. While keeping the central theme the same, they vary in usage of technologies.

Distributed-assisted smart parking systems are the second category. Here many services are connected and controlled by a single server. A vehicular network where one vehicle is connected to others can realise this approach well. Transit-based information system (Idris et al., 2009), opportunistically-assisted parking search (Kokolaki et al., 2012), and mobile storage node-opportunistically assisted parking search (Kokolaki et al., 2013) fall in this category. These approaches vary in the information transformation mechanism between vehicles.

The other category is non-assisted parking search (Delot et al., 2013). In this approach, no information is exchanged. The decision is solely based on driver observation. They wander around a parking lot and park whenever they find an available spot. At a broad level, a smart parking system implements mainly three use cases (Al-Turjman and Malekloo, 2019): the smart payment system, the parking reservation system, and the e-parking system.

A smart payment system (Chinrungrueng et al., 2007) is an integrated IoT system with advanced technologies to assure reliability and fast payment as opposed to conventional slow parking meters. Parking reservation systems (Mouskos, 2007) allow drivers to secure a parking spot in advance prior to their journey, especially in peak hours. E-parking (Sauras-Perez et al., 2014) allows users to obtain information about parking availability electronically.

In Alkenazan et al. (2021), various security aspects of smart parking system are presented. An identification card along with a private complex password is issued to each user. Authorization checking is performed at the entry of the parking lot. The authors tested every different scenario for the proposed adaptive framework and established with proven results.

In Li et al. (2017), a thorough study of a state-of-art of smart parking system is elaborated. This chapter presents insight to the details of all different categories of technologies and solutions related to smart parking. The authors focused on a smart parking ecosystem, as it becomes a vital issue with the increase of urban population and traffic congestion. It is also established that smart parking ecosystems are multi-disciplinary, and three macro-themes need to be integrated—namely, information collection, system deployment, and service dissemination for better sustainable solution in the cities.

At the outset, the proposed RecoPark enables privacy preserving data analysis for parking service allocators. The distributed consortium blockchain-based architecture provides faster response, controls central failure, and provide security with a smart contract. Moreover, RecoPark will predict the availability of a parking space and offer reward-based smart parking. Finally, in crowded and busy cities, prediction-based hourly basis parking space bookings will keep users calm, even during rush hour. This feature will enhance more reliability and dependability of RecoPark.

9.3 NECESSITY OF NETWORK-BASED SMART PARKING

In the smart era there is a general tendency to explore every facility through the internet and to be knowledgeable, which makes life smarter and definitely saves time. Therefore, researching information on car parking before reaching the destination becomes common to keep pace and match the rhythm of life in a busy daily schedule. Smart people utilise their network for getting advance information and smart life-style facilities are available through internet easily. It provides great relief to drivers and a mental peace before they start their trip.

During the pandemic, the preferred mode of travel was self-driven cars or rental cars. Latest statistics show that vacation trips by car are increasing day by day with busy lifestyles. In the smart era, vacations by train are decreasing compared to the vacations by car or plane. This is due to lot of factors, like the reservation of tickets, choice of tickets, proper vacation planning in busy lifestyle, etc. Instead, people may travel by their own car for sudden plans or necessity. However, this will be easier if the driver of the car is comfortable and knowledgeable with detailed parking information.

In this context, it can be cited that weekend trips are mostly travelled by car. Parking is not challenging if people visit remote lonely places, but on the other hand, if they visit a busy city, it is always preferrable to know where and when car parking will be available. Travelers can make their itineraries according to the car parking schedule and recommendation. It is worth mentioning that parking is challenging for visitors of residents or people attending any kind of marriage ceremony, banquet dinner, conferences for 2 to 3 days in crowded and unfamiliar city.

To provide the solutions for these problems, it is absolutely necessary to recommend a smart parking system. The system includes various factors such as the location of the parking lot, the distance from the parking lot to the destination, the approaching roads near the parking lot, the parking rate, the availability at the required time, the duration, and advanced booking options. Advanced booking options prioritise recommendations or the reputation of the driver. This feature is required to confirm the parking lot before they reach the place, specifically for inter-city travel itineraries. Therefore, networked-based or distributed smart parking is necessary to deliver a peaceful solution.

This chapter proposes a reward-based recommender system for smart parking to encourage drivers not to extend the parking time, but rather to vacate the parking space as early as possible. The proposed recommendation system will prioritise those drivers for future booking. The reputation or recommendation of the drivers will absolutely expedite the system in terms of time, cost, and quality of life.

9.4   EVOLUTION OF IOT-INTEGRATED SYSTEM

The internet allows users to access information and services electronically, regardless of their geographic position. Improvement of device configuration and demands for user mobility has made portable computing a reality.

Electrical and electronic gadgets are becoming smarter and intelligent. Devices such as sensors, actuators, and RFIDs are becoming part of our world. The increased pervasiveness has resulted in thing-to-thing communication along with human-to-thing communication. The digital world is witnessing impact of IoT-enabled devices. The IoT global arena is growing exponentially.

The internet was developed with data created by people, while the IoT is about data created by things (Madakam et al., 2015). The term IoT is now widely used, but there is no common definition of understanding of what the IoT encompasses (Wortmann and Flüchter, 2015).

Although there is no *standard* definition for IoT, it has been defined and explained numerous times in the literature (Huang et al., 2016; Lund et al., 2014; Ben-Daya et al., 2017; Madakam et al., 2015; Ornes, 2016). In a broad sense, the objective of IoT is similar despite variations in the definition. In general, it is about a network of networks of uniquely identifiable endpoints or "things" that capture and share data. The main goal of IoT technologies is to simplify processes to ensure a better efficiency of systems and improve life quality. It is applied in different fields.

The efficient implementation of IoT applications is linked with the available speed and coverage of the wireless network (Wi-Fi). There is a noticeable increase in Wi-Fi network coverage and speed.

During the period from 2017 to 2022, the global increase in Wi-Fi speed is expected to more than double, i.e. from about 24 Mbps to more than 54 Mbps (Nižetić et al., 2020). The biggest increase is expected is the Asian region, and the lowest increases are expected in the Latin America, Middle East, and Africa regions. This has a direct impact on IoT application deployment in those areas.

Based on current available technical solutions the most represented application sectors of IoT applications are shown in Figure 9.1.

The most promising application areas of IoT are related to industry (Osterrieder et al., 2020) and the smart city concept (Sivanageswara Rao et al., 2020) with respect to the number of realised projects. There are other areas like transportation (Porru et al., 2020), smart energy management in buildings (Douglas et al., 2020), management of power networks (Martín-Lopo et al., 2020), and the agriculture sector (Villa-Henriksen et al., 2020) where IoT is showing promising potential.

Development of IoT applications in specific areas strongly depends on several key factors (Nižetić et al., 2020) such as availability of advancements in electronic components, availability of software solutions and user-friendly surrounding, solutions

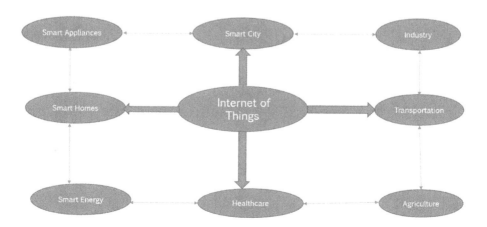

FIGURE 9.1 Applications of IoT.

related to sensor technologies, quality of network, sufficient energy supply for production, and operation of IoT devices.

One of the key objectives of IoT is to improve quality of life. Most of the people need to travel every day. According to the British National Travel Survey, a typical household drives 361 hours a year (Anon., 2020), and on average the vehicle is parked for 95% of its lifetime (Cogill et al., 2014). Normally, people tend to travel using their own vehicles due to a higher rate of comfort and availability (Shoup, 2006).

Parking locations and spaces are selected based on human-to-vehicle ratio. About 31% of the total land is used for parking in San Francisco, 16% in London, 18% in New York, and 81% in Los Angeles (Manville and Shoup, 2005; Pierce and Shoup, 2013). If the driver has prior information about availability of parking slots, fuel consumption will be less (Rajabioun and Ioannou, 2015).

IoT, along with cloud computing, can be applied in developing an automated valet parking and smart cities (Huang et al., 2018). These services include real-time processing, location awareness, and data and load management for environment sensing and coordination, which may have a direct effect on human mobility and future transportation systems (Ni et al., 2019).

A broad structure of IoT solutions is presented in Figure 9.2, which includes smart sensors, apps, IoT solutions, perform data analytics, and storage analytics across the wide area network.

In IoT, the "things" are different sensors and actuators. They are connected to the internet through Wi-Fi. "Things" get connected to an application through an end Edge. The edge is responsible for authenticating the data that is coming from different "things;" after authenticating the data it sends the data to the application. The application is hosted in a cloud. Last but not least, in broad terms, IoT solutions follow this structure.

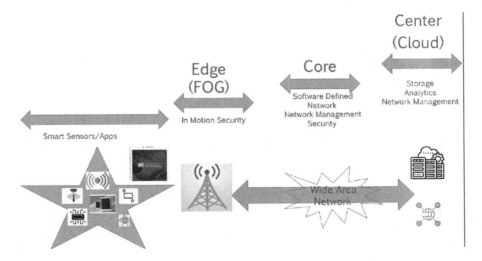

FIGURE 9.2   Broad IoT solutions including sensors, applications, Data Analytics etc.

Next, this chapter presents machine learning-based recommender system followed by the architecture of the proposed recommendation system.

9.5 BRIEF OVERVIEW OF RECOMMENDER SYSTEM

In today's world users are overwhelmed with overloaded information. It is difficult for users to find items of interest. Recommender systems are software applications that helping with this. Recommender systems are one of the most visible success stories of artificial intelligence in practice. The main objective of such systems is to direct users to potential topic of interest. Recommender systems not only help users in information overload situation (Ricci et al., 2015) but also can significantly contribute to the business success of service providers (Jannach et al., 2021).

In the recent years, recommender systems have grown exponentially, and its applications have spread over various domain of life including online shopping for books, home appliances, movies, and electronic gadgets and recommendations for doctors and hospitals for patients, institute recommendation for students and teachers, hotel recommendations for tourists, and many more (Sohail et al., 2017). The success of recommender is the human tendency to rely upon experiences of neighbours and friends prior to making any kind of decision.

9.5.1 CLASSIFICATION

Usually, recommender systems can be categorised on several bases (Adomavicius and Tuzhilin, 2005). The main categorisations are based on a) approaches used, b) area of application for which the recommendation is made, and c) data mining techniques applied, etc.

On the contrary, broadly eight categories of recommender systems are identified (Sohail et al., 2017).

1. Collaborative filtering-based recommender systems
2. Reclusive methods-based recommender systems
3. Demographic filtering based recommender systems
4. Knowledge based-recommender systems
5. Hybrid recommender systems
6. Context aware recommendation system
7. Social network-based recommender systems
8. Soft computing techniques-based recommender systems

The collaborative filtering approach makes use of the recommendations from other customers whose choices are like the customer for whom the recommendation is made. It is one of the most successful and frequently used techniques since the appearance of first recommender system in mid 1990s.

The reclusive approach exploits the features of the objects and requires its representation (Yager, 2003). Reclusive approaches are complementary to collaborative techniques. Its emphasis is on finding similarities between objects (about which recommendations are asked for) rather than finding similarities between users.

The demographic approach also uses similarity measures like the collaborative approach. But while considering the neighbour users, it tries to find similarity between the user's demographic information like age, sex, occupation, etc. According to the preference of the customer, the system recommends alike items to a new user having the similar age, sex, occupation, etc. to the customer.

Apart from collaborative and reclusive approaches, a recommender can also be thought of as knowledge-based approach. A knowledge-based approach places importance on the user's requirements and characteristics of the recommended products/services.

The hybrid approach is a different combination of reclusive and collaborative approaches. The context aware approach is a kind of knowledge-based approach where the context of the product/services is also considered as knowledge.

The details of a recommender applied over a social networking environment has been extensively studied and presented (Zhou et al., 2012) because people mostly consult the recommendations from social networking due to the huge information flow in the social network.

Increasingly, the soft computing techniques have been used in recommender systems for incorporating collaborative recommendations, reclusive recommendations, and hybrid recommendations (Sohail et al., 2017).

9.5.2 FUNCTIONAL ARCHITECTURE

In a broader sense, recommender systems work on available data and respond to users with the required recommendations. Figure 9.3 represents a functional block diagram of a recommender in today's context.

A recommendation system exposes different application programming interfaces (APIs) to provide different recommendations through various mobile apps or web apps. Apps call the APIs to get the recommendation. Recommendation systems work on different available data from different datastores to generate the recommendation.

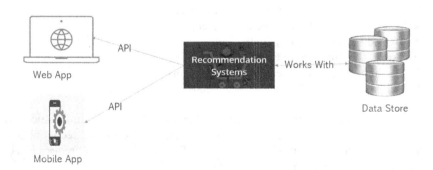

FIGURE 9.3 Functional block diagram of recommender system.

Recent recommender systems use users' previous behaviours to predict their current preferences as well. This is achieved through the handshaking of machine learning and recommender systems.

The next section illustrates the proposed smart parking recommender architecture briefly.

9.6 PROPOSED SMART PARKING RECOMMENDER ARCHITECTURE

This section proposes an integrated smarter parking system, RecoPark. It aims at flexibility to make sure the proposed solution can autonomously adapt to different usage scenarios of smarter parking. The solution is targeted to be usable in terms of user experience and ease of operation. The proposed system is layered and integrated with various IoT devices and various smarter technologies, like blockchain, cloud, etc. For ease of understanding, the section elaborates on the hierarchical structure, architecture, and functionalities with a top-level use case diagram.

9.6.1 HIERARCHICAL STRUCTURE

This proposed system will connect various states and cities across the country. The proposed solution is capable of hierarchically scaling up. Many localities/cities can be part of a state/county; states can be part of country; countries can be part of a subcontinent/continent. A hierarchical view of the proposed smart parking system is presented in Figure 9.4 to explain one such situation of a state.

Therefore, the system can connect all the parking lots of a locality or city or different states. A city may have multiple parking lots, and each parking lot consists of many parking spaces. Each parking lot is managed by *manager*, and the parking

FIGURE 9.4 Hierarchical structure of the proposed system.

space is managed by an *allocator*. Parking lots may be managed by different organisations; hence, a manager is solely responsible for the specific parking lot and communicates to the allocator of a particular parking space. Simultaneously, an allocator is responsible for allotting parking to the driver in the specific parking space. Our current scope is restricted to a technical scope, and as a result, we are not including the ownership aspect of parking lots.

In this scenario, a state consists of multiple cities. The city contains multiple parking lots. We have only shown this for one city for the simplicity of the diagram. Other cities also have multiple parking lots. A parking lot contains multiple parking spaces. For a similar reason, we have detailed only one parking lot here.

The same picture can be extended to depict the entire hierarchy up to a continent.

9.6.2 ARCHITECTURE

A layered architecture to implement smarter parking solution is proposed to maintain productivity with enhanced maintainability. The proposed architectural principles are influenced by IEEE Internet of Things Reference Architecture.

Moreover, different layers from IBM Internet of Things Reference Architecture (IoT Cloud Architecture Centre) are also adopted. Layers are created to enhance separation of concern and loose coupling. Each layer is dependent on the service from its adjacent right layer. For example, the user layer always depends on the interaction layer, and the interaction layer depends on the application layer. Implementation of each layer can be changed anytime while keeping the interfaces between the layers the same. Each layer is accessed through a gateway or façade kind of service. The gateway/façade ensures that there is only one entry point to a layer. It increases the security of each layer. The gateway/façade services leverage other services to provide the required layer functionality.

Figure 9.5 illustrates the overview of the proposed architecture.

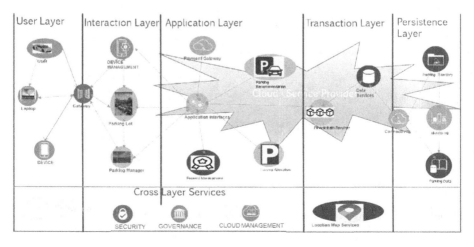

FIGURE 9.5 Proposed smart parking architecture.

The architecture of the proposed smart parking system, RecoPark, consists of five different layers: *user layer, interaction layer, application layer, transaction layer,* and *cloud layer.* The user layer allocates demand-based parking space in the specific location. In order to achieve this, the user needs to communicate with RecoPark through the interaction layer. The interaction layer is solely responsible for timely instantaneous communication between the user and parking recommender. Next, the application layer provides the actual allocation of space with charges per hour or per day.

A driver of the car will search location-based available parking lots through their devices, such as a smart phone. The gateway will check the nearby or surrounding parking lots for available space. The gateway communicates with the smart parking application, RecoPark, for further recommendations. Next, the gateway is solely responsible for providing the free parking lot to the user through his or her device. The moment the driver parks the vehicle in the allocated space, RecoPark will automatically update the information. The updated information will also be available to the parking manager for spot allocation.

The user layer describes the users of our application. As it is a smarter parking system, it will be used by different vehicles. Based on user preference, the driver can use a laptop, handheld device, or built-in interfaces in the vehicle. We assign a unique identifier to the device used by a particular vehicle, and that identifier is used to identify the vehicle in our system. In case a device is changed, e.g. the driver decides to use a handheld device instead of a built-in interface, the vehicle need to be re-registered. There would be a provision to use the previous ID.

The user layer interacts with the interaction layer through a gateway. The gateway acts as an edge between the users and our application. The gateway authenticates the device and forwards the request to the interaction layer. The interaction layer mainly provides three kind of interaction ability. Device management helps in registering or authorising a device (vehicle). It provides a capability of interacting with a parking lot when a vehicle enters or departs a parking lot. Vehicles can also interact with a parking manager to find or reserve parking. Parking lots are registered with the parking manager. Based on the number of places we deploy our solution, we may have more than one parking manager specific to a place.

The interaction layer interacts with the application layer through application interfaces. We propose application interfaces as a façade in the application layer, and to provide the services, it takes help from different helper services. The payment gateway helps process payment while reserving a parking space. Parking recommendation services provide recommendations about the nearest parking or better time slots to get proper parking with an affordable cost. Once the proposed system has data for few months, the parking recommendation service can use artificial intelligence capabilities to provide better recommendations. Parking allocation services help allocate the parking. The reward management service helps manage rewards for vehicles. The rewards can be based on different rules like frequent parking, flexible parking time, etc. Application interfaces also interact with the transaction layer.

The application layer interacts with the transaction layer to manage data persistence. As the proposed solution is meant to be used in multiple places, it is likely to be used by different parking operators. To build trust among them, we propose using blockchain services to persist data. The transaction layer has a local data store as a helper. Block chain services can operate in the local data store to validate the data.

Validated data is stored at persistence layer. The persistence layer is accessed through a connectivity service as a gateway. There are different data stores for parking lots and parking. There is a monitoring service that monitors data periodically.

The application layer, transaction layer, and persistence layer can be deployed in a cloud and implemented using cloud services. To increase portability, we can implement these layers within a container, and deploy the containers in a cloud. That way the layers can be deployed in any cloud. Our architecture provides this flexibility.

We have few cross-layer services that are applicable to all layers. To keep provisions in deploying the solution in cloud, it has a cloud management service. It monitors for availability, memory, etc. and invokes remedial functions like autoscaling when required. Security services take care of the application security. Location map services helps identify nearby parking and provide directions. We have flexibility to use any available map service. Governance services help to monitor the various health parameters of the application.

9.6.3 Functionalities

Based on the detailed described architecture, the major functionalities of RecoPark from the user point of view is depicted in Figure 9.6, which is a top-level use case diagram. Broadly, we envisage four kinds of users of the proposed RecoPark, such as administrators, managers, allocators, and drivers. Administrators are responsible for setting up the infrastructure of the system. Managers and allocators are responsible for a particular parking lot and parking space, respectively. Drivers use the system for managing their parking. We also propose to reward the drivers for maintaining discipline in parking.

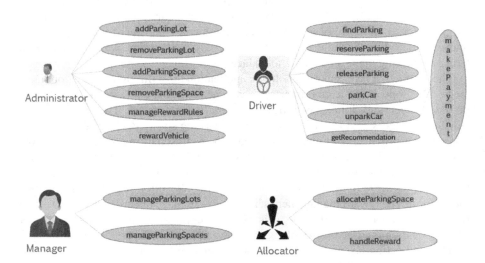

FIGURE 9.6 Top-level use case diagram of the proposed system.

Administrators are responsible for setting up the structure of the system. They can add and remove a parking lot. They can add or remove a parking space to a parking lot. Administrators can manage the rules for rewards such as using the same parking lot or leaving a parking space before time, etc. Administrators also reward the drivers based on their disciplined performances.

A user may reserve the parking space in advance based on recommendation. Recommendation of distance-based parking space and parking fees is always inversely proportioned. For example, the drivers need to pay less if they can park their vehicle in a distant place. This is advantageous if the vehicle or car is parked for a longer duration. The authors propose machine learning-based nearest parking lot predictions for the specific region, while remembering that RecoPark will have a significant amount of dataset in the near future. Furthermore, RecoPark will provide smarter parking solutions across cities. So, a reservation of a parking lot in another city is always advantageous to the users before they reach the actual place.

The user is always encouraged to utilise the space as much as possible through a reward-based system. To be listed as exemplary, the user booked the parking lot for 2 hours, but he/she left before the 2 hours. In practice, users have paid for 2 hours parking, but since the user has made available the reserved space before 2 hours, suppose within 1 hour 30 minutes, this user would earn reward points for 30 minutes. So in case of early departure of the parking lot, reward points will be earned, and the redemption of accumulated rewards points is also provisioned.

Hence, the administrator will mainly provide the recommendation of parking space and reward points to the users. The manager may have one or many parking lots. Thus, each manager needs to complete registration of the parking lots, and available parking lots or spaces will be notified after certain interval dynamically to the system. The allocator is solely responsible for allocating parking space for the specific region to the driver. The allocator is working as the person who takes care of the on-spot parking facility in a traditional parking system. Finally, the user or driver may do advance booking based on recommendation. The driver will make payments securely and may earn reward points through releasing the parking space early. A point to be noted is that the reward points can be redeemed in the next turn.

The vehicles need to be parked in various places in the same city or in different cities, as well as utilising the smart parking system and traditional parking system. In the case of the traditional parking system, the details of the car and driver are not stored for further retrieval. However, in the case of the smart parking system, the detailed and important information needs to be stored electronically for further access and retrieval. So an electronic consent management system can take care the risk of sharing this vital information through multiple service providers such as a parking recommender, parking allocator, and parking lot managers. Hence, it can expedite personal care and enhance security by reducing the threat to the driver or the chances of stealing or damaging car.

9.7   CONCLUSION

A secured smart parking system can make smart city project the successful. Providing physical parking spaces for any vehicle on an on demand basis, smart parking not only reduces traffic congestion and air pollution, but it also enhances mental peace to the drivers because they can reserve the parking space in advance without facing any hazards in less time. This chapter proposed a secured integrated smarter parking solution through the smart application, RecoPark. It also provisioned reward points to encourage users to utilise parking lots in optimum ways. Future scope of this research is enormous. The authors will complete the execution of a real-life case study through proper implementation of RecoPark. In due course the authors will execute a recommendation system with real-life datasets, which will confirm the prediction of distance-based parking spaces for a crowded area. This feature confirms provisioning of cheaper and secured smarter parking in smart city.

REFERENCES

Adomavicius, G., and Tuzhilin, A. (2005). "Toward the Next Generation of Recommender Systems: A Survey of the State-of-the-art and Possible Extensions," *IEEE Transactions on Knowledge and Data Engineering*, vol. 17, no. 6. pp. 734–749.

Al Amiri, W., Baza, M., Banawan, K., Mahmoud, M., Alasmary, W., and Akkaya, K. (2020). "Towards Secure Smart Parking System Using Blockchain Technology," in *IEEE 17th Annual Consumer Communications and Networking Conference (CCNC)*, pp. 1–2.

Alkenazan, W. A., Taha, A. A., Alenazi, M. J. F., and Abdul, W. (2021), "An Enhanced Framework for Secure Smart Parking Management Systems," *International Transaction Journal of Engineering, Management, & Applied Sciences & Technologies*, vol. 12, no. 7, 12A7B, pp. 1–13.

Al-Turjman, F., and Malekloo, A. (2019)."Smart Parking in IoT-enabled Cities: A Survey, Sustainable Cities and Society," vol. 49 [online], https://www.sciencedirect.com/science/article/pii/S2210670718327173 (Accessed 28th September 2021).

Anon, K. (2020). *British National Travel Survey*, https://assets.publishing.service.gov.uk. (Accessed 20th March 2022).

Ben-Daya, M., Hassini, E., and Bahroun, Z. (2017). "Internet of Things and Supply Chain Management: A Literature Review," *International Journal of Production Research*, pp. 1–24, https://doi.org/10.1080/00207543.2017.1402140.

Bong, D. B. L., Ting, K. C., and Lai, K. C. (2008). "Integrated Approach in the Design of Car Park Occupancy Information System (COINS)," *IAENG International Journal of Computer Science*, vol. 35, no. 1.

Chen, M., Chang, B., Xu, C., and Chi, Ed H. (2021). "User Response Models to Improve a REINFORCE Recommender System," in *Proceedings of the 14th ACM International Conference on Web Search and Data Mining (WSDM '21)*. Association for Computing Machinery, New York, NY, pp. 121–129, https://doi.org/10.1145/3437963.3441764.

Chinrungrueng, J., Sunantachaikul, U., and Triamlumlerd, S. (2007). "Real Time Driver Drowsiness Detection System Using Image Processing," *International Symposium on Applications and the Internet Workshops*, 66, www.scopus.com.

Cogill, R., et al. (2014). "Parked Cars as a Service Delivery Platform," in *2014 International Conference on Connected Vehicles and Expo (ICCVE)*, pp. 138–143, https://doi.org/10.1109/ICCVE.2014.7297530.

Cookson, G. (2017). *Parking Pain—INRIX Offers a Silver Bullet, INRIX—INRIX* [Online], http://inrix.com/blog/2017/07/parkingsurvey/ (Accessed 24th April 2022).

Delot, T., Ilarri, S., Lecomte, S., and Cenerario, N. (2013). "Sharing with Caution: Managing Parking Spaces in Vehicular Networks," *Mobile Information Systems*, vol. 9, no. 1, pp. 69–98.

Huang, C., Lu, R., Lin, X., and Shen, X. (2018). "Secure Automated Valet Parking: A Privacy-Preserving Reservation Scheme for Autonomous Vehicles," *IEEE Transactions on Vehicular Technology*, vol. 67, no. 11, pp. 11169–11180, https://doi.org/10.1109/TVT.2018.2870167.

Huang, X., Craig, P., Lin, H., and Yan, Z. (2016). "SecIoT: A Security Framework for the Internet of Things," *Security and Communication Networks*, vol. 9, no. 16, pp. 3083–3094.

Hui-ling, Z., Jian-Min, X., Yu, T., Yu-Cong, H., and Ji-Feng, S. (2003). "The Research of Parking Guidance and Information System Based on Dedicated Short Range Communication," in *Proceedings of the 2003 IEEE International Conference on Intelligent Transportation Systems*, vol. 2, pp. 1183–1186, https://doi.org/10.1109/ITSC.2003.1252671.

IBM Cloud Architecture Center. *IBM Internet of Things Reference Architecture*, https://www.ibm.com/cloud/architecture/files/iot-high-level.pdf last (Accessed 28th March 2022).

Idris, M. Y. I., Leng, Y. Y., Tamil, E. M., Noor, N. M., and Razak, Z. (2009). "Car Park System: A Review of Smart Parking System and its Technology," *Information Technology Journal*, 8, pp. 101–113 [Online], https://scialert.net/abstract/?doi=itj.2009.101.113 (Accessed 28th September 2021).

IEEE Internet of Things Reference Architecture Reference Architectures for the Internet of Things | *IEEE Journals & Magazine* | IEEE Xplore.

IoT Cloud Architecture Centre. *IBM Internet of Things Reference Architecture*, https://www.ibm.com/cloud/architecture/files/iot-high-level.pdf.

Jannach, D., and Jugovac, M. (2019). "Measuring the Business Value of Recommender Systems," *ACM Transactions on Management Information Systems*, vol. 10, no. 4, pp. 1–23.

Jannach, D., Manzoor, A., Cai, W., and Chen, L. (2021). "A Survey on Conversational Recommender Systems," *ACM Computing Surveys*, vol. 54, no. 5, Article 105, 36 pages, https://doi.org/10.1145/3453154.

Kokolaki, E., Karaliopoulos, M., and Stavrakakis, I. (2012). "Opportunistically Assisted Parking Service Discovery: Now It Helps, Now It Does Not," *Pervasive and Mobile Computing*, vol. 8, no. 2, pp. 210–227 [Online], http://www.sciencedirect.com/science/article/pii/S1574119211000782 (Accessed 28th September 2021).

Kokolaki, E., Kollias, G., Papadaki, M., Karaliopoulos, M., and Stavrakakis, I. (2013). "Opportunistically-Assisted Parking Search: A Story of Free Riders, Selfish Liars and Bona Fide Mules," *2013 10th Annual Conference on Wireless On-demand Network Systems and Services (WONS)*, pp. 17–24, https://doi.org/10.1109/WONS.2013.6578315.

Kuran, M. Ş., Viana, V. A., Iannone, L., Kofman, D., Mermoud, G., and Vasseur, J. P. (2015). "A Smart Parking Lot Management System for Scheduling the Recharging of Electric Vehicles," *IEEE Transactions on Smart Grid*, vol. 6, no. 6, pp. 2942–2953, https://doi.org/10.1109/TSG.2015.2403287.

Li, X., Chuah, M. C., and Bhattacharya, S. (2017). "UAV Assisted Smart Parking Solution," in *International Conference on Unmanned Aircraft Systems (ICUAS)*, pp. 1006–1013.

Lund, D., MacGillivray, C., Turner, V., and Morales, M. (2014). *Worldwide and Regional Internet of Things (IoT) 2014–2020 Forecast: A Virtuous Circle of Proven Value and Demand*. Framingham, MA: Int. Data Corp. Tech. Rep. 248451.

Madakam, S., Ramaswamy, R., and Tripathi, S. (2015). "Internet of Things (IoT): A Literature Review," *Journal of Computer and Communications*, vol. 3, no. 5, pp. 164–173. https://doi.org/10.4236/jcc.2015.35021.

Manville, M., and Shoup, D. (2005). "Parking, People, and Cities," *Journal of Urban Planning and Development*, vol. 131, no. 4, pp. 233–245.

Martín-Lopo, M. M., Boal, J., and Sánchez-Miralles, A. (2020). "A Literature Review of IoT Energy Platforms Aimed at End Users," *Computer Networks*, vol. 171, p. 107101, ISSN 1389–1286, https://doi.org/10.1016/j.comnet.2020.107101.

Mendes, D. L. S., Rabelo, R. A. L., Veloso, A. F. S., Rodrigues, J. J. P. C., and dos Reis Junior, J. V. (2020). "An Adaptive Data Compression Mechanism for Smart Meters Considering a Demand Side Management Scenario," *Journal of Cleaner Production*, vol. 255, p. 120190, ISSN 0959-6526, https://doi.org/10.1016/j.jclepro.2020.120190.

Mouskos, K. C. (2007). "Technical Solutions to Overcrowded Park and Ride Facilities," City Univ. New York, New York, NY, USA, Tech. Rep. FHWANJ-2007-011.

Ni, J., Lin, X., and Shen, X. (2019). "Toward Privacy-Preserving Valet Parking in Autonomous Driving Era," *IEEE Transactions on Vehicular Technology*, vol. 68, no. 3, pp. 2893–2905, https://doi.org/10.1109/TVT.2019.2894720.

Nižetić, S., Šolić, P., López-de-Ipiña González-de-Artaza, D., and Patrono, L. (2020). "Internet of Things (IoT): Opportunities, Issues and Challenges Towards a Smart and Sustainable Future," *Journal of Cleaner Production*, vol. 274, p. 122877, ISSN 0959–6526, https://doi.org/10.1016/j.jclepro.2020.122877.

Ornes, S. (2016). "The Internet of Things and the Explosion of Interconnectivity," in *Proceedings of the National Academy of Sciences: 113*, pp. 11059–11060.

Osterrieder, P., Budde, L., and Friedli, T. (2020). "The Smart Factory as a Key Construct of Industry 4.0: A Systematic Literature Review," *International Journal of Production Economics*, vol. 221, p. 107476, ISSN 0925-5273, https://doi.org/10.1016/j.ijpe.2019.08.011.

Pierce, G., and Shoup, D. (2013). "Getting the Prices Right: An Evaluation of Pricing Parking by Demand in San Francisco," *Journal of the American Planning Association*, vol. 79, no. 1, pp. 67–81.

Porru, S., Misso, F. E., Pani, F. E., and Repetto, C. (2020). "Smart Mobility and Public Transport: Opportunities and Challenges in Rural and Urban Areas," *Journal of Traffic and Transportation Engineering*, vol. 7, no. 1, pp. 88–97.

Rajabioun, T., and Ioannou, P. A. (2015). "On-Street and Off-Street Parking Availability Prediction Using Multivariate Spatiotemporal Models," *IEEE Transactions on Intelligent Transportation Systems*, vol. 16, no. 5, pp. 2913–2924, https://doi.org/10.1109/TITS.2015.2428705.

Ricci, F., Rokach, L., Shapira, B., and Kantor, P. B. (2015). *Recommender Systems Handbook* (2nd ed.). Springer-Verlag.

Sarwar, B. M., Karypis, G., Konstan, J. A., and Riedl, J. T. (2000). "Application of Dimensionality Reduction in Recommender System—A Case Study," *Architecture*, vol. 1625, pp. 264–268.

Sauras-Perez, P., Gil, A., and Taiber, J. (2014). "ParkinGain: Toward a Smart Parking Application with Value-Added Services Integration," in *2014 International Conference on Connected Vehicles and Expo (ICCVE)*, pp. 144–148.

Shoup, D. C. (2006). "Cruising for Parking," *Transport Policy*, vol. 13, no. 6, pp. 479–486, ISSN 0967-070X, https://doi.org/10.1016/j.tranpol.2006.05.005.

Sivanageswara, R. G., Raviteja, K., Phanindra, G., and Vignesh, D. (2020). "Analysis of Internet of Things Concept for the Application of Smart Cities," *International Journal of Advanced Science and Technology*, vol. 29, no. 3, pp. 3691–3704.

Sohail, S. S., Siddiqui, J., and Ali, R. (2017). "Classifications of Recommender Systems: A Review," *Journal of Engineering Science & Technology Review*, vol. 10, no. 4.

Villa-Henriksen, A., Edwards, G. T. C., Pesonen, L. A., Green, O., Sørensen, C. A. G. (2020), "Internet of Things in Arable Farming: Implementation, Applications, Challenges and Potential," *Biosystems Engineering*, vol. 191, pp. 60–84, ISSN 1537–5110, https://doi.org/10.1016/j.biosystemseng.2019.12.013.

Weyrich, M., and Ebert, C. (2016). "Reference Architectures for the Internet of Things," *IEEE Software*, vol. 33, no. 1, pp. 112–116, https://doi.org/10.1109/MS.2016.20.

Wortmann, F., and Flüchter, K. (2015). "Internet of Things," *Business & Information Systems Engineering*, vol. 57, no. 3, pp. 221–224, https://doi.org/10.1007/s12599-015-0383-3.

Yager, R. R. (2003). "Fuzzy Logic Methods in Recommender Systems," *Fuzzy Sets and Systems*, vol. 136, no. 2, pp. 133–149.

Zhou, X., Xu, Y., Li, Y., Jøsang, A., and Cox, C. (2012). "The State-of-the-Art in Personalized Recommender Systems for Social Networking," *Artificial Intelligence Review*, vol. 37, pp. 119–132, https://doi.org/10.1007/s10462-011-9222-1.

10 Classification of Road Segments in Intelligent Traffic Management System

Md Ashifuddin Mondal and Zeenat Rehena

CONTENTS

10.1 INTRODUCTION

With every passing day, the city dimension is increasing throughout the world. By the end of 2050, 70% of the population will live in cities.[1] The municipalities and city administrators are facing the daunting task of providing the citizens the quality of living with the limited resources that they have. The smart city idea can handle the difficulties associated with the management of many city components such as transportation, energy, health, and buildings, among others.[2] A smart city is an initiative that employs information and communication technology (ICT) to efficiently manage different city resources, increase public information sharing, and improve the quality of government services and citizen welfare. A smart city is a kind of urban strategy that will improve the standard of living of the citizens in urban areas by offering quality services.[3] Smart mobility is one of the important features of smart city initiatives.[4] Due to socio-economic development and the migration of people from rural to urban areas, the number of automobiles on the road is rapidly growing. According to Rawal and Devadas (2015), the number of registered vehicles in India climbed from 300,000 in 1951 to 142 million in 2011. [5] However, the capacity of current road infrastructure is insufficient to handle the growing number of automobiles. This causes severe traffic congestion on city streets and results in road accidents, air pollution, and the waste of inhabitants' precious time. Expanding or building additional infrastructure (roads, flyovers, etc.) to handle the enormous number of cars is one way to minimize traffic congestion. However, owing to a variety of circumstances, including a lack of physical space to build new roads over old ones and a lack of financial backing, this is not a practical option.[6, 7]

The conventional traffic management system is incapable of efficiently managing traffic on a city's road network because it lacks a real-time traffic data collection method, smart data processing, and adequate distribution of traffic information to residents. For traffic data collection, traffic monitoring, and traffic control, it mostly depends on human resources (traffic sergeants). As a result, to control traffic in a vast geographic region, the conventional traffic management system requires a significant number of human resources. As a result, it lacks scalability. This leads to the necessity of developing an intelligent traffic management system (ITMS), and it is one of the important areas of smart city. With the advancement in information and communication technology (ICT) and Internet of Things (IoT), the existing traffic management system can be improved and upgraded into an intelligent system. It enables the existing traffic infrastructure to become smarter and helps the traffic authority in managing the traffic and provides traffic information in advance to the users. The aim of this chapter is to present a framework in an intelligent traffic management system for better management of traffic. The framework utilizes wireless sensor network (WSN) technology for on-site real time traffic data collection.[8] Different types of vehicle detection sensors, inductance loop, and video cameras need to be deployed on the roadside for traffic data collection, and they are wirelessly connected with the remote data processing server. The data processing server hosting different types of algorithms, and techniques process these sensed traffic data and infer meaningful information about traffic conditions and make proper decisions toward traffic congestion control. Different business application modules are in the framework like a smart parking management system,[9] route recommendation system, road traffic congestion state identification system,[10] adaptive traffic signal control, and classification of roads based on traffic data. All these modules assist the commuters as well as traffic authority in making proper decisions and taking measures to minimize traffic congestion. Out of these modules, a smart parking management system and road traffic congestion state identification system are implemented in the work Rehena et al. (2018) and Mondal and Rehena (2019) respectively.[9, 10] Another important module is classification of roads based on traffic data. This chapter also focuses on different machine-learning techniques for classification of road segments based on road traffic data like traffic density and average speed on a particular road.

The rest of the chapter is organized as follows: Section 10.2 discusses the related work regarding the ITMS framework and different machine-learning techniques for classification. The framework in ITMS for congestion control and road classification techniques is presented in Section 10.3. Simulation results and analysis are discussed in Section 10.4. Finally, Section 10.5 concludes the chapter.

10.2 RELATED WORK

In recent times, intelligent traffic management systems are gaining importance to researchers due to the importance of traffic congestion control. In Rehena and Janssen (2018), researchers proposed a framework for context aware intelligent traffic management system for smart cities.[11] They discussed different challenges that need to be address while designing the smart traffic management system and different components of the framework. In Rawal and Devadas (2015) and Mondal and Rehena (2019), the authors discussed the details of the classification of an intelligent transportation system (ITS) and different components of ITS.[5, 6] In Djahel et al. (2015), the authors presented a detailed review on different technologies that have been used in designing traffic management systems (TMSs) and gave an overview of future TMSs.[8] In this work, they have also mentioned the use of smart cars and social media for fast and accurate traffic congestion detection. In Knorr et al. (2012), traffic jam related issues are discussed.[12] They presented a strategy to reduce traffic congestion by using vehicle-to-vehicle communication. Related to the traffic jam issue, the Kammoun et al. (2011) proposed a hybrid method based on an ant colony and hierarchical fuzzy system, which will adjust road traffic intelligently according to the real-time changes in the road network and suggest an alternate path to the destination.[13] In a similar type of work, Shashikiran et al. (2011) used Kruskal's algorithm to suggest an optimal path based on various parameters like the speed of vehicles and traffic rate at a particular road network. [14] A VANET-based distributed, collaborative traffic congestion detection system has been proposed in Jayapal and Roy (2016).[15] They used users' mobile phones to detect location through GPS, and the information was relayed to the server, which detects traffic congestion. If congestion is detected, the information is disseminated to the users' phone via roadside unit. In Misbanhuddin et al. (2015), the authors presented an IoT-based traffic management solution for smart cities where transport authorities can monitor and control the traffic flow through their smart phone.[16] They proposed a smart traffic light system. The smart traffic light reacts to the data analysis of the obtained traffic data from cars, road sensors, and social network.

A lot of research work has been carried out on finding traffic patterns. In Wen et al. (2014), the authors studied traffic congestion patterns of Beijing city. [17] To calculate the congestion intensity, they used traffic performance index (TPI) and used a clustering method to identify congestion pattern. The k-means clustering technique has been used for analyzing the traffic data and clusters the road accident data.[18] In a similar type of work, Yu et al. (2013) used a support vector machine technique to determine the traffic condition.[19] Based on three attributes, namely traffic volume, average speed and occupation ratio, their paper classified the transport condition. In Kumar and Toshniwal (2016), the authors used a k-means clustering approach for identification of accident-prone areas in different road segments.[20] They grouped together the accident-prone roads based on frequency of road accidents. They also further analyzed these data to find the main cause of accident.

As far as congestion control is concerned, these works each focus on one particular application to solve the problem. But no framework in intelligent traffic management system has been presented. Therefore, this chapter presented a framework in intelligent traffic management system for managing the traffic flow and controlling the traffic congestion. As far as traffic data analysis is concerned, the chapter implements different machine-learning techniques to classify and cluster the road segments based on traffic parameters.

10.3 PROPOSED FRAMEWORK

This section presents the proposed framework in intelligent traffic management system (ITMS) and road segments classification method based on traffic density and average speed.

10.3.1 OVERVIEW OF THE FRAMEWORK

As mentioned earlier, the traditional traffic management system is not sufficient to manage ever increasing traffic congestion because it lacks the ability to collect real-time road traffic information like traffic flow, traffic density, average speed, etc. The traditional traffic management system does not have an intelligent data processing module and proper dissemination of information to the commuters. To overcome the shortcomings of the traditional system, ITMS needs to be used. ITMS basically utilizes the advancement of information and communication technology (ICT) in the context of traffic management. Hence, this chapter introduces a framework in intelligent traffic management in view of managing traffic congestion. The proposed framework integrates different technologies like information sensing, communication, data processing, and data mining. The framework has five components: (i) data acquisition module, (ii) roadside unit, (iii) data pre-processing module, (iv) intelligent data processing module, and (v) business application module. The framework is shown in Figure 10.1.

10.3.1.1 Data Acquisition Module

This module is a very important module in any intelligent traffic management system. The proper traffic status monitoring and accurate timely decision making is very important for better management of traffic flow, and traffic data is one of the imperative factors for this. The more accurate traffic data will be collected, the more accurate decisions and actions can be taken towards the management of traffic flow. Real-time traffic data like traffic density, traffic flow, etc. from the roadside need to be collected and based on this data; the data processing module will provide meaningful insight into the traffic status. The framework considers heterogeneous data sources (such as different types of sensors, GPS, satellite system, etc.) for collecting

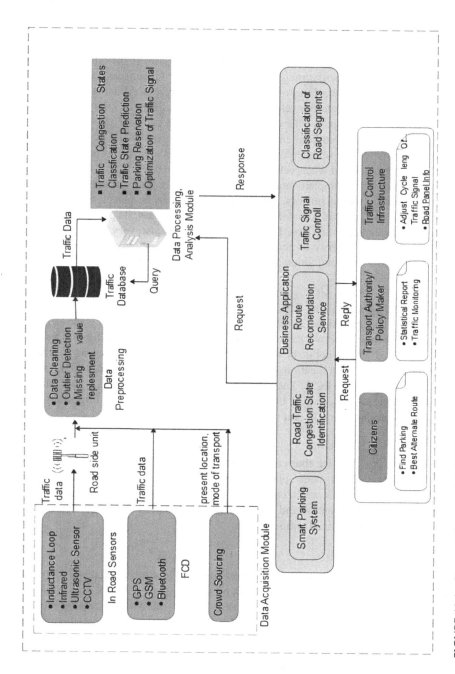

FIGURE 10.1 Proposed framework in ITMS.

traffic data. Following are the three data acquisition techniques that can be used for data collection:

10.3.1.1.1   In Road Detector

Different types of detectors can be placed on the roadside. It includes pneumatic tubes, piezoelectric sensors, magnetic loops, ultrasonic sensors, and infrared. Pneumatic road tubes are a kind of rubber tube that are placed across the road to detect the vehicle. It detects the vehicles from pressure changes in the tube that are generated when vehicles pass. The drawback of this technology is that its efficiency is hampered due to bad weather, temperature, and traffic conditions. A loop detector is another alternative for vehicle detection. It detects the vehicle on the basis of the induced current generated when vehicle passes over the detector. This technology is widely accepted, but its implementation and maintenance cost are high. The better alternatives are the use of sensors. Ultrasonic sensors can be placed over the lane, and it emits ultrasound waves to detect the vehicles. But again, its performance may hamper in bad weather conditions. Infrared technology is also very good and can be used. It uses infrared energy to detect the vehicles.[21–23] Better solutions are the use of RFID technology and video cameras for capturing traffic information.

10.3.1.1.2   Floating Car Data

Floating car data (FCD) is the best alternative for a source of high-quality accurate traffic data. In this technique, traffic data are collected by monitoring the vehicles with the help of mobile network or GPS over the entire road network. Every vehicle must be equipped with a mobile phone or GPS system, which act as a sensor. A wide variety of data like vehicle location, current speed, direction of movement, and traffic flow is collected through FCD. The advantages of this technique are high accuracy and a wide range of data can be collected; thus, it has become an important data acquisition technique in intelligent traffic management systems.

10.3.1.1.3   Crowd-Sourcing

Crowdsourcing is a practice that engages crowds or groups together for a common goal.[24] Different social media platforms like Facebook and Twitter can be used to collect traffic information. Citizens traveling along the road may capture a traffic incident in a particular location and send it to a dedicated system, and the system can infer meaningful knowledge from it.

10.3.1.2   Roadside Unit

A roadside unit (RSU) is placed on the roadside, and it acts as a gateway between the data acquisition module and remote data processing server. Traffic data collected from the heterogeneous data source are transmitted to the data processing module through RSU. Communication between RSU and the remote data processing module is either wired or wireless.

10.3.1.3   Data Pre-Processing Module

The raw data that is collected by the data acquisition module is not directly used for processing or data mining as it contains erroneous data or missing data. The presence of such erroneous data or missing data leads to a misinterpretation, and thus it hampers the performance of data processing module in terms of inferring actual traffic conditions. That is why the raw data need to be passed through the data pre-processing module before they feed into the data processing module. Data pre-processing includes the replacement of missing values and detection of abnormal data in the form of outlier detection.

10.3.1.4 Data Processing Module

The data processing module is the brain of this ITMS, and it actually makes the system the intelligent one. This module can process the traffic data collected from the field and provides meaningful insight about the traffic condition to the traffic authority, which helps them make proper decisions on traffic regulation. Also, this module provides the commuters with helpful information like whether or not a particular road is congested, the optimal route toward a destination, etc. In this module, different types of algorithms and techniques are used for the classification of data, prediction, and decision making, which includes multi-criteria decision analysis (MCDA) technique, the artificial neural network (ANN), long short-term memory (LSTM), and many more machine-learning techniques. Dedicated algorithms are hosted in this module for traffic congestion state identification,[10] future traffic prediction, parking reservation,[9] traffic signal optimization, etc.

10.3.1.5 Business Application Module

The framework has different business application modules, which are used by commuters as well as by the transport authority. Smart parking systems are one of the business applications that are already implemented in our previous work and can be used by commuters for finding and reserving the most suitable parking slots in the city.[25] On the other hand, the classification of road segments based on traffic data is a business application that helps the traffic authority identify and group together the similar types of road segments on the basis of traffic data. The next section discusses different machine-learning classification techniques.

10.3.2 CLASSIFICATION TECHNIQUE

This section discusses the classification of road segments and clusters them based on traffic parameters, namely traffic density and average speed of the particular road. Each cluster will contain similar types of roads in terms of traffic density and average speed. This kind of clustering of roads on the basis of traffic patterns will help the traffic authorities in decision-making regarding traffic rules and regulations on those road segments. The steps of classification of road segments are shown in Figure 10.2.

Step 1: Initially, road traffic data need to be acquired using a *data acquisition module* and the traffic parameters on which classification has to be performed needs to be identified. In that case, the two parameters are traffic density and average speed on a road segment.

Step 2: As explained earlier, before performing data processing (i.e., classification of roads based on average speed and traffic density), the acquired traffic data are pre-processed by the data pre-processing module to detect outlier data. The outlier is

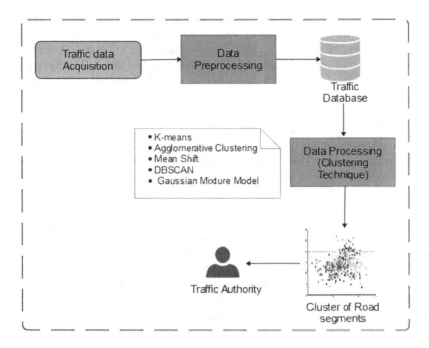

FIGURE 10.2   Classification of road segments.

defined as "an observation (or set of observations) which appears to be inconsistent with the remainder of that set of data".[26, 27] In another way, we can say that an outlier is an observation that deviates significantly from another set of observations. In this work, the outlier needs to be detected in acquired road traffic data. As this chapter considers two traffic parameters, namely traffic density and average speed on a road segment, a multivariate outlier detection needs to be applied. In this work, a density-based spatial clustering (DBSCAN) technique has been used.

DBSCAN is a popular machine-learning tool for data analysis and clustering to visualize the outlier in the data set. It is a density-based clustering technique. Here cluster is defined as the maximal set of densely connected points in the feature space. In DBSCAN, two hyper-parameters are used:

- *eps*: It is the radius of the neighbourhoods around a data point p and represented by ϵ.
- *min_samples*: The minimum number of data points that needs in a neighbourhood to form a cluster.

Based on these two hyper-parameters, DBSCAN classify the data points into three categories:

- *Core point*: A data point is core point if its neighbourhoods contain at least same or more number of data points than *min_samples*.

- *Border point*: A data point is a border point that lies in a cluster and its neighbourhood does not contain more points than *min_samples.*
- *Outlier*: A point is an outlier point if it is neither a core point nor a border point.

Step 3: After detecting and eliminating the outlier data points, the remaining data points are stored in the traffic data base.

Step 4: The classification of road segments is performed in the data processing module using different machine learning techniques. This work focuses on different machine-learning techniques, namely k-means clustering, agglomerative clustering, mean shift, DBSCAN, and the Gaussian mixture model for clustering of road segments.

Step 5: The output of data processing module gives a clear insight about the road segments that are of similar types in terms of traffic density and average speed.

10.4   SIMULATION RESULTS

This section simulates the proposed classification technique of road segments. The sample traffic data of road segment 'R1' is shown in Table 10.1, and Figure 10.3 shows the plotting of these data points.

TABLE 10.1
Sample Traffic Data of Road Segment 'R1'

Date	Traffic Density (no. of car/km)	Avg. speed (km/hr)
11.1.2021	80	20
12.1.2021	73	20
13.1.2021	75	19
14.1.2021	60	25
15.1.2021	65	25
16.1.2021	83	18
17.1.2021	86	18
18.1.2021	85	16
19.1.2021	79	17
20.1.2021	77	17
21.1.2021	84	18
22.1.2021	88	15
23.1.2021	86	15
24.1.2021	69	19
25.1.2021	71	21
26.1.2021	73	19
27.1.2021	65	22
28.1.2021	83	16
29.1.2021	10	10
30.1.2021	150	0
31.1.2021	90	15

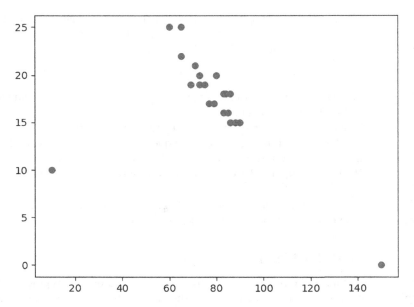

FIGURE 10.3 Acquired traffic data of road segment 'R1'.

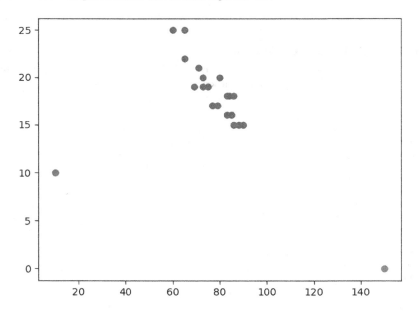

FIGURE 10.4 Detection of outlier of road segment 'R1'.

Suppose present day (i.e., 31.1.2021) traffic data is: traffic density = 90 and average speed = 15km/hr. First, it needs to identify whether this data point is outlier data or not. For that, this chapter uses the DBSCAN technique. Figure 10.4 presents the detection of outlier data points using the DBSCAN technique. The red point represents an outlier data point whereas the blue point represents normal/valid data points. From Figure 10.4, it is seen that the traffic data (10, 10) and (150, 0) on 29.1.2021 and 30.1.2021, respectively, are outlier data for road segment 'R1'. Hence these outlier data are eliminated from the data set. The removal of outlier data has to be performed for the rest of the road segments.

Then a clustering technique has to be applied to classify and cluster the road segments for a particular day. In this chapter, different clustering techniques like k-means clustering, agglomerative clustering, mean shift, DBSCAN, and the Gaussian mixture model have been used. To simulate the mentioned clustering techniques, Python has been used. The intention of this work is to form four clusters based on density and average speed: high density-low speed (cluster 1), medium density-low speed (cluster 2), medium density-moderate speed (cluster 3), and low density-high speed (cluster 4). Table 10.2 shows the sample traffic data of different road segments on a particular day, which are fed into the data processing module for the classification of road segments. Figure 10.5 shows the initial graphical presentation of traffic data.

First the k-means clustering technique was applied. The value of k in k-means clustering algorithm is 4. Based on Table 10.2 data, it forms four different groups of road segments using the k-means clustering technique. Figure 10.6 shows the clusters of different road segments formed using k-means clustering algorithm. Figure 10.6 depicts four clusters of road segments with different colours. The colour black indicates high density-low speed (cluster 1), red indicates medium density-low speed (cluster 2), magenta represents medium density-moderate speed (cluster 3), and blue represents low density-high speed (cluster 4).

Then agglomerative clustering has been applied on the same traffic data set shown in Table 10.2. As the intention was to form four clusters, the hyper-parameter $n\_clusters$ in agglomerative clustering algorithm is set to four. The $n\_clusters$ denotes the

TABLE 10.2
Sample Traffic Data of Different Road Segments

Date	Road Segment	Traffic Density (no. of car/km)	Avg. speed (km/hr)
31.1.2021	R1	90	15
31.1.2021	R2	60	30
31.1.2021	R3	60	30
31.1.2021	R4	55	33
31.1.2021	R5	75	20
31.1.2021	R6	80	18
31.1.2021	. . .	. . .	. . .
31.1.2021	. . .	. . .	. . .
31.1.2021	R64	26	90
31.1.2021	R65	20	88
31.1.2021	R68	57	35
31.1.2021	R69	42	65
23.1.2021	R70	21	91

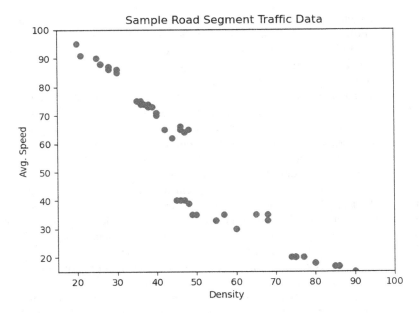

FIGURE 10.5   Sample road segment traffic data.

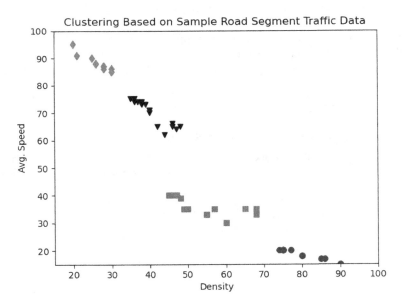

FIGURE 10.6   Clustering of road segments using k-means.

number of clusters. Figure 10.7 shows the formation of cluster of road segments using the agglomerative clustering technique.

Also, a spectral clustering technique has been applied for clustering on the same dataset as shown in Table 10.2. As the intention is to form four clusters, the hyper-parameter *n_clusters* in the spectral clustering algorithm is set to four. Figure 10.8 shows the formation of clusters of road segments using the spectral clustering technique.

Then, on the same data set, mean shift clustering has been applied. In the mean shift algorithm hyper-parameter "*n_clusters*" is absent, hence we cannot mention the

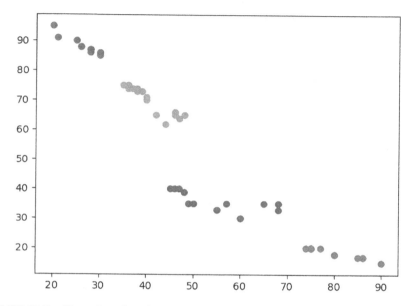

FIGURE 10.7 Clustering of road segments using agglomerative clustering.

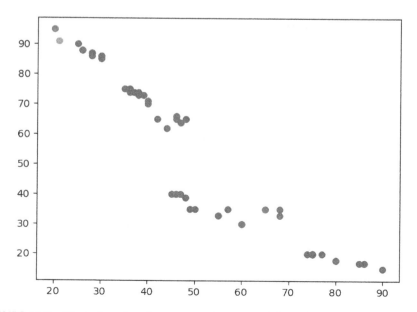

FIGURE 10.8 Clustering of road segments using spectral clustering.

number of clusters we require. Figure 10.9 shows the formation of clusters of road segments using the mean shift clustering technique.

The same dataset is also fed into the Gaussian mixture model. Here the hyper-parameter *n_clusters* is present, and it is set to four. Figure 10.10 shows the formation of clusters of road segments using the Gaussian mixture model technique.

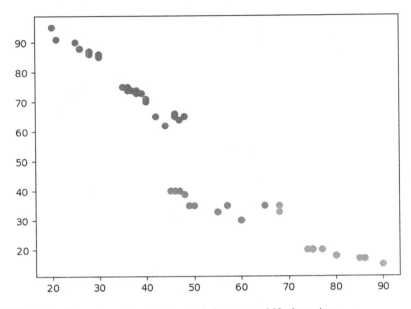

FIGURE 10.9   Clustering of road segments using mean shift clustering.

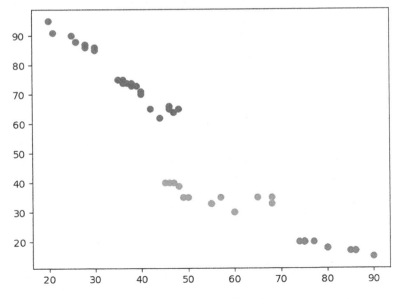

FIGURE 10.10   Clustering of road segments using Gaussian mixture model.

From the simulation, it has been observed that the performance of k-means, agglomerative clustering, Gaussian mixture model, and mean shift clustering are quite similar; whereas the performance of spectral clustering is not good. Generally, the k-means technique forms the clusters as spherical or round shape. The data points that are close to each other are put in the same cluster. But the spectral clustering technique does not follow a fixed pattern. This technique follows the graph theory approach where the grouping of nodes, i.e., data points, in the graph is done based on whether they are connected with each other through edges or not. Here, data points are put in the same cluster even if they are distant apart, but they are connected. Similarly, data points that are close to each other in terms of distance may be put into different clusters if they are not connected.

10.5 CONCLUSION

This chapter introduced a framework for an intelligent traffic management system for better management of traffic flow. The framework has many business application modules. Some modules help the citizens during their journey by helping them finding a proper parking space or by suggesting best routes, etc. It also assists the traffic authorities in making proper decisions and regulations regarding traffic management by providing meaningful insight about traffic situations. Also, this chapter discussed one of the important business application modules, which is the classification and clustering of road segments based on traffic parameters like traffic density and average speed. Different machine-learning techniques have been discussed, and their performance was evaluated.

REFERENCES

[1] B. Clara, R. Dameri, B. D'Auria, Smart Mobility in Smart City. *Action Taxonomy*, ICT Intensity and Public Benefits, 2016, https://doi.org/10.1007/978-3-319-23784-8_2.

[2] A. Gaur, B. Scotney, G. Parr, S. McClean, Smart City Architecture and its Applications Based on IoT. In: *The 5th International Symposium on Internet of Ubiquitous and Pervasive Things*, vol. 52. Elsevier, 2015, pp 1089–1094. https://doi.org/10.1016/j.procs.2015.05.122.

[3] P. Hall, Creative Cities and Economic Development. *Urban Studies*, 37, 633–649, 2000.

[4] L. Staricco, Smart Mobility, Opportunità e condizioni. *Tema-Journal of Land Use, Mobility and Environment*, 3, 289–354, 2013.

[5] T. Rawal and V. Devadas, Intelligent Transportation System in India – A Review. *Journal of Development Management and Communication*, 2, 3, April 2015.

[6] M. A. Mondal, Z. Rehena, An IoT-Based Congestion Control Framework for Intelligent Traffic Management System. In: *International Conference on Artificial Intelligence and Data Engineering*, Springer, 2019.

[7] N. Shah, S. Kumar, F. Bastani, I.-L. Yen, Optimization Models for Assessing the Peak Capacity Utilization of Intelligent Transportation Systems. *European Journal of Operational Research*, 239–251, 2012. https://doi.org/10.1016/j.ejor.2011.07.032 (Elsevier).

[8] S. Djahel, R. Doolan, G.-M. Muntean, J. Murphy, A Communications-oriented Perspective on Traffic Management Systems for Smart Cities: Challenges and Innovative Approaches. *IEEE Communication Surveys and Tutorials*, 17(1), 2015, First quarter. https://doi.org/10.1109/COMST.2014.2339817.

[9]   Z. Rehena, M. A. Mondal, M. Janssen, A Multiple-Criteria Algorithm for Smart Parking: Making Fair and Preferred Parking Reservations in Smart Cities. In: *Proceedings of the 19th Annual International Conference on Digital Government Research: Governance in the Data Age, DG.0 2018, Delft*, The Netherlands, pp 40:1–40:9. https://doi. org/10.1145/3209281.3209318.

[10] M. A. Mondal and Z. Rehena, Intelligent Traffic Congestion Classification System using Artificial Neural Network. In: *Companion Proceedings of the 2019 World Wide Web Conference (WWW '19)*. Association for Computing Machinery, New York, NY, . 2019, 110–116. https://doi.org/10.1145/3308560.3317053.

[11] Z. Rehena, M. Janssen, Towards a Framework for Context-Aware Intelligent Traffic Management System in Smart Cities, 893–898, 2018. https://doi.org/10.1145/3184558. 3191514.

[12] F. Knorr, D. Baselt, M. Schreckenberg, M. Mauve, Reducing Traffic Jams via VANETs. *IEEE Transactions on Vehicular Technology*, 61(8), 3490–3498, 2012. https://doi. org/10.1109/TVT.2012.2209690

[13] H. M. Kammoun, I. Kallel, A. M. Alimi, J. Casillas, Improvement of the Road Traffic Management by an Ant-Hierarchical Fuzzy System. In: *2011 IEEE Symposium on Computational Intelligence in Vehicles and Transportation Systems (CIVTS) Proceedings*, 2011, 38–45. https://doi.org/10.1109/CIVTS.2011.5949535.

[14] V. Shashikiran, T. T. S. Kumar, N. S. Kumar, V. Venkateswaran, S. Balaji, Dynamic Road Traffic Management Based on Krushkal's Algorithm. In: *2011 International Conference on Recent Trends in Information Technology (ICRTIT)*, 2011, 200–204. https://doi.org/10.1109/ICRTIT.2011.5972263

[15] C. Jayapal, S. S. Roy, Road Traffic Congestion Management Using VANET. In: *2016 International Conference on Advances in Human Machine Interaction (HMI)*, 2016, 1–7.

[16] S. Misbahuddin, J. A. Zubairi, A. Saggaf, J. Basuni, S.-A. Wadany, A. Al-Sofi, IoT Based Dynamic Road Traffic Management for Smart Cities. In: *2015 12th In-Ternational Conference on High-capacity Optical Networks and Enabling/Emerging Technologies (HONET)*, 2015, 1–5.

[17] H. Wen, J. Sun, X. Zhang, Study on Traffic Congestion Patterns of Large City in China Taking Beijing as an Example. *Procedia—Social and Behavioral Sciences*, 138, 482–491, 2014, the 9th International Conference on Traffic and Transportation Studies (ICTTS 2014).[Online]. http://www.sciencedirect.com/science/article/pii/ S1877042814041469.

[18] P. A. Nandurge, N. V. Dharwadkar, Analyzing Road Accident Data Using Machine Learning Paradigms. In: *International Conference on I-MAC*, 2017.

[19] R. Yu, G. Wang, J. Zheng, H. Wang, Urban Road Traffic Condition Pattern Recognition Based on Support Vector Machine. *Journal of Transportation Systems Engineering and Information Technology*, 13, 130–136, 2013.

[20] S. Kumar, D. Toshniwal, A Data Mining Approach to Characterize Road Accident Locations. *Journal of Modern Transportation*, 24(1), 2016.

[21] G. Leduc, Road Traffic Data: Collection Methods and Applications. In: *Working Papers on Energy, Transport and Climate Change N.1*, 2008.

[22] J. Lopes, J. Bento, E. Huang, C. Autonious, M. Ben-Akiva, Traffic and Mobility Data Collection for Real-time Applications. In: *13th International IEEE Annual Conference on Intelligent Transportation Systems*, Madeira Island, Portugal, 2010.

[23] A. Sumalee, H. W. Ho, Smarter and More Connected: Future Intelligent Transportation System. In: *IATSS Res*, 67–71, 2018. https://doi.org/10.1016/j.iatssr.2018.05.005 (ScienceDirect)

[24] G. Chatzimilioudis, A. Konstantinidis, C. Laoudias, D. Zeinalipour-Yazti, Crowdsourcing with Smartphones. *IEEE Internet Computing*, 16(5), 3644, 2012. https://doi.org/10.1109/MIC.2012.70

[25] M. A. Mondal, Z. Rehena, M. Janssen, Smart Parking Management System with Dynamic Pricing. *Journal of Ambient Intelligence and Smart Environments*, 13(6), IOS Press, 2021.

[26] T. L. Vic Barnett, *Outliers in Statistical Data*, Wiley, 1994.

[27] M. A. Mondal, Z. Rehena, Road Traffic Outlier Detection Technique Based on Linear Regression. *Procedia Computer Science*, 2547–2555, 2020.

11 Facial Gestures-Based Recommender System for Evaluating Online Classes

Anjali Agarwal and Ajanta Das

CONTENTS

DOI: 10.1201/9781003319122-11

11.1 INTRODUCTION

Automated learning analytics is quickly becoming a critical topic in the educational field, which requires efficient systems to track student progress and offer feedback to teachers. The computer vision based surveillance system is used to accurately monitor students' attendance on a daily basis. An automated facial gestures-based recommender system is a development in the realm of automation that has replaced the old evaluation method.[1] It is now possible to direct and conduct daily lessons and regular exams for students at educational institutions remotely, thanks to the internet and modern technology. With the current change in working life for students and instructors in the online arena, this has become even more crucial. However, unlike physical homeroom learning, web-based learning lacks the intuitive human interaction and correspondence that physical homeroom learning provides. Instructors may find it beneficial to have some sort of mechanism to inform them when a student looks to be losing attention during online sessions in order to improve the web-based learning experience.

Students' attitudes regarding the knowledge and activities being employed must be tracked in order to adjust content and teaching approaches for each student.[2] Teachers' lives have been made simpler by the facial gesture tracking technology, which has made monitoring marking a breeze. Face detection and identification is crucial in a variety of applications, including the attendance management system, online evaluation system, and so on. This system involves the detection of a human face through a high-definition camera with image detection performed using the Viola Jones algorithm.[3]

Face recognition technology is progressively growing into a universal biometric solution because, as compared to other biometric solutions, it needs little effort from the user. Biometric face recognition is primarily employed in three areas: time attendance and staff management, visitor management systems, and authorization and access control systems. Gesture recognition, a relatively new concept in human-computer interaction (HCI), is used in a variety of applications ranging from simple home automation to navigation and monitoring.[4] This eye-gazing technology and facial feature movement can be used to communicate between students and teachers.

In the future generation, the basic nonverbal interaction of eye blinking and facial movement will change. Intelligent video surveillance techniques may be utilized to tackle the aforementioned problem, thanks to the rapid progress of information technology. We provide a unique paradigm for measuring learning engagement in this chapter, which uses facial expression recognition to record learners' emotional fluctuations in real time. Experiments show that our recommended method for evaluating learners' learning engagement is effective.

The purpose of this study was to create an automated system that would allow faculty to capture and summarize student actions in the classroom as part of data collection for decision making. The technology captures the whole session, determines when pupils in the classroom are paying attention, and then sends a report to the facilities. Our studies and design reveal that our approach is more adaptable and accurate than past efforts.

11.2 TRADITIONAL MONITORING SYSTEM

Student tracking systems are traditionally taken manually using an attendance form provided by faculty members in class, which is a time-consuming process. Furthermore, in a big classroom setting with scattered branches, it is extremely difficult to check whether or not authorized students are attentively listening and studying.

The tracking of students' performance is still an important aspect of every educational institution. Students' attendance in class has an influence on their academic success. It is becoming more difficult for schools to monitor their attendance as the number of students grows. Due to the manual registration of names and distribution of the paper-based attendance sheet for students to sign, the traditional attendance monitoring method takes a long time. Fake results and time waste are common with paper-based attendance tracking methods and certain existing automated solutions such as mobile apps, radio frequency identification (RFID), Bluetooth, and fingerprint attendance models.

The shortcomings of traditional tracking systems prompted the use of computer vision to fill the void. Biometric candidate systems such as iris recognition and facial recognition can be used to track student's engagement in online classes. Face recognition has the most promise among these because it is non-intrusive. Despite the fact that several automated monitoring methods have been developed, inadequate system modelling has a detrimental impact on the systems.

This chapter suggests a smart facial gestures-based monitoring system that employs face recognition to track students' activities during online classes in order to increase the success of automated evaluation systems. Using computer vision, we can develop an algorithm which can assess learning engagement that employs facial expression recognition to track students' behavioral variations in real time. All that is required to use this technology is good eye and vision control. By exploiting the application's interaction features, known as interacts, and using Haar cascade through OpenCV,[4] we may expand the options for monitoring pupils. A multi-camera system is also proposed to ensure proper student capture.

11.3 RELATED WORK

In Ngoc Anh et al. (2019), for the face detection module, the authors have used the single stage headless (SSH) face detector, which is essentially a hybrid of O-Net and L-Net multi task cascaded convolutional neural networks (MTCNN), ArcFace for facial representation, and Hopenet for gaze estimation.[5] Different learning methods were used to complete the face categorization challenge. Rather than requiring particular technologies and being limited by their limits, they were able to deal with a more realistic situation. The authors focused on the real educational setting where classrooms contain a broader variety of recording devices and a bigger number of students, despite the fact that there was a restricted range of behaviors that have been identified.

In Richardson and Abraham (2013), two surveys of university students' study habits and grade point averages were conducted to assess theory-based models (GPA).[6] The personality systems interaction (PSI) hypothesis and the theory of planned behavior (TPB) were put to the test. When it came to self-reported statistics, the TPB worked well, but when it came to GPA, it wasn't as effective. Although the results for study behavior vs GPA varied, there was some evidence for the PSI theory. In Study 1, when TPB factors and previous activities were controlled for, an interaction between volitional competency and subjective norm explained distinctive variance in study patterns. After controlling for TPB factors and previous accomplishment in Study 2, implicit attention control had a direct impact on GPA. The implications of initiatives aimed at boosting tertiary academic success are examined.

The impact of utilizing an electronic device for a non-academic purpose during class on later exam performance was investigated in this study Glass and Kang (2019).[7] Electronic devices were allowed in half of the lectures in a two-section college course; therefore, the effect of the gadgets was evaluated in a within-student, within-item counterbalanced experimental design. As judged by within-class exam questions, dividing attention between an electronic device and the classroom lecture did not affect understanding of the presentation. Instead, split attention hampered long-term recall of the classroom lecture, which resulted in poor performance on following unit and final exams. In each lesson, students self-reported whether or not they utilized an electronic device. Both students who used and did not use electronic devices during the exam performed much lower than the no-device control condition.

It is possible to simplify the monitoring and analysis of students' performance in the classroom by using IoT devices and computational methods such as computer vision techniques, machine learning, and data analysis.[8] It can do automatic real-time surveillance of the student's behavior across the network in preparation and react quickly to critical situations if necessary. Nonetheless, the long-term performance of pupils may be documented, and the data can be used for future ongoing evaluation. The authors have presented an IoT framework based on three analytic modules: face recognition, motion analysis, and behavior understanding to efficiently conduct classroom monitoring tasks such as collecting attendance, identifying entering and exiting actions, and analyzing students' concentration levels.

Agarwal et al. (2005) proposed a unique detection approach that combines many of the core characteristics of rapid eye movement (REMs) while needing few parameter adjustments.[9] In the proposed technique, a single parameter might be used to control the REM detection sensitivity and specificity tradeoff. The approach developed utilizing training data that has been manually graded. The method's performance is compared to manual REM episode rating, and validation results are provided using a different data set.

Budi et al. (2018) outline a low-cost method for keeping track of student attendance.[10] Students' faces are automatically located using a face detection algorithm, and students merely identify their faces on the records to register their attendance.

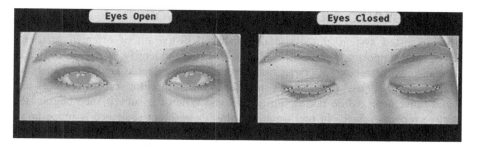

FIGURE 11.1   An example of eyes open and eyes closed.

As the major interfaces to engage with the system, mobile applications were built for both students and instructors.

Mery et al. (2019) have released a full-annotated dataset of photos from a classroom with roughly 70 pupils captured over the course of 15 weeks in 25 sessions.[11] Using a procedure that takes into consideration the amount of face photographs per subject included in the gallery, 10 face recognition algorithms based on learnt and created characteristics are assessed. FaceNet, a system based on deep learning features, performed best in tests by attaining over 95% accuracy with only one enrollment image per individual. We think that the facial recognition-based automated student attendance system can save time for both teachers and students while also preventing fraudulent attendance.

Yang et al. (2016) demonstrated that existing face detection performance falls short of real-world needs.[12] The WIDER FACE dataset, which is 10 times larger than previous datasets, can aid future face detection research. Occlusions, postures, event categories, and face bounding boxes are among the many annotations in the collection. Faces in the proposed dataset are exceedingly difficult to work with because of enormous changes in scale, position, and occlusion, as seen in Figure 11.1. Furthermore, the WIDER FACE dataset is an effective face detection training source. We compare the performance of many typical detection systems to provide an overview of current state-of-the-art performances and provide a technique for dealing with large-scale variances. Finally, we go through several typical failure scenarios that should be studied further.

Thus far, these applications have only been beneficial for drivers monitoring how dizzy they are; but, with our unique technology, educational institutions will be able to interface with the computer just by facial gestures. Section 11.4 proposes a recommender framework for implementing this facial gesture-based online evaluation system. Section 11.5 constitutes of all the materials required, which is followed by Section 11.6's approach for implementing the framework. Section 11.7 contains the experimental data and discussions, and the limitations of this system are in Section 11.8. Section 11.9 brings the chapter to a close where we discuss future work.

11.4   PROPOSED RECOMMENDER FRAMEWORK

The suggested system employs the Haar-based histogram of oriented gradients (HOG) and support vector machine (SVM) classifier to identify face gestures in real time through a webcam as input, then processes it to enable keyboard capability using facial motions, which allows the user to smart monitor student postures and facial movements while taking online lessons. When the surveillance begins, the camera records images in real time, and the image input sequence is made up of these frames from the webcam.[13] Using a Haar-based HOG and a linear SVM classifier, this system detects the student's face, followed by their eye and lips. The eye blink comes next, which aids in determining if the children are dozing or active. This is explained in Figure 11.1 for both the cases, *eyes open* and *eyes closed*. We also recorded lip movement to see if the students were actively learning or conversing with their classmates.

The proposed recommender framework is as follows:

Step 1: Take a picture from a camera as input.
Step 2: Create a region of interest (ROI) around the face in the image.
Step 3: Use the ROI to find the eyeballs and input them to the classifier.
Step 4: The classifier will determine whether or not the eyes and lips are open.
Step 5: Examine to see if the students are sleepy or inattentive.

In general, the system is set to propose a protocol when the eye aspect ratio and lip ratio are greater than their respective thresholds, at which point the keys are triggered and the teacher learns which students are actively participating and which students are not; otherwise, if the ratio is less than the threshold, there is no movement and no further computation. This is fully dependent on the ratio in which the movement is executed, as well as whether it is a blink or a lip movement.

The keyboard keys are activated as soon as the system identifies any blink that is consistent for a specific time interval or any lip movement, indicating if a learner is dozing or conversing. As a result, the instructor will be alerted and will be able to take appropriate action. Teachers can also document it and grade the students on their day-to-day activities and alertness in online classes. The intended architecture as a whole is represented in diagram form in Figure 11.2.[13]

11.5   MATERIALS

Real-time face recognition developed a prototype model of a system using the descriptive research approach to meet the study's goals. The prototype model is used to achieve the system development method, which includes gathering requirements, creating a rapid design, and creating a prototype. User assessment was used to test the prototype, and it was then reworked, improving it as needed until an acceptable prototype was developed and maintained from which the entire system could now be utilized.

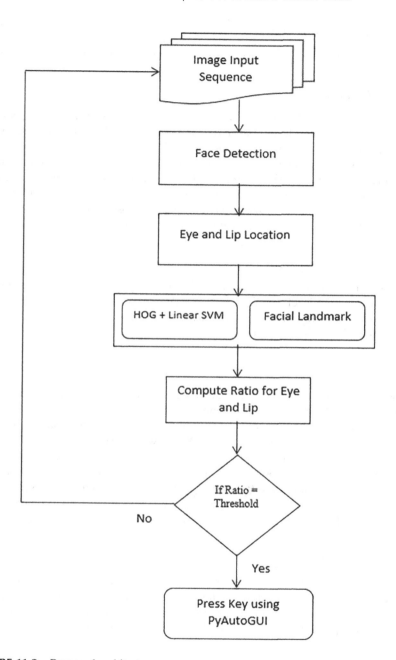

FIGURE 11.2 Proposed architecture.

11.5.1 Visual Studio Code

It's an open-source framework that's used to create the dynamic app.

11.5.2 Python

Python is a dynamically semantic, interpreted, object-oriented high-level programming language. Its high-level built-in data structures, together with dynamic typing and dynamic binding, making it ideal for rapid application development and as a scripting or glue language for connecting existing components. Python's concise, easy-to-learn syntax prioritizes readability, which lowers software maintenance costs. Modules and packages are supported by Python, which fosters program modularity and code reuse. The Python interpreter and its substantial standard library are free to download and distribute in source or binary form for all major platforms.

11.5.3 Computer Vision

Computer vision is an interdisciplinary topic concerned with how computers may be made to obtain high-level comprehension from digital photos or movies.[14] The goal is to automate activities that human visual systems can perform, such as recognizing that a human face is being detected.

11.5.4 OpenCV

OpenCV is a software library for computer vision that Gary Bradsky started working on in 1999 at Intel, and the initial version was released in 2000. It is said to support a broad range of programming languages, including C++, Python, Java, and X Vector, as well as a variety of platforms including Windows, Linux, and others. All pictures in OpenCV are transformed to NumPy arrays, making it easy to connect them with other NumPy libraries. In addition, all of the photos will be specified as a matrix.[14] OpenCV will read it as a NumPy array, which means that Python stores the photos as a NumPy array to a matrix of integers, such as a 3D matrix if it's a colored image; if it's a grayscale image it will be a 2D matrix.

11.5.5 PyAutoGUI

PyAutoGUI is a program that allows you to operate your computer's mouse and keyboard to do a range of activities. It's a platform-agnostic Python GUI automation package for humans. Call the press() method and provide it a string from the PyAutoGUI to press the appropriate keys on the keyboard.[15]

11.6 METHODOLOGY

11.6.1 Face Detection

It's a piece of code that can distinguish human faces in any image or video. Face recognition software such as OpenCV and Dlib are widely used to recognize faces using a number of methods. A linear classifier with a conventional HOG feature make up the detector. A facial landmarks detector is used in Dlib to recognize facial features like eyes, ears, and nose.

11.6.2 FACIAL LANDMARK EXTRACTION

The problem of face landmark detection is a subset of the problem of shape prediction.[16, 17] Given an input image, a shape predictor attempts to locate significant places of interest along a form (and typically an ROI that identifies the item of interest). Our goal is to find essential facial features on the face using shape prediction algorithms. As a result, identifying facial landmarks requires two steps:

Step 1: Identify the face on the camera.
Step 2: On the face ROI, find the major facial structures.

The position of 68 (x, y)-coordinates that correspond to face structures is estimated using the Dlib library's pre-trained facial landmark detector. The 68-point iBUG 300-W dataset was used to train the Dlib face landmark predictor, and these annotations are from it.[18] The indices of the 68 coordinates are shown in Figure 11.3.

11.6.3 EYE AND LIP DETECTION

Following the recognition of the face, facial landmark features are used to identify the eye and lip region. Using the facial landmarks dataset,[14] we can identify 68 landmarks on the face. Each landmark is assigned an index. These indices are used to determine the face's target area. After the eye region has been removed,

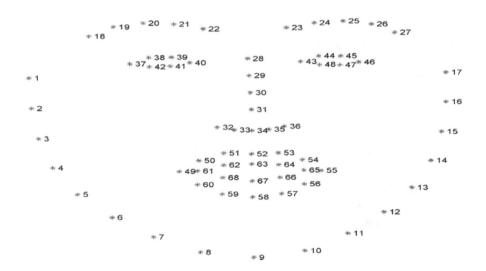

FIGURE 11.3 68 facial landmarks coordinates.

it is analyzed to determine eye blinks and lip movement. The 68 facial landmarks coordinates shown in Figure 11.3 can be used to calculate the eye and lip index.[13]
For two eyes index:

Left eye index: (37, 38, 39, 40, 41, 42)
Right eye index: (43, 44, 45, 46, 47, 48)

For both lip index:

Upper lip Index: (63)
Lower lip index: (67)

11.6.4   EYE ASPECT RATIO

The eye aspect ratio (EAR) is a single scalar value that represents whether the eye is open or closed. The distance between vertically aligned eye landmarks and horizontally aligned eye landmarks is calculated using the eye aspect ratio function.[19] To determine the eye aspect ratio, we must compute the Euclidean distance between the facial landmark's points for each video frame as depicted in equation 1. As a result, the number obtained for the eye aspect ratio when the eye is open is nearly constant. In the case of an eye blink, the value will rapidly decrease until it hits zero. The eye aspect ratio achieves a near-constant value when the eye is closed, which is much smaller than when the eye is open. As a result, the aspect ratio drop indicates that the eyes are blinking.

$$\text{EAR} = \frac{\|p2 - p6\| + \|p3 - p5\|}{2\|p1 - p4\|} \tag{1}$$

where p1, p2, p3, p4, p5, and p6 are the 2D landmark locations, depicted in Figure 11.4. The numerator of this equation assesses the distance between vertical eye landmarks, while the denominator indicates horizontal eye landmarks, appropriately weighting the denominator.

11.6.5   EYE BLINK AND LIP MOVEMENT MONITORING

We can distinguish blinks in the specific eye location with the help of two lines. The one on the left is drawn horizontally, while the one on the right is drawn vertically,

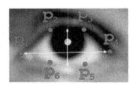

$$\text{EAR} = \frac{\|p_2 - p_6\| + \|p_3 - p_5\|}{2\|p_1 - p_4\|}$$

FIGURE 11.4   Eye landmark coordinates.

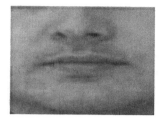

FIGURE 11.5   Lip landmark coordinates.

establishing a separation between the eyes. Blinking is a natural action that involves the momentary closure of the eyes and movement of the eyelids. We must determine what happens when one of the eyes blink. We may presume that the eye is closed/blinked when the eyeball is not visible or the eyelid is closed. We may assume these motions are blinks if they stay between 0.3 and 0.4 seconds; if they persist longer, we can assume they are closed eyelids.[13]

With an open eye, both vertical and horizontal lines are almost identical, but with a closed eye, the vertical line shrinks or vanishes totally. A ratio is calculated using the horizontal line as a point of reference in relation to the vertical line. We'll need to set a threshold here, and if the ratio is more than that, we'll think the eye is closed; otherwise, it'll be open. The EAR calculates the threshold value.

Similarly, we can recognize the lip region. We've just looked at the vertical line so far. The distance between the upper and lower lip indexes must be greater than the threshold to determine that the student is inattentive in the classes. The threshold is equal to the absolute value of the upper lip index value minus the lower lip index value, as illustrated in Figure 11.5.

11.6.5.1 Access Keyboard

The keyDown(), which simulates pressing and then releasing a key, is wrapped in the press() function. When the system detects a blink or lip movement from the students, the keyDown() key is pressed alerting the user to take some necessary actions against the students.

11.7 EXPERIMENTAL RESULTS AND DISCUSSIONS

The authors have tested the system through its trials in real-time and analyzed the outcomes. Our computer vision-aided algorithm was put to the test in a real-life situation, and the results were recorded. Based on preliminary testing of the prototype system, it has been discovered that the face detection OpenCV Python module is a huge help to developers because it eliminates the need for them to manually write the function of detecting photos. The system's testing has shown expected results, and the procedure of monitoring students has gone well. As a result of the system's features, the design may be improved even further. Our system is completely efficient and user-friendly. We utilized a low-cost, lightweight Python alternative to commercial systems so that the code could be run on any device and apps with limited computational resources. Though eye blinks and lip movement are more precise in tracking a student's performance and engagement in studies and day-to-day activities during online classes, natural blink can sometimes be detected instead of a voluntary blink. These drawbacks can be mitigated by utilizing a high-resolution camera. Its usability is efficient for people who operate remotely or in any location or circumstance that prevents traveling, and its applicability can be a solution to a problem in the event of a pandemic.

11.7.1 Eye and Lip Movement Detection

Within seconds of opening the program, the camera starts recording your facial motions, mostly eye blinks and lip movements, and feeds a live feed to the app using OpenCV, a computer vision library. The face is detected using a linear SVM classifier and a Haar-based HOG with the video as the source.[20] The eye region is recognized using the Dlib library 68 facial landmarks feature detector once the face has been detected. We were able to detect both the lip and eye movement easily, which further helped the user in assessing student's attention in the online classes.

11.7.2 Facial Movement Monitoring

The major purpose of the technology is to allow professors to keep a close watch on students' attention during online sessions. We have applied the threshold to the eyeball after identifying the eye region to increase the capture accuracy. To distinguish between natural and voluntary eye blinks, a metric called eye aspect ratio is utilized. The key for that frame is triggered if the observed ratio exceeds the threshold. The eye threshold in our system is 0.26, although it may vary based on the camera's quality and the region in which it works. Similarly, the key is activated if the difference between the top and lower coordinates of the lip is greater than the threshold. Our method uses a lip threshold of 0.30 to determine if the student is talking or silent.

When the eye is open in Figure 11.6, [19] the top-left is a representation of eye landmarks. Eye landmarks while the eye is closed are in the top-right. In the bottom, the eye aspect ratio throughout time is plotted. A blink is indicated by a decrease in the eye aspect ratio. An eye is completely open in the top-left, with the eye facial landmarks mapped. There's a closed eye in the top-right corner. The eye aspect ratio is shown over time at the bottom. As can be seen, the eye aspect ratio remains constant (showing that the eye is open), then swiftly decreases to zero, then rises again, indicating that a blink has occurred.

The system successfully detected all the blink or lip movement which were constant over a particular time interval; the keyboard keys were also engaged, which indicated that the learner was either dozing or talking. As a consequence, the teachers were notified and were able to take the necessary actions.

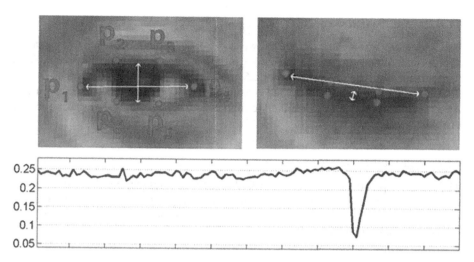

FIGURE 11.6   Eye blink graph.

11.7.3   GESTURE RECOMMENDER SYSTEM ADVANTAGES

The prototype system OpenCV has been developed. The following are examples of real-time facial gesture tracking systems:

- It might be a solution to keep track of attendance while courses are in online sessions.
- It can help teachers keep track of which students are actually attending online class.
- It's simple to keep track of students' activities, and it prevents interruptions or human mistake.
- It can assist educators and users who work from home or remotely save money.
- It saves the professor or user time and effort.

11.8   LIMITATIONS

11.8.1   ADEQUATE ILLUMINATION

Due to poor lighting, the framework is sometimes unable to distinguish the eyes. As a result, it generates an inaccurate outcome that must be managed. 56 circumstance infrared setting enlightenments should be used consistently to avoid unfavorable lighting conditions.

11.8.2   Optimal Range

Issues emerge when the distance between the face and the webcam isn't exactly appropriate. When the face is too close to the camera, the framework is unable to recognize it from the image (less than 25 cm). The setting light is not there to appropriately edify the face when the face is more than 80 cm distant from the camera. As a result, eyes are no longer linked to high accuracy, and sluggishness is no longer visible.

11.8.3   Face Alignment

The face is typically seen when it is tilted to a certain degree, but the framework is unable to distinguish the face beyond that. When a person's face isn't recognized, the eyes aren't either. The framework will return an incorrect result if the camera recognizes more than one face.

11.8.4   Eyewear

If the user is wearing spectacles, the system may fail to recognize their eyes, which is the most serious flaw in these systems. This problem has yet to be overcome, and it is a test for almost all current eye detection systems.

11.9   CONCLUSION AND FUTURE WORK

Using OpenCV, PyAutoGUI, and the Dlib package, we have exhaustively covered the system's capabilities and operation in this chapter. The students' attendance will be tracked and documented on a daily basis in online classes. Many organizations and institutions will profit from the computer vision-based attendance tracking system since it will save them time. For every learning management institution, an automatic attendance management system is a must-have tool. The teachers were able to recognize all of the students' faces and could also track their eye and lip movement using the real-time camera. The teachers could easily determine whether the students were dozing or not by their eye blinks and could identify if they were discreetly studying or conversing between themselves from their lip movement. The teacher could assess both activities and, based on those, evaluate the students' performances and involvement in their studies during online sessions.

The majority of existing solutions are time intensive and require the teacher or pupils to perform semi-manual tasks. By incorporating facial recognition into the process, we hope to overcome the problems. Even while this method has drawbacks, such as the inability to recognize a huge number of faces, there is still a lot of space for development. We may enhance different modules until we obtain an acceptable detection and identification rate since we use a modular strategy. The system may be improved such that the accuracy, detection rate, and recognition rate are all raised, allowing for a greater number of students to be discovered and recognized in the class.

11.10   KEY TERMS AND DEFINITIONS

Eye aspect ratio—The eye aspect ratio can be used to assess whether or not a person is blinking in a video frame.

Eye gaze—It's an electrical gadget that lets you operate a computer or tablet by staring at text or commands shown on a video screen.

Facial Gesture—It is an automatic and indirect mode of communication that allows us to communicate our feelings.

Facial Landmarks—Face landmark detection is a computer vision job that involves detecting and tracking significant features on a human face.

Region of Interest—Let's imagine you want to recognize people's faces from a snapshot. You don't need the hat or the clothes; all you need is a close-up of their face.

Threshold—Thresholding is the process of assigning values in respect to a certain threshold value.

REFERENCES

1. Bradski, G., and Kaehler, A. (2008). *Learning OpenCV Computer Vision with the OpenCV Library*. O'Reilly.
2. Agarwal, A., and Das, A. (2021, in press) An innovative marks prediction tool for regular courses using machine. *Accepted and presented in the International Conference on Recent Trends in Science and Technology (ICRTST 2021), held on 8th–9th July 2021.*
3. Viola, P., and Jones, M. J. (2004). Robust real-time face detection. *International Journal of Computer Vision, 57*(2), 137– 154.
4. Laganiere, R. (2011, May). *OpenCV 2 Computer vision Application Programming Cookbook*. PACKT Publication.
5. Ngoc Anh, B., Tung Son, N., Truong Lam, P., Le Chi, P., Huu Tuan, N., Cong Dat, N., . . . and Van Dinh, T. (2019). A computer-vision based application for student behavior monitoring in classroom. *Applied Sciences, 9*(22), 4729.
6. Richardson, M., and Abraham, C. (2013). Modeling antecedents of university students' study behavior and grade point average. *Journal of Applied Social Psychology, 43*(3), 626–637.
7. Glass, A. L., and Kang, M. (2019). Dividing attention in the classroom reduces exam performance. *Educational Psychology, 39*(3), 395–408.
8. Lim, J. H., Teh, E. Y., Geh, M. H., and Lim, C. H. (2017, December). Automated classroom monitoring with connected visioning system. In *2017 Asia-Pacific Signal and Information Processing Association Annual Summit and Conference (APSIPA ASC)* (pp. 386–393). IEEE.
9. Agarwal, R., Takeuchi, T., Laroche, S., and Gotman, J. (2005). Detection of rapid-eye movement in sleep studies. *IEEE Transactions on Biomedical Engineering, 52*(8), 1390–1396.
10. Budi, S., Karnalim, O., Handoyo, E. D., Santoso, S., Toba, H., Nguyen, H., and Malhotra, V. (2018, December). IBAtS-Image based attendance system: A low cost solution to record student attendance in a classroom. In *2018 IEEE International Symposium on Multimedia (ISM)* (pp. 259–266). IEEE.
11. Mery, D., Mackenney, I., and Villalobos, E. (2019, January). Student attendance system in crowded classrooms using a smartphone camera. In *2019 IEEE Winter Conference on Applications of Computer Vision (WACV)* (pp. 857–866). IEEE.

12.   Yang, S., Luo, P., Loy, C. C., and Tang, X. (2016). Wider face: A face detection benchmark. In *Proceedings of the IEEE Conference on Computer Vision and Pattern Recognition* (pp. 5525–5533).

13.   Agarwal, A., and Das, A. (2021, in press). Facial gesture recognition based real time gaming for physically impairment. *Accepted and Presented in the International Symposium on Artificial Intelligence (ISAI 2021), held on 17th–19th February 2021.*

14.   Vignesh, C. P., and Sriram, R. (2020). Eye blink controlled virtual interface using opencv and dlib. *European Journal of Molecular & Clinical Medicine, 7*(8), 2119–2126.

15.   AlSweigart, *PyAutoGUI* [Online]. Available: https://pypi.org/project/PyAutoGUI/

16.   *Face Landmark Detection in an Image.* Available: https://docs.opencv.org/3.4.2/d2/d42/ tutorial_face_landmark_detection_in_an_image.html (accessed on 10 August 2019).

17.   *Face Landmark Detection.* Available: http://dlib.net/face_landmark_detection.py.html (accessed on 10 August 2019).

18.   Rosebrock, A. (2021, April 12). *Facial Landmarks with Dlib, OpenCV, and Python* [Online]. Available: https://www.pyimagesearch.com/2017/04/03/facial-landmarks-dlib-opencv-python/

19.   Soukupova, T., and Cech, J. (2016). Eye blink detection using facial landmarks. *21st Computer Vision Winter Workshop*, Rimske Toplice, Slovenia.

20.   Rosebrock, A. (2021, April 12). *OpenCV Haar Cascades* [Online]. Available: https:// www.pyimagesearch.com/2021/04/12/opencv-haar-cascades/

ADDITIONAL READINGS

21.   Karnalim, O., Budi, S., Santoso, S., Handoyo, E. D., Toba, H., Nguyen, H., and Malhotra, V. (2018, November). Face-face at classroom environment: Dataset and exploration. In *2018 Eighth International Conference on Image Processing Theory, Tools and Applications (IPTA)* (pp. 1–6). IEEE.

22.   Mothwa, L., Tapamo, J. R., and Mapati, T. (2018, November). Conceptual model of the smart attendance monitoring system using computer vision. In *2018 14th International Conference on Signal-Image Technology & Internet-Based Systems (SITIS)* (pp. 229–234). IEEE.

23.   Olagoke, A. S., Ibrahim, H., and Teoh, S. S. (2020). Literature survey on multi-camera system and its application. *IEEE Access, 8*, 172892–172922.

24.   Strueva, A. Y., and Ivanova, E. V. (2021, September). Student attendance control system with face recognition based on neural network. In *2021 International Russian Automation Conference (RusAutoCon)* (pp. 929–933). IEEE.

25.   Su, M. C., Cheng, C. T., Chang, M. C., and Hsieh, Y. Z. (2021). A video analytic in-class student concentration monitoring system. *IEEE Transactions on Consumer Electronics, 67*(4), 294–304.

26.   Cronjé, L., and Sanders, I. (2021). Semiautomated class attendance monitoring using smartphone technology. *Journal of Artificial Intelligence and Technology, 1*(1), 9–20.

27.   Ngoc Anh, B., Tung Son, N., Truong Lam, P., Le Chi, P., Huu Tuan, N., Cong Dat, N., . . . and Van Dinh, T. (2019). A computer-vision based application for student behavior monitoring in classroom. *Applied Sciences, 9*(22), 4729.

28.   Raj, A., Raj, A., and Ahmad, I. (2021). Smart attendance monitoring system with computer vision using IOT. *Journal of Mobile Multimedia*, 115–126.

29.   Malhotra, M., and Chhabra, I. (2021, September). Automatic invigilation using computer vision. In *3rd International Conference on Integrated Intelligent Computing Communication & Security (ICIIC 2021)* (pp. 130–136). Atlantis Press.

30. Torricelli, D., Goffredo, M., Conforto, S., and Schmid, M. (2009). An adaptive blink detector to initialize and update a view-basedremote eye gaze tracking system in a natural scenario. *Pattern Recognition Letters*, *30*(12), 1144–1150.
31. Zhang, L., Wu, B., and Nevatia, R. (2007, October). Detection and tracking of multiple humans with extensive pose articulation. In *2007 IEEE 11th International Conference on Computer Vision* (pp. 1–8). IEEE.
32. Divjak, M., and Bischof, H. (2009, May). Eye blink based fatigue detection for prevention of Computer Vision Syndrome. In *MVA* (pp. 350–353).
33. QiangJi, X. Y. (2002, October). Real-time eye, gaze, and face pose tracking for monitoring driver vigilance. *Journal of Real-Time Imaging*, *8*(5), ISSN: 10772014, http://doi.org/10.1006/rtim.2002.0279.

12 Application of Swarm Intelligence in Recommender Systems

Shriya Singh, Monideepa Roy, Sujoy Datta, and Pushpendu Kar

CONTENTS

12.1 INTRODUCTION

We need to make decisions at every stage of our daily lives. Whenever we want to buy something, the first thing we do is to gather as much information as we can about that particular item before we make a decision. The source of this information may be from the internet, past buyer reviews or even gut feelings.

Among these items, there are many common lifestyle activities, such as shopping for clothes, eating out and going to the movies, that depend highly on the individual

DOI: 10.1201/9781003319122-12

tastes of a person. In such cases it is difficult to recommend something to a person if the other person is not aware of the personal likes and dislikes of person. So people usually ask friends for their suggestions and inputs. Such recommendations were useful when the number of options was limited. But with the vast number of choices for everything today, it is not possible to get the best recommendations with just suggestions from friends and relatives. So this has led to the advent of various recommendation algorithms, which can recommend the best options to the users from a very large selection of items by considering various factors in just a few seconds.

However, the traditional cognitive approaches are yet to achieve the desired levels of accuracy. This led to the development of recommendation engines,[1, 2] which were based on deep learning algorithms that solved these accuracy problems. So deep learning recommendation systems are now popular because of their high performance and accuracy. Apart from the fact that we need to identify products that are likely to be purchased, there are several other parameters that also play a crucial part in generating better recommendations. Some of them are appropriate selling price, ability to pay, sell or non-sell decisions based on inventory and demand forecasting. So effectively there may be hundreds of such different combinations of such parameters in such a complex ecommerce system.[3, 4] Executing these algorithms in real time within a few seconds is the next big challenge.

Swarm intelligence is one such concept that is particularly useful in the development of complex systems based on multi-agent frameworks.

This chapter focuses on how the particle swarm optimization (PSO) algorithm can be used to fine-tune a profile-matching algorithm within a recommender system so that it is tailored to satisfy the preferences of the individual users. This makes the recommender system capable of making more accurate predictions about the likes and dislikes of a user and, thus, succeed in making better recommendations to users. The PSO technique was invented by Eberhart and Kennedy in 1995 and was inspired by behaviours of social animals such as a group of birds or a school of fish. It is a simple algorithm and only a few parameters need to be adjusted, after which it can be applied for a variety of applications. PSO is receiving a lot of attention these days because researchers think it has great potential for application in diverse fields. The rest of the chapter is organised as follows: Section 12.2 is a background work on what recommendation systems are, Section 12.3 discusses the scope of swarm intelligence, Section 12.4 discusses some basic concepts in recommender systems, Section 12.5 discusses the swarm intelligence techniques, Section 12.6 gives the conclusion and future scope, and the references in Section 12.7.

12.2 BACKGROUND

12.2.1 RECOMMENDATION SYSTEMS

The terms "recommender system", "collaborative filtering" and "social filtering" are used interchangeably by some researchers. Recommender systems use collaborative filtering (CF) and content-based filtering (CBF), also known as the personality-based approach, in addition to other systems like a knowledge-based systems. The collaborative filtering method uses the past behaviour of a user to build a model, i.e. items which have been previously bought or selected are given numerical ratings, as well as users who have made similar choices. Then this model is used for the prediction/ratings of items that the user may be interested in. The content-based filtering method, on the other hand, uses a set of pre-tagged characteristics of an item so that it can recommend more items with similar properties.

MovieLens is one such movie recommendation website that uses the collaborative filtering method to send recommendations.[5, 6] It captures user preferences and builds a profile by asking the user to rate the movies. It will then search for users with similar profiles, i.e. users who have similar choices, and will use them to generate new recommendations. The dataset that has been collected through the MovieLens website is available for the purposes of research.

Using the ratings collected from the users, the probabilities of the words being in hot or cold documents are determined. Web Watcher is another system that monitors the behaviours of the users and their choices of the links of their web pages visited to recommend web page links that the user is likely to visit in the future. CBF is not as complex compared to CF because in the former only an analysis of the items that an independent user has either bought or seen needs to be done. The creation of sufficient sets of features might not always be possible, so each item is described by its features in CBF.

In the demographic filtering method (DF), users having similar demographic characteristics are placed in the same categories and the cumulative buying behaviour or the preferences of these users in the categories are tracked.

If there is a new user, then the first step is to find out the category he or she belongs to, after which the cumulative buying preferences of users who were previously in the group are recommended to the new user. The demographic technique also uses correlations between people like the collaborative technique, but it uses data which is dissimilar. Both CF and CBF need a history of the ratings of the user, which is not needed by the demographic method.

Genetic algorithms (GAs) are adaptive heuristic search algorithms and fall in the category of evolutionary algorithms. GAs follow the process of natural selection and genetics. GAs are useful in generating superior quality solutions for optimization and search problems.

GAs simulate the natural selection process, i.e. the concept of "survival of the fittest", to solve a problem. It means the species that are capable of survival and adapting to the environment changes are taken as the sample population for the simulation parameters. The representation of every individual is done as a string of characters or integers or a float or a bit.

12.2.2   Particle Swarm Optimization (PSO)

The PSO technique is similar to the genetic algorithms because it is a population-based evolutionary technique, but the difference is that in PSO every particle has a position, velocity and acceleration.

When the velocity and acceleration change, the particle can explore the space of all possible solutions and does not use the existing solutions to reproduce. The movement of the particles in space enable them to sample various locations. There

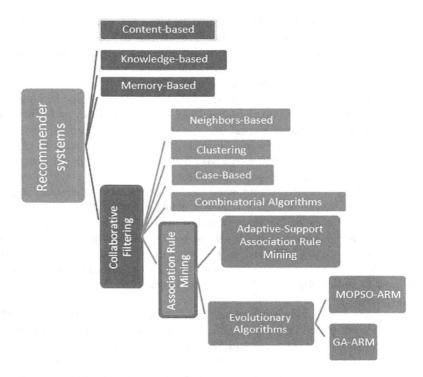

FIGURE 12.1   Application scenarios of PSO in recommender systems.

is a fitness value for every location depending on how well it satisfies the objectives, which are determined by the user preferences.

Following the rules of the swarm process, the particles will be eventually found to swarm around the area which contains the best solutions. So PSO is gradually becoming a popular technique for application in various fields.

The original PSO and the cooperative particle swarm optimiser (CPSO) were applied by Van der Bergh in the training of neural networks. The CPSO technique uses multiple swarms where a swarm is used for the handling of a part of the vector that is going to be optimised. Figure 12.1 shows possible ways of application of PSO in recommender algorithms.

12.3   SCOPE OF SWARM INTELLIGENCE

RSs assist users in finding their relevant items of choice, in a personalised way, from a very large information space. Matches or close matches of choices of users are recommended to the users.

There were several important challenges in the practical application of RSs that have been identified in the last decade. Firstly, when learning about user preferences, the prediction models are obtained by optimizing one or more objective functions, which are generally some measurable quality parameters.[3] However, in the real world, the performance of a RS also depends heavily on subjective or user perceived data, which can only be derived through multi-objective optimization techniques.

Secondly, the user preferences may have contextual dependence. This means that the judgement of a user may vary based on the current context. Some contexts like time, location and other contexts need to be considered in the recommendation process, and suitable weights for them also need to be decided.

Thirdly, real world RSs deal with a huge amount of data, which only grow over time. So the scalability of the RS is another issue.

Another challenge came with the emergence of the social networks. The common collaborative filtering and content-based approaches are not adequate for the representation of the graph-based nature that is present in social networks. So social relations also need to considered in RS.

Swarm intelligence (SI) techniques are decentralised and self-organising by definition, and therefore they offer a good solution for multi-objective optimization of black box functions. The previously mentioned challenges can be handled reasonably well using SI.

Swarm intelligence is based on the PSO technique. It is used to determine the optimal solution in a high dimension solution space, i.e. either maximization or minimization problem. There can be multiple maxima or minima for a function, but there will only be a global maxima or minima. If we have a complex function, it can be very difficult to determine the global maxima or minima. With the help of PSO, we can try to capture the points close to the global maxima or minima, even though it is not able to determine the exact global maxima or minima. Hence PSO is actually a heuristic model.

Here we consider a function to show why it is sometimes very difficult to determine the global maxima or minima.

Suppose we take the function: $y=f(x)=\sin(x)+\sin(x^2)+\sin(x)*\cos(x)$, which is shown in Figure 12.2.

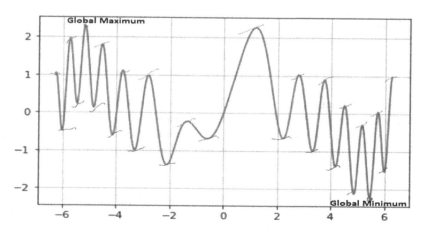

FIGURE 12.2   Graph showing the growth of function $y=f(x)=\sin(x)+\sin(x^2)+\sin(x)*\cos(x)$

As we can see, the function has one global minimum and maximum each. If the function is considered in the interval (-4 to 6 in the X-axis), the maxima will not be the global maxima. It depends on the interval chosen. If we observe only a part of a continuous function, we will not get the correct results. Moreover, in dynamic systems there may not be a static function that will work.

In addition, data analytics is power hungry and needs huge volumes of data to train a model properly. Although we can use statistical sampling, it still may not give exact values. If we develop a mathematical function based on a real-life scenario, it may have multiple variables or higher dimensional vector space, e.g. the growth of bacteria in a jar. It depends on various factors like temperature, humidity, etc. Then it becomes even more challenging to find the global maximum or minimum, e.g. the following function:

$$z = f(x, y) = \sin(x^2) + \sin(y^2) + \sin(x)*\sin(y)$$

If more variables are added, it becomes even more complex. To deal with such complex problems, swarm intelligence techniques are being tested for recommender systems and are giving very promising results.

12.4   SOME BASIC CONCEPTS OF RS

In this section some basic concepts of recommender systems are defined, which will help in a better understanding of the rest of the chapter.

12.4.1   USER, ITEM AND FEEDBACK

Let $\mu = \{u1, \ldots, un\}$ be the set of users where each user is represented by a set of characteristics, e.g. age, nationality or location, as well as a number of domain-specific user features. However, some characteristics may be difficult to obtain if they are sensitive characteristics. Similarly, let $L = \{i1, \ldots, im\}$ be the set of items where each item is represented by its unique identifier and some item characteristics. The characteristics of the items are usually domain-specific in most of the cases; for example, for movies the characteristics are title, genre, director, budget etc. Although such types of information are not sensitive, it needs to be inserted into a database by a human and is a costly and time consuming process.[7]

The third important aspect in RSs is the user's feedback on items, which can be seen as a utility (or preference) measure for user-item pairs. It maps $f : \mu \times L \rightarrow$ from the pairs of user-item to the set F of possible feedback values. If the feedback is explicit type, then the user evaluation of items is done explicitly by the user on the basis of some rating scale. The process of explicit feedback puts a burden on the user because the user has to evaluate an item, and it may affect the behaviour pattern of the user. But for implicit feedback, only the past interactions of the user with the objects are recorded. Implicit feedback is easy for collection, but its main drawback is that there is no negative feedback.

12.4.2 The Recommendation Task

Given the past users' feedback and some domain knowledge (if available), to learn a model F: $\mu \times L \rightarrow \mathbb{R}$ such that acc(f, $\hat{f}$, Φ) is maximal or err(f, $\hat{f}$, Φ) is minimal. Accuracy or error measures express the quality of the learned model $\hat{f}$ w.r.t., the feedback of the users Φ on so-far "unseen" items.

12.4.2.1 Rating Prediction

Rating prediction is the explicit feedback and is used for the prediction of the ratings of users on items. So the widely used mean squared error (MSE), e.g. in Bao et al. (2012), is defined as follows:[1]

$$\text{err}^{\text{mse}}(f, \hat{f}, \Phi) = 1 / |\Phi| \sum\nolimits_{(ui,ij,f(ui,ij)) \in \Phi} (f(ui, ij) - \hat{f}(ui, ij))^2 \qquad (1)$$

The model $\hat{f}$ under which err^{mse} is minimal is then used for recommendation. In the most common case of top-k recommendation, items $i_{j1}, \ldots, i_{jk}$ with the highest predicted ratings are recommended to the user ui.

12.4.2.2 Item Ranking

Item ranking provides the personalised rankings of items to the users.[8] There are many types of accuracy measures and many of them are taken from information retrieval. The value of $\hat{f}(u_i, i_j)$ represents a ranking score of the item i_j for the user u_i. If the ranking score is high, it means there is a higher likelihood that a user prefers that item. But the ordering of recommendations can be done by a family of rank-based metrics, e.g. mean average precision (MAP) or normalized discounted cumulative gain (nDCG). nDCG accommodates varying relevance levels and is particularly suitable for explicit feedback datasets as well. The discounted cumulative gain (DCG) is defined as:

$$\text{acc}^{\text{DCG}}\left(u_i, k, f, \hat{f}, \Phi\right) = \sum\nolimits_{j=1}^{k} \frac{f\left(u_{i,i_{rank(j)}}\right)}{\log_2\left(j+1\right)} \qquad (2)$$

where rank(j) function returns the index of j-th best object according to the model $\hat{f}$.

12.4.3 Recommendation Techniques

The two most popular recommendation techniques are content-based filtering (CBF) and collaborative filtering (CF).

12.4.3.1 Content-Based Filtering

Content-based filtering uses the features of items for recommending other items that are similar to what a user likes, based on their previous actions or some explicit feedback.

12.4.3.2   Collaborative Filtering

This method filters out items that a user might like based on the reactions of users with similar profiles. It searches a large group of people and finds a smaller set of users who have tastes similar to a particular user.

12.4.3.3   Hybrid Methods

There are many hybrid models which use both CF and CBF techniques, such as the neighborhood-based CF models that can be easily extended by merging the features of CF and CBF, e.g. weighted similarity metric.

12.4.4   CLUSTERING IN RECOMMENDER SYSTEMS

The two main factors in RS are ssparsity and scalability. High sparsity (also known as the cold-start problem) of available feedback, i.e. situations, where a large fraction of $f(u_i, i_j)$ is unknown, leads to hindrance in the application of CF. The scalability of RS is the ability of the system to maintain a reasonable query response time when the volume of input data (both $|U|$, $|I|$ and $|\Phi|$) increases. Cluster analysis or clustering is the process where entities are grouped into clusters so that the entities in the same cluster are more similar to each other as compared to those in other clusters. Clustering techniques are utilised in RS to overcome scalability and sparsity issues. Instead of learning the predicted rating/ranking for each user-item pair directly, users are first mapped into clusters $\hat{g} : U \rightarrow C_u$, where $|C_u| \ll |U|$. Then the predicted rating/ranking is learned for each cluster-item pair $\hat{f}_{cl} : C_u \times I \rightarrow \mathbb{R}$. In this way, the time complexity of the learning function f_{cl} is bounded by the volume of clusters and the sparsity of cluster-feedback matrix $C_u \times I$ is much smaller than the sparsity of user-feedback matrix $U \times I$. So clustering may help in the reduction of the cold-start problem as well as scalability issues,
 but there will be less individual personalization.

12.4.5   EVALUATION OF RECOMMENDATION TECHNIQUES

Recommender systems are used in a variety of domains; it's still not clear to what extent the recommender systems have some commercial value. It's challenging to build a reliable product suggestion system. But it is also challenging to define what is meant by reliability. Any predictive model relies heavily on data to make reliable predictions. Therefore, the best recommender systems come from organizations who have large volumes of data, such as Google, Amazon, Netflix or Spotify. Machine learning thrives on data, and to train the model, the more data the system has, the better will be the results it will give.

12.5   SWARM INTELLIGENCE TECHNIQUES

The swarm intelligence technique belongs to evolutionary computing (EC), and artificial neural networks (ANN) and fuzzy systems belong to the family of the computational intelligence (CI) method. CI methods are, in general, a set of approaches that are nature inspired and aim to address complex optimization problems where mathematical or traditional models are not very effective. The main paradigm of SI is an application of a *population* of simple *agents* for the task. Agents interact with one another as well as with the surrounding environment; so SI approaches are decentralized and self-organized systems.

Let $f : \mathbf{X} \rightarrow \mathrm{R}$, where $\mathbf{X} = \mathbf{X}_1 \times \mathbf{X}_2 \cdots \times \mathbf{X}_k$, is a a *fitness function* that has to be optimized. f can be a black-box function for which the analytic form is not known. X is denoted as the space of possible solutions to the optimization problem, and for each position $\mathbf{x} \in \mathrm{X}$, we denote its fitness value as $f(\mathbf{x}) = r_\mathbf{x}$.

In general, SI approaches start with a randomly chosen initial population of s agents, $\mathbf{A} = \{ai(\mathbf{x}i , i) \,|\, i \in \{1, \dots, s\}\}$, where i is an inner state of agent ai.

12.5.1 ANT COLONY OPTIMIZATION (ACO)

ACO is a probabilistic technique for solving computational problems which can be reduced to finding best paths through graphs.[9] ACO was inspired by the foraging behaviour of real ants who form and maintain a line to their food source by laying a trail of *pheromone*, i.e. a chemical compound that attracts other ants. Whenever an ant finds a source of food, it returns to its nest by following its own path and deposits a certain amount of pheromone. Other ants are more attracted to the shorter routes leading to the equally valuable food sources and mark such paths with additional pheromone. Soon nearly all the ants choose the shortest routes to the best food sources.

For each iteration of the algorithm, each ant $a_i \in A$ will aim to find a suitable food source via exploring the graph's nodes. It will start at the source node n_s, and each ant constructs a set of feasible transitions to new nodes $s = \{n_j[1], \dots, n_{jk}[k]\}$. Each node $n_j[1], \dots, nj[k]$ has assigned a transition probability $ps_,j[1], \dots, ps_,j[k]$ respectively. The next transition of an ant is a node nj chosen randomly based on the $p_{s,j}[1], \dots, p_{s,j}[k]$ probabilities. Each ant will iterate over feasible nodes until it finds a food source. A probability $p_{i,j}$ of a transition from n_i to n_j depends on the combination of two values resembling prior and posterior desirability of the move. The updated pheromone concentration on the path $n_a \rightarrow n_b, \tau_{a,b}^{[it+1]}$ will be:

$$\tau_{a,b}^{[it+1]} = (1 - \rho) \times \tau_{a,b}^{[it]} + \sum_{i=1}^{|A|} \left(\mu_i^{a,b} * \frac{c}{l_i} \right)$$

where the prior concentration of pheromone is denoted as $\tau_{a,b}^{[it]}$ and the evaporation coefficient as. Indicator $u_i^{a,b}$ indicates whether the ant a_i uses the edge $n_a \rightarrow n_b$ in its current path to a food source. The amount of pheromone that is added depends on the quality of the food source (usually a constant c) and the length of the path to it, l_i.

12.5.2 PARTICLE SWARM OPTIMIZATION (PSO)

PSO follows the example of how birds move in flocks.[10] PSO assumes a real-valued k-dimensional solution space X, where the inner state of each agent (particles) i will contain its prior velocity $\mathbf{v}_i = v_1, \ldots, v_k$, personal best solution X_i^{best} and has the access to the swarm's up-to-date best solution $\mathbf{x}^{best} : \delta_i = \{\mathbf{v}_i, x_i^{best}, \mathbf{x}_{best}\}$. For every iteration, the velocity of each particle is updated towards the position of its personal and global best, and the particle moves w.r.t. its current velocity.

$$v_i^{[it+1]} = v_i^{[it]} + \alpha \times rand() \times (x_i^{best} - \mathbf{x}_i) + \beta \times rand() \times (x^{best} - x_i)$$

Hyper parameters and control local and global convergence respectively and $rand()$ function generates random numbers from uniform [0, 1] distribution. After the velocity adjustment, particles move to their new positions:

$x_i^{[it+1]} = x_i^{it} + v_i^{[it+1]}$ and best solutions are updated.

Decision-making is a very important aspect of our everyday lives. So before we make any decision, we make sure that we have gathered sufficient information about it. The source of this information can be predefined rules, surveys or even gut-feelings. With the advent of recommendation systems, we can circumvent this problem by the suggestion of items or products to the customer based on his/her preferences. e-commerce websites make use of these systems quite widely as marketing tools for increasing their revenues by presenting products to a customer that he/she is likely to buy. So a site on the internet may use a recommender system to find the likes and dislikes of a customer and to understand the individual needs of a customer and thereby increase the customer loyalty. Here we have seen how we can use a RS along with a PSO algorithm to learn the personal preferences of users and provide custom-made suggestions.

12.6 CONCLUSION AND FUTURE SCOPE

In this chapter it was discussed how PSO techniques can be applied to recommender systems to fine tune the existing algorithms to customize them for fitting the individual preferences of users. Experiments show that the PSO technique outperforms the non-adaptive approach and gives a better accuracy in the prediction as compared to GA and Pearsons algorithms in a majority of the cases.

For this, if we use the large scale and publicly available datasets for the experiments and use the recommendation or machine-learning algorithms that are publicly available, then we can compare among the state-of-the-art baselines.

In addition to this, the PSO algorithms have reached the final solution significantly faster as compared to GA.

As a future scope of work, SI-based recommendation systems may be used for complex types of recommendation problems, and we can also try to solve the long tail problem and increased diversity, novelty and serendipity in recommendations by using multi-criteria optimization techniques using agents.

REFERENCES

1.   J. Bao, Y. Zheng, M.F. Mokbel, Location-based and preference-aware recommendation using sparse geo-social networking data, in: *ACM SIGSPATIAL 2012*, ACM, 2012, pp. 199–208, https://doi.org/10.1145/2424321.2424348.

2. G. Guo, J. Zhang, N. Yorke-Smith, A novel bayesian similarity measure for recommender systems, in: *Proceedings of the 23rd International Joint Conference on Artificial Intelligence (IJCAI)*, 2013, pp. 2619–2625.
3. K. Goldberg, *Jester Data*, 2003, http://eigentaste.berkeley.edu/dataset/, accessed: 2nd September 2015. O. Celma, *Last.fm Dataset 1k Users*, 2006, http://www.dtic.upf.edu/ocelma/MusicRecommendationDataset/lastfm-1K.html, accessed: 2nd September 2015.
4. H. Khrouf, R. Troncy, Hybrid event recommendation using linked data and user diversity, in: *ACM RecSys 2013*, ACM, 2013, pp. 185–192, https://doi.org/10.1145/2507157.2507171.
5. GroupLens, *Movielens 100k Data*, 1998, http://grouplens.org/datasets/movielens/, accessed: 2nd September 2015.
6. GroupLens, *Movielens 1m Data*, 2003, http://grouplens.org/datasets/movielens/, accessed: 2nd September 2015.
7. S. Ujjin, P.J. Bentley, Learning user preferences using evolution, in: *Proceedings of the 4th Asia-Pacific Conference on Simulated Evolution and Learning*, Singapore, 2002.
8. K. Lakiotaki, N.F. Matsatsinis, A. Tsoukias, Multicriteria user modeling in recommender systems, *IEEE Intelligent Systems* 26 (2) (2011): 64–76, https://doi.org/10.1109/MIS.2011.33.
9. R. Sharma, H. Banati, P. Bedi, Adaptive content sequencing for e-learning courses using ant colony optimization, in: *SocProS 2011*, Springer, 2012, pp. 579–590.
10. H.C. Chen, K.K. Huang, C.C. Hsu, Y.M. Huang, A personalized video learning system by artificial bee colony algorithm on Facebook, *Internet Technology* 16 (5) (2015).

13 Application of Machine-Learning Techniques in the Development of Neighbourhood-Based Robust Recommender Systems

Swarup Chattopadhyay, Anjan Chowdhury, and Kuntal Ghosh

CONTENTS

DOI: 10.1201/9781003319122-13

13.1 INTRODUCTION

Generally speaking, recommender systems (RSs) are information processing tools that attempt to recommend the most appropriate items (products or services) to specific users (individuals or businesses). They do so by predicting a user's interest in an item based on related information about the items, the users, and the interactions between the items and the users. The objective of developing RSs is to alleviate information overload by extracting the most pertinent information from a large dataset and offering individualised services. The most critical characteristic of RSs is their capacity to predict a user's likes and interests through analysis of their activity in order to create customised suggestions. There are many types of e-service personalization that use RSs that have been studied by many researchers in the last two decades. Collaborative filtering (CF), [1] content-based (CB), [2] and hybrid techniques [3] are some of the most commonly used techniques for making recommendations. Each recommendation method has its own pros and cons. For example, CF is simple, scalable, and easy to start, but CB has too many specific recommendations.

There are several ways to build RSs that make better recommendations or suggestions to users based on machine-learning techniques. There are a number of machine-learning approaches or algorithms in the literature that can figure out how important the user's previous choice was in relation to the products that are still available and make better suggestions.[4, 5–7] Machine learning (ML) is one of the most exciting and rapidly expanding areas of research in almost every field. ML approaches are being used in practically every area of computing. For example, the approaches have been successfully applied to book recommender systems (BRSs) in order to improve the systems' prediction and recommendation accuracy. The task of these ML approaches is to extract the important features and classify the book's characteristics. Several other approaches from the ML area have also been used to provide recommendations. Among these, the majority are probabilistic in nature, while some might be seen as classification problems. [8] Other well-known ML techniques, such as the Markov decision methods,[9] artificial neural networks,[10] clustering,[11] Bayesian classifiers,[12] support vector machines,[13] ånd deep neural networks [14] were also used to recommend items to the user in the RSs. Bayesian networks are a common ML approach that is widely used to build models for content-based RSs.[15] This chapter discusses how ML techniques may be used to improve the accuracy of RSs. The current research integrates a novel network clustering strategy, a popular ML approach, and a CF technique to create a robust neighbourhood-based RS that provides better and more efficient suggestions.

CF is a valuable recommender system technique that has been employed in a number of successful RSs on the internet.[1] The majority of collaborative filtering-based RSs create a neighbourhood of clients that share similar interests. Once a user's neighbourhood has been established, these systems employ a variety of algorithms to provide suggestions. The objective of this chapter is to incorporate a community discovery approach with neighbourhood-based RSs in order to improve their effectiveness. During the last decade, numerous academics have tackled critical problems such as user recommendations of items, user opinions on various items, user buying behaviour patterns, etc. by clustering individuals or objects into meaningful groupings. Many researchers have utilised community identification algorithms to cluster users based on their ratings or purchases and then used these clusters to make suggestions for them.

The goal of community detection is to partition a network into groups of vertices with a high edge density inside each group and a low edge density between groups. Numerous graph theoretic and probabilistic approaches are used to discover communities in real-world and artificial networks. Modularity is a frequently used goodness metric that accurately quantifies the robustness of a network's community structure.[16] The Louvain method is a widely used heuristic-greedy approach for detecting disjoint communities by optimising network modularity.[17] Raghavan et al. (2007) introduced a label propagation algorithm (LPA) for detecting both disjoint and overlapping communities through the propagation of labels denoting community membership across nodes in a network.[18] The Infomap approach breaks down the network into communities or clusters by condensing a description of the probability flow, which is used as a proxy for information flows in the real world. [19] We also introduce and integrate a nodality-based clustering (NBC) approach in the development of neighbourhood-based robust RS.[20] The detailed procedures of the NBC algorithm for network community detection are discussed in Section 13.7. As a result, community discovery algorithms look for clusters in a graph where the amount of interaction inside a cluster is more than the amount of interaction outside of it. We think that these dense clusters present in a network will help us build better user neighbourhoods in a RS.

Sarwar et al. (2002) also applied the clustering technique to generate the neighbourhood information and used this to increase the performance of neighbourhood-based RSs.[21] Adsorption is one example of such a neighbourhood-based algorithm that is used in applications like recommending YouTube videos, movies, and sentiment analysis of text data, among such others.[22] The adsorption algorithm is a random walk-based method that spreads preferences through graphs. The algorithm is based on the idea that a user's preferences for items are likely to match those of other users who are similar to them. Parimi et al. (2014) recently employed the modularity-based community detection approach to create a neighbourhood for users, and then used collaborative filtering to the neighbourhood to recommend collaborators and books to the users.[23] They have combined the detected communities with neighbourhood-based RSs, notably the adsorption algorithm, which uses implicit user preferences to recommend things. Following the same lines of thinking, this chapter discusses the same strategy that combines several important network clustering techniques with the adsorption algorithm to construct robust neighbourhood-based RSs that provide better and more efficient recommendations. The empirical results from DBLP, [24] Book Crossing,[25] Amazon Photo,[26] and MovieLens [27] datasets demonstrate the efficacy of the integrated neighbourhood-based RSs, which may be useful for other e-commerce applications as well.

13.2 STRUCTURE OF A RECOMMENDER SYSTEM

A recommender system, also known as a recommendation engine or platform, is a type of information filtering system that attempts to forecast a user's rating or preference for an item. RS was first used on e-commerce sites to propose items to customers and boost merchant revenue by selling more.[28] The core notion of friendship and likeliness guided the development of recommenders in a RS. RSs usually consists of three parts: **user information**, such as what the user likes and what he or she has bought, user ratings, and user reviews; **item information**, such as what the items look like and how they work and features of the item; and **filtering techniques** that use this user and item information to find items that match the user's interests.

The information provided by the user is highly vital and crucial in the construction of the user profile, which in turn assists the RS in filtering the ideas provided by the user. The features or attributes of an item, on the other hand, are also an important aspect of the recommendation system used to evaluate and recommend a new item to the user. The values of certain features remain constant throughout time, whereas the values of others fluctuate over time. Suppose we are looking at a mobile phone. The product's brand, colour, and so on are fixed for a specific model, but the ratings and suggestions for that product vary over time. Both the user and item information are required in order to construct user-item interactions, which are the actions made by the user while interacting with the system for a particular item. The involvement might take the shape of a search for a certain item or providing comments on a specific item. The activity log of the recommendation system keeps track of all of these actions. Finally, the filtering algorithms employed by RS take into account the user-item interactions along with the user information and the item information as input and provide a suggestion for a new item for the users to consider.

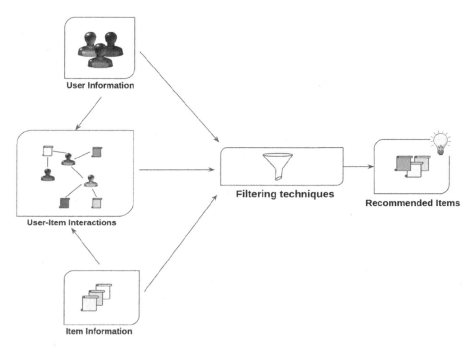

FIGURE 13.1   Basic architecture of a recommender system.

The user information, the item information, and the information about their interactions utilised in filtering approaches are all included into the core structure of the RS, as illustrated in Figure 13.1.

13.3   OBJECTIVE OF A RECOMMENDER SYSTEM

The main reason for the development of RSs was to cut down on the amount of information and processing costs by working with personalised information and data. This is done by looking at the user's interests and behaviour to figure out what he or she likes and doesn't like.[29] It is good for both users and service providers. Today, many companies, such as Google, Twitter, LinkedIn, Netflix, and Amazon, use recommendation systems to make decisions about how to make more money or cut down on their risk.[30, 31]

The major objective of the RSs is to alleviate information overload caused by the exponential proliferation of information on the web. This giant of information is built up by giving customers a lot of different sources of information about things like goods, hotels, and restaurants to use.[32, 33] To attain this core purpose, RSs take numerous common objectives into account, including relevance, correctness, originality, serendipity, and variety.

The goal of RSs is to present the user with items that are relevant to their choices. The accuracy of RSs is measured by how relevant the item is to the user's perception.[34] This shows up in things like precision, recall, mean absolute error (MAE), root mean squared error (RMSE), mean average precision (MAP), and the F1-score, which show how well RS predictions work. One of the most important factors in a product's ability to be recommended is its uniqueness.[35] To put it another way, the uniqueness of a RS is how well it can produce new suggestions for consumers.

13.4 APPROACHES OF A RECOMMENDER SYSTEM

The RSs methodologies may be classified broadly into four broad categories: collaborative filtering (CF), content-based filtering (CBF), hybrid filtering, and knowledge-based filtering strategy. Figure 13.2 illustrates various RSs methodologies.

13.4.1 COLLABORATIVE FILTERING (CF)

CF is the most commonly utilised approach for designing recommender systems.[36] The standard CF recommendation approach works by analysing previous user-item rating data to identify additional like-minded users for recommending items and making suggestions. It anticipates the behaviour of a user based on their previous habits, or in other words, it discovers a link between two or more similar users based on their previous activities in order to make a recommendation.[37] These users, who are similar to one another, are referred to as "neighbours". In recommender systems, the CF method is employed in practically every field of data, though it is suffering from a cold-start problem.[38, 39] Collaborative techniques may be grouped into memory-based and model-based filtering techniques.

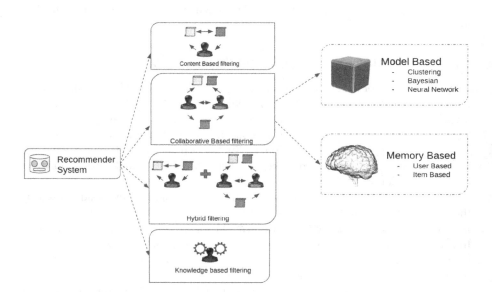

FIGURE 13.2 Major approaches in a recommender system.

13.4.1.1 Memory-Based Filtering

Memory-based filtering techniques are simple and straightforward to build. They predict preferences by referring to comparable users or items. This method is used to determine the degree of similarity between users or items, which has a significant impact on the precision and effectiveness of neighbourhood approaches. Memory-based strategies are divided into two categories: **user-based** and **item-based**.[40]

13.4.1.2 Model-Based Filtering

Model-based filtering methods employ data mining and machine-learning techniques to anticipate a user's preference for an item in a RS. Decision trees,[4] artificial neural networks,[41] clustering,[11] Bayesian classifiers,[12] association rule mining,[42] support vector machines,[13] matrix factorization,[5] and deep neural networks [14] are examples of these approaches.

13.4.2 CONTENT-BASED FILTERING (CBF)

The CBF recommender system is built up based on a user's prior history. It assumes that if a person preferred an item in the past, they will continue to like it in the future. The similarities between two items are measured by evaluating the individual features corresponding to the items.

The CBF technique concentrates its efforts primarily on these extracted features of the individual items in a RS and generates recommendations for an item to a user within that RS based on these extracted features. CBF sometimes suffers from the limited content analysis that is caused by the inability to extract meaningful content from data items.[43] Therefore, the performance of the CBF recommender system falls due to the presence of this lack of sufficient content information. As a result of this constraint, CBF is rarely examined in its real form in a practical context. Instead, CBF may be used to tackle the real problem by integrating it with the other methodologies for RSs, which are sometimes referred to as hybrid approaches.

13.4.3 HYBRID FILTERING

Despite the difficulties of a cold start, which is a problem when there is a lack of information in a RS, the CF technique of recommendation is the most frequently employed approach. On the other hand, the CBF technique, too, suffers from insufficient content analysis. To address these challenges, researchers have come up with several other approaches and developed hybrid systems that combine CF and CBF techniques.[3] Hybrid approaches combine the best aspects of each and attempt to solve the challenges. Several hybrid approaches may be created by combining CF and CBF in different ways. Saquib Sohail et al. (2017) talked about seven different types of hybrid approaches for RSs.[44] The hybrid approaches have become very popular and effective in increasing the performance of the recommender systems. As a result, hybrid methods have been employed in almost every field of recommendation, from movies and books to e-commerce, hotels, and tourism.[45, 46]

13.4.4 KNOWLEDGE-BASED FILTERING

Knowledge-based (KB) filtering makes use of back-end knowledge or information about users, things, and their relationships in order to filter out irrelevant information. Some recommendation systems in e-learning take a knowledge-based approach to making recommendations. Knowledge-based filtering systems illustrate how a certain item satisfies the criteria of a specific customer. It is necessary to acquire domain-specific knowledge about people and things in order to employ the KB technique effectively. Techniques for knowledge-based filtering include context-based and ontology-based methods,[47] among others.[48] In the context of e-learning, KB systems make use of relational information in order to locate learning resources that are relevant to the individuals who use the systems.[49]

13.5 ML APPROACHES FOR RECOMMENDER SYSTEMS

Machine learning (ML) is one of the most important and rapidly growing areas of computer science. Recommenders' prediction and recommendation accuracy have been enhanced by the use of ML techniques. Various ML techniques are employed by RSs to anticipate a user's preference for an item. A wide range of approaches are available to aid in the development of ML, including decision trees,[4] artificial neural networks,[41] clustering,[11] Bayesian classifiers,[12] support vector machines,[13] matrix factorization,[5] deep neural networks,[14] and many others.

An artificial neural network (ANN) is a group of nodes and links with different weights that are based on the structure of the biological brain. It is possible to build model-based RSs with an ANN.[15] Hsu et al. (2007) used an ANN to make a TV recommendation system.[50] Christakou et al. (2007) proposed a hybrid RS that combines CB and CF in order to produce exact suggestions for movies.[51] The usage of ANN has also been shown to increase the accuracy of several RSs. A study by Xin et al. (2013) used CF and ANN approaches to help in finding or suggesting books in academic libraries.[52] Hussain et al. (2018) employed a variety of machine learning algorithms to forecast students' difficulties in following sessions of an online course. [53] Trifa et al. (2019) improvised the RS by utilising semantic correlation and a dynamic key value memory network.[54] The support vector machine (SVM) is a popular supervised machine learning technique that can be used to solve classification and regression problems.[13] In recommending books in book recommendation signage (BRS), Mikawa et al. (2011) employed the SVM approach.[55] A probabilistic matrix factorization approach was combined with social context and trust information for recommendation making by Ma et al. (2011).[56] Many researchers have used the Bayesian classifier approach, an important approach of ML, in the development of models for content based RSs.[15]

Deep learning is another important aspect of ML that is currently widely used in a variety of sectors for a variety of purposes, including object and speech recognition, natural language processing (NLP), as well as advertising and RSs.[57] Zhang et al. (2018) came up with a deep-belief networks model that can be used with massive open online courses to help students be more efficient.[58] Association rule mining (ARM) is another ML technique for discovering associations between objects in a large dataset that is both efficient and effective. It falls within the domain of unsupervised machine learning approaches. ARM is the most commonly used ML approach in the BRS community. The ARM technique is also used to develop an intelligent RS for books in Lina et al. (2013).[59]

Clustering is an unsupervised ML approach that uses distance metrics to group things with similar features.[11] Xue et al. (2005) demonstrated a typical application of clustering in RSs.[60] Their strategy makes use of clusters to smooth out the unrated data for individual users. Lina and Zhiyong (2013) used k-means clustering in conjunction with association rule mining to generate personalised book suggestions.[59] A clustering technique is used to alleviate the problem of cold starts in RSs by grouping things together.[61] Clustering methods were also employed by Ghazanfar and Prügel-Bennett (2014) to locate and resolve the issue with gray-sheep users in RS.[62] GA-based k-means clustering algorithms are used to identify market segments for personalised recommendation systems in the online purchasing sector. [63] Khanal et al. (2020) used a k-mean clustering technique to extract the learning sequence in accordance with the CF method.[64]

13.6   IMPORTANCE OF ML APPROACHES

Machine-learning algorithms have a wide range of applications in several areas, not limited to computer science, but including business, marketing, advertising, and medicine, to name a few examples. Several machine-learning methods are currently available in the literature. They can be grouped according to their learning processes. The four main learning styles are supervised, unsupervised, semi-supervised, and reinforced. Algorithms are supervised when supplied with training data and the correct replies. The supervised ML algorithm learns from training data and then applies that learning to real-world data. Unsupervised learning, on the other hand, requires no training data. They are given real-world information and asked to learn from it. They seek to identify hidden patterns in data. The semi-supervised learning techniques are between the two. Semi-supervised learning systems must learn from a training set containing missing data. Finally, reinforcement learning algorithms learn from external input such as external thoughts or the environment. The variety of learning methods therefore enhances the machine learning system, making it more computationally efficient and successful when applied to unstructured raw data in the real world.

The ML approaches learn from training data and design mathematical models to draw the inference and predict outcome from testing data. Due to their efficiency and accuracy of prediction, they have been implemented in all types of tasks which need data processing. As a result, the relevance or importance of ML approaches employed across several domains in real-world systems arises from their wide range of applicability, computing efficiency, extensive learning potential, and increasing precision or accuracy. As previously stated, ML algorithms are also used in recommendation systems to provide users with better recommendations or ideas based on their prior purchases. In addition, ML approaches assist the RS in efficiently extracting user and item information from enormous volumes of unstructured data in order to analyse it further. As new machine-learning algorithms are constantly proposed in the literature, the efficiency of a RS in terms of time and assessment metrics continues to improve.

13.7   INTEGRATION OF ML APPROACHES

Thus, we have seen that ML approaches are useful in making better RSs, and many researchers opt for this in order to recommend a better user rating or preference for an item. Network clustering techniques are one such ML approach which may be used for generating a better user neighbourhood in a RS. In this chapter, we will consider some popular network clustering approaches and integrate them with the neighbourhood-based RSs for the purpose of generating better and more effective recommendations. These are introduced briefly in the following.

13.7.1   APPROACH 1: MODULARITY (MODU)

The modularity in a network can be defined as a property measuring the degree to which densely connected nodes can be decoupled into separate communities. The modularity (modu) in a network G can be mathematically defined as:

$$Modu = \frac{1}{2m} \sum_{uv} \left[A(u,v) - \frac{d_u d_v}{2m} \right] \delta \left(C_u, C_v \right)$$

Where A is the adjacency matrix of G, m is the number of edges in G, d_x is the degree of node x, $\delta(C_u, C_v)$ is 1 if u and v are in the same community C else 0.

The modularity function can be optimized to find the communities inside a network, for example, the Louvain method.[65]

13.7.2   APPROACH 2: INFOMAP (INFO)

Infomap is based on popular map equation.[19] It finds optimal partitions (hence, communities) inside a network by calculating an upper bound of the length of a random walk for each partitions.

13.7.3   APPROACH 3: LABEL PROPAGATION ALGORITHM (LPA)

Label propagation is a popular semi-supervised ML algorithm that is used to find communities inside a network.[66] Starting with a very few labelled nodes and by propagating the message (labels) to the neighbours of each node, it produces several communities inside a network where each community is labelled uniquely.

13.7.4   APPROACH 4: NODALITY-BASED CLUSTERING (NBC)

13.7.4.1   Computation of Nodality

In this chapter, another measurement of similarity called **nodality** is put forth to compute the similarity between two nodes, which is analogous to the co-citation index used in bibliometric research.[20, 67] The similarity metric compares all nodes in a network exhaustively in order to establish the link between two nodes. The nodality of two nodes is measured by their connections to all other nodes in the network. Thus, the nodality function is used to determine the degree of resemblance or link between two nodes in a network that are connected. Let $D(i,j)$ represents a score which defines between nodes i and j in the following way:

$$D(i,j) = \left| Nbd(i) \cup Nbd(j) \right| - \left| Nbd(i) \cap Nbd(j) \right|, \forall i,j,$$

where $Nbd(i)$ and $Nbd(j)$ correspond to the set of neighbours of nodes i and j. Thus, the nodality between nodes i and j can be defined as:

$$nodality(i,j) = \begin{cases} M - D(i,j) & \text{if } i \text{ and } j \text{ are connected} \\ -1 & \text{otherwise} \end{cases}$$

Here the value of M corresponds to the total number of nodes in the network. If two nodes, i and j are connected to each other and to every other node in the network, they have a maximum nodality of M. However, this is an ideal case and rarely occurs in real-world networks. Nodality attains the minimum value zero when $D(i,j) = M$. The nodality measure, in contrast to other measures of node similarity, considers the neighbours of nodes i and j while calculating the relationship between them.

The nodality is used to figure out how far two communities are from each other in the first step of the NBC method for detecting communities.

13.7.4.2   NBC Algorithm for Detecting Communities

To calculate the distance between two communities in a network, a distance function, say *comm dist*, is constructed. It calculates the distance between two communities, C_x and C_y, for example. Let S_{xy} denote a multi-set which consists of the nodality values between nodes x and y such that $x \in C_x$ and $y \in C_y$, with the following definition: $S_{xy} = \{nodality(x,y) : nodality(x,y) > 0, \forall x \in C_x \text{ and } y \in C_y\}$. Then the distance between two communities C_x and C_y present in a network is defined by the following function *comm_dist*.

$$comm\_dist(C_x, C_y) = \begin{cases} \infty & \text{if } S_{xy} = \phi \\ M - \max(S_{xy}) & \text{otherwise} \end{cases}$$

The maximum value of the multi-set S_{xy} determines the distance between two communities, C_x and C_y, and is returned when the function *comm dist()* is called. **Algorithm 13.1** depicts the phases of the NBC algorithm for community detection. Each node is first viewed as a community, and the process starts with M distinct communities. In the first stage, a $M \times M$ distance matrix CD is constructed, with the $(x, y)^{th}$ entry $CD[x][y]$ denoting the distance between communities C_x and C_y. It's a square matrix with M rows and M columns for M communities, with each row or column representing one of them. The method combines two communities with the smallest distance between them in each iteration, updating the nodality matrix. This technique is repeated until there are no more communities with a non-negative distance between them. In other words, the algorithm stops when the distance between any two communities becomes infinite. Notably, the nodality function is able to identify the underlying structure of a network in addition to determining the relationships between nodes. The nodality values between each pair of nodes inside a community should ideally be very high, and the distance between each pair of communities should be infinite at the end of the process.

13.7.5 INTEGRATED NEIGHBOURHOOD-BASED RSS

Network communities are a systematic approach to clustering vertices in a graph. As a consequence, such tightly linked clusters of users or items would yield superior neighbourhoods when compared to those generated in a straightforward manner for certain applications. One such straightforward way to generate a neighbourhood in a RS is by calculating the common neighbours (CN) of a user or item in RSs. The CN approach produces the neighbourhood in RS by selecting the n-nearest neighbours according to the following weights between two user u and v:[23]

$$W(u,v) = \frac{|N\,Item(u) \cap N\,Item(v)|}{|N\,Item(u)| + |N\,Item(v)|}, \tag{1}$$

where *NItem(u)* and *NItem(v)* corresponds the set of items chosen or favoured by user u and user v, respectively. It makes sense to think that two customers who choose many things and have many things in common must be different from two customers who choose many things and have few things in common. We have used this CN approach for our experimental purpose to generate n-nearest neighbours. Other such competitive approaches include modularity, LPA, and Infomap community detection methods for generating the n-nearest neighbours of a user or item in a RS. In

---

Input : A set of communities $C = \{C_1, C_2, ..., C_M\}$.
Output: A modified set of communities C.
/* Calculate all pair community distance matrix.   */
1 $CD \leftarrow \text{getCD}(C)$
/* Calculate the number of communities.   */
2 $no\_of\_comm \leftarrow |C|$
/* repeat until no_of_comm > 0   */
3 **while** $no\_of\_comm > 0$ **do**
   | /* find minimum distance communities and their indices */
4 | $minDist, i, j \leftarrow getMinDistAndIndex(CD)$
5 | **if** $minDist > 0$ **then**
6 | | $C_i \leftarrow C_i \cup C_j$
7 | | $CD \leftarrow Merge(CD, i, j)$
8 | | $no\_of\_comm \leftarrow no\_of\_comm - 1$
9 | **else**
10 | | $Break$

ALGORITHM 13.1 NBC Algorithm for Detecting Communities

this way, the identification of communities in a network of users or items may be significant for creating the n-nearest neighbours and, as a result, for providing better recommendations in a RS. One of the purposes of this study is to investigate the performance of the NBC community detection approach when it comes to constructing the n-nearest neighbours of specific users or items. In the following step, the nearest neighbours that have been chosen will be employed in the adsorption algorithm to generate recommendations in a variety of recommender datasets used in this chapter for e-commerce applications. Therefore the NBC integrated neighbourhood-based RS is performing as follows:

- Compute the weight $W(u,v)$ corresponding to every pair of users u and v according to the weight equation (Eq. 13.1) in a dataset and normalized the value between 0 and 1.
- Construct the user-user or item-item graph according to the varying threshold $t \in [0,1]$.
- Apply the approaches mentioned earlier (Approach 1–4) for community discovery algorithms over the user-user or item-item graph to produce distinct communities.
- Generate the n-nearest neighbour of a user in a community by selecting top-n neighbours based on the sorted weight values belongs to the same community.
- Perform adsorption algorithm to generate recommendation.

The algorithmic structure of the steps of the NBC integrated neighbourhood-based RS is shown in **Algorithm 13.2**. Subsequently, we have compared the effectiveness of the n-nearest neighbours generated through competitive approaches to the effectiveness of the n-nearest neighbours discovered using the NBC algorithm in a

---

Input : A network $G(V, E)$, A threshold t, A value K.
Output: Item recommendation vector for each user.
```
/* Calculate all pair weight matrix for users.          */
```
1 $W \leftarrow$ getAllPairWeight(G)
```
/* Construct user-user graph using W and t.             */
```
2 $UsrGraph \leftarrow getUsrUsrGraph(G, W, t)$
```
/* apply community detection algorithms on user-user graph
   */
```
3 $Comm \leftarrow getCommProp(UsrGraph)$
```
/* Build top-K neighbors matrix based on the communities */
```
4 $UserNbdMatrix \leftarrow buildTopK(Comm, UsrGraph, K)$
```
/* Using top-K neighborhoods for each users, compute
   preference vectors (item recommendations) for each user
   by applying adsorption algorithm.                     */
```
5 $UserRecomMatrix \leftarrow ApplyAdsorption(UsrGraph, UserNbdMatrix)$

ALGORITHM 13.2   Algorithm for Integrated Neighbourhood-Based RSs

RS using MAP and MAE values. Experimental results over DBLP, Book Crossing, Amazon Photo, and MovieLens datasets show the potential of the NBC-integrated neighbourhood-based RS compared to the competitive model as discussed elaborately in Section 13.10.

13.8   EVALUATION MEASURES

Several measures have been proposed by the researchers to evaluate the performance of a RS based on the actual (Y) and predicted $(\hat{Y})$ preference vector corresponding to a user u.[68, 40] These set of RS evaluation metrics may be broken down into two groups:[68] predictive accuracy and rank accuracy metrics. To this end, we have computed MAP and MAE values as a performance measure of a RS for all the competitive approaches discussed in this chapter.

13.8.1   PREDICTIVE ACCURACY

The mean absolute error (MAE), normalized mean absolute error (NMAE), and root mean square error (RMSE) are used to evaluate a RS method's effectiveness in prediction accuracy.[68] The following equations may be used to determine the MAE, NMAE, and RMSE, respectively, if there are N items and Y_i represents the actual rating and $\hat{Y}_i$ represents the predicted rating of item i. A 1.6 value is taken as the normalising constant by assuming a uniformly distributed actual and predicted rating. The better the performance, the lower the MAE, NMAE, or RMSE.

$$MAE = \frac{\sum_{i=1}^{N}\left|Y_i - \hat{Y}_i\right|}{N}$$

$$NMAE = \frac{\sum_{i=1}^{N}\left|Y_i - \hat{Y}_i\right|}{1.6N}$$

$$RMSE = \frac{\sum_{i=1}^{N}\left(Y_i - \hat{Y}_i\right)^2}{N}$$

13.8.2   RANK ACCURACY

The rank accuracy measure is used to determine the degree of correlation between a recommender's rating and the actual rank of an item. Here we have used MAP at L for a ranked list of length L to measure the rank accuracy of a RS.[68] The adsorption method produces a list of *(item, preference score)* tuples that represents the user's recommendation in the data set.[22] Note that the preference score relates to the quality of a user's (u) choice for an item (i) and is defined as:

$$preference\_score(u,i) = \sum_{v \in users(i)} W(u,v)$$

Subsequently, we generate an ordered list of L tuples, which is sorted in descending order based on the value of *preference score*. From this ordered list, we determine the average precision at the top L rankings for each user, and then we aggregate these results to compute the MAP@L for the entire group.[23]

13.9   DATASETS

A set of real-world datasets are used in our experiment. The dataset descriptions are given in Table 13.1. The Book Crossing dataset is a bipartite graph consisting of users and books as nodes. There is a link between a user node and a book node if the user read that book. In the Amazon Photo dataset, the nodes represent goods and a link between two nodes represents these two goods are purchased together. In DBLP graph, the nodes represent users and a link between two nodes represents two users collaborated together. Like the Book Crossing network, the MovieLens network is a bipartite network where the nodes in one set represents users and other set represents movies. There is a link between a user node and a movie node if the user rated the movie.

13.10   EXPERIMENTAL SETUP AND ANALYSIS

13.10.1   PRE-PROCESSING

For the Book Crossing and MovieLens datasets, we filtered out the subgraph by removing the user nodes having a degree less than 4, which implies that we trimmed out the users who do not read more than four books (in the case of the Book Crossing dataset) or who did not rated more than four movies (in the case of the MovieLens

TABLE 13.1
Dataset descriptions

Network	# Vertices	# Edges
Book Crossing [25]	440k	1.1M
Amazon Photo [26]	7K	119K
DBLP [24]	1.3M	18.9M
MovieLens [27]	138K	19M

TABLE 13.2
Dataset Split Description

Subset	Trainingdata	TestData
s1	T1 U T2	T3
s2	T2 U T3	T4
s3	T3 U T4	T5
s4	T4 U T5	T6

dataset). For the DBLP network, we use a subgraph of this large graph by capturing only the links having timestamp in between 1992 and 2012.

13.10.2 Dataset Splits

We split each dataset into six sets as shown in Table 13.2. Using these splits, we obtained four subsets (s1, s2, s3, and s4). Each of the subsets are split into training and testing sets. For Book Crossing datasets, we use approximately 20% of preferences in each of the split. For the DBLP dataset, the data from each split are based on 3 years. Each split in the MovieLens datasets is done uniformly based on the user rating. Finally, the splitting criterion for Amazon Photo is done uniformly based on the product category.

13.10.3 Competitive Methods and Hyperparameters

We have designed and analysed the robust neighbourhood-based RSs by integrating five competitive network clustering approaches, viz., common neighbors (CN), modularity (modu), Infomap (Info), label propagation algorithm (LPA), and nodality-based clustering (NBC), with the adsorption algorithm. We varied the number of neighbourhoods n as 5, 10, and 15. For each case, we applied four subsets. We have tested the evaluation measures on various user-user graphs generated by varying the threshold value t between 0.0 to 0.80 corresponding to the NBC algorithm. In the adsorption algorithm, we fixed P_{inj}, P_{term}, and P_{cont} to 0.10, 0.65, and 0.25 respectively. The value of K is fixed to 10 for the top-K recommendations.

13.10.4 Analysis of Result

Table 13.3 represents the performance of the competitive approaches corresponding to the Book Crossing dataset in terms of the evaluation metrics MAE and MAP scores by varying neighbourhood size n. In a similar way, Table 13.4, Table 13.5, and Table 13.6 respectively denote the performance of the competitive approaches in terms of the MAE and MAP score values corresponding to the Amazon Photo, DBLP coauthor, and MovieLens datasets. In the NBC method, we varied the threshold t to vary the structure of the generated user-user graph and obtain the results for all the generated graphs. As can be seen from these tables, the value of MAP and MAE scores are first increased and then decreased when we increased the values of t starting from 0.0 to 0.80. The reason for this is when the threshold t increases, the generated user-user graph become sparser, and it is very difficult to find meaningful communities in the highly sparse graph leading it to the low value of the MAP and MAE scores.

The **bold font** of the average values of the evaluation metrics of each table indicates that the corresponding competitive approach outperforms the other for a given threshold value t. The performance of the integrated neighbourhood-based RS corresponding to the NBC algorithm varies less across all neighbourhood sizes investigated, and it converges on the best solution, which corresponds to a threshold value t that lies between 0.2 and 0.4. From Table 13.5, it is clear that as n increases, the average MAE value of the CN method decreases as opposed to the Infomap method. The average MAP score of the adsorption algorithm employing the NBC approach, on the other hand, increases as the number of neighbours grows. For instance, when n is increased from 5 to 15, the MAP score for all the subgroups increases for $t = 0.2$, as shown in Table 13.5. The same pattern for the NBC method corresponding to the other datasets is also observed for varying threshold value t, as depicted in other tables (Table 13.3–Table 13.6). The Infomap community detection algorithm performs better in almost all the datasets compared to the competitive approaches in terms of all the evaluation metrics, as clearly seen from Table 13.3–Table 13.6. Again, as the value of n increases, the performance of the Infomap and LPA algorithms also increases, corresponding to all the datasets in terms of MAP and MAE values. The NBC-integrated RS performs similarly to the Infomap and better than the other competitive for certain threshold values of t (=20 or 30) corresponding to the DBLP and MovieLens datasets. As a result, we can infer that the NBC approach for community discovery may be suitable for neighbourhood construction in the coauthor domain and may result in a more accurate suggestion of a user's collaborators in a DBLP coauthor dataset. The performance of modularity and CN is always inferior to the performance of the NBC approach in most of the datasets except one. For varying n corresponding to the Book Crossing dataset, the CN performs competitively, and sometimes better than the others in terms of MAP and MAE values. On the other hand, as the neighbourhood size increases, the performance of the NBC-integrated RS also sometimes becomes effective compared to the others corresponding to the Book Crossing and MovieLens datasets. The empirical results suggest that the performance of the LPA and Infomap methods are quite similar to each other in almost all datasets for varying t and n. The experimental results as depicted in Table 13.3–Table 13.6 also suggest that when the Infomap method is used

TABLE 13.3
MAP and MAE Scores for the Book Crossing Dataset

NBD	Subset	CN	Modu	Info	LPA	CA					
						NBC					
						t=0	t=0.2	t=0.3	t=0.4	t=0.6	t=0.8
MAP											
5	s1	0.0072	0.0072	0.0074	0.0073	0.0073	0.0071	0.0070	0.0071	0.0067	0.0065
	s2	0.0071	0.0073	0.0073	0.0073	0.0073	0.0072	0.0071	0.0073	0.0067	0.0064
	s3	0.0074	0.0072	0.0074	0.0071	0.0072	0.0072	0.0073	0.0073	0.0069	0.0063
	s4	0.0075	0.0073	0.0072	0.0072	0.0073	0.0071	0.0073	0.0071	0.0069	0.0065
	Avg	**0.0073**	0.0072	**0.0073**	0.0072	0.0072	0.0071	0.0071	0.0072	0.0068	0.0064
10	s1	0.0075	0.0072	0.0073	0.0074	0.0073	0.0073	0.0074	0.0074	0.0071	0.0062
	s2	0.0074	0.0072	0.0075	0.0072	0.0073	0.0073	0.0071	0.0072	0.0069	0.0066
	s3	0.0075	0.0074	0.0074	0.0073	0.0073	0.0073	0.0071	0.0071	0.0068	0.0065
	s4	0.0073	0.0074	0.0074	0.0073	0.0072	0.0071	0.0073	0.0072	0.0069	0.0063
	Avg	**0.0074**	0.0073	**0.0074**	0.0073	0.0072	0.0072	0.0072	0.0072	0.0069	0.0064

(Continued)

TABLE 13.3
(Continued)

CA

NBD	Subset	CN	Modu	Info	LPA	NBC					
						t=0	t=0.2	t=0.3	t=0.4	t=0.6	t=0.8
15	s1	0.0071	0.0072	0.0074	0.0074	0.0071	0.0074	0.0073	0.0072	0.0071	0.0062
	s2	0.0074	0.0073	0.0074	0.0073	0.0069	0.0073	0.0072	0.0071	0.0069	0.0067
	s3	0.0075	0.0072	0.0075	0.0075	0.0070	0.0072	0.0073	0.0074	0.0072	0.0065
	s4	0.0076	0.0075	0.0073	0.0074	0.0067	0.0073	0.0074	0.0071	0.0071	0.0062
	Avg	**0.0074**	0.0073	**0.0074**	**0.0074**	0.0069	0.0073	0.0073	0.0072	0.0070	0.0064
MAE											
5	s1	0.643	0.596	0.641	0.644	0.514	0.643	0.631	0.611	0.593	0.544
	s2	0.653	0.614	0.642	0.652	0.488	0.644	0.634	0.611	0.593	0.546
	s3	0.637	0.612	0.646	0.636	0.494	0.623	0.623	0.626	0.586	0.513
	s4	0.646	0.588	0.646	0.646	0.494	0.634	0.632	0.633	0.614	0.525
	Avg	**0.644**	0.602	0.643	**0.644**	0.497	0.636	0.630	0.620	0.596	0.532
10	s1	0.665	0.591	0.666	0.666	0.494	0.642	0.662	0.631	0.626	0.536
	s2	0.673	0.596	0.676	0.676	0.494	0.636	0.663	0.635	0.625	0.547
	s3	0.678	0.61	0.671	0.674	0.513	0.637	0.666	0.646	0.615	0.545
	s4	0.675	0.612	0.671	0.676	0.518	0.641	0.668	0.614	0.597	0.534
	Avg	0.672	0.602	0.671	**0.673**	0.504	0.639	0.664	0.631	0.615	0.540
15	s1	0.663	0.596	0.676	0.673	0.537	0.641	0.671	0.636	0.634	0.543
	s2	0.665	0.614	0.672	0.668	0.515	0.653	0.657	0.655	0.614	0.523
	s3	0.676	0.611	0.676	0.676	0.524	0.653	0.666	0.667	0.618	0.547
	s4	0.678	0.588	0.669	0.675	0.513	0.647	0.665	0.663	0.625	0.545
	Avg	0.670	0.602	**0.673**	**0.673**	0.522	0.648	0.664	0.655	0.622	0.539

The NBC approach used a threshold (t) on edge weight ranging from 0.0 to 0.8. The size of the neighbourhood (n) is changed between 5 and 15, and the number of recommendations, i.e., the value of k is set at 10.

Neighbourhood size (NBD); clustering approaches (CA); common neighbours (CN); modularity (modu); nodality-based clustering (NBC); Infomap (Info); label propagation algorithm (LPA).

to detect communities, it outperforms the other competitive, making it a good choice for neighbourhood-based RSs in the vast majority of cases. Note that the performance of the NBC integrated neighbourhood-based RS is also sometimes effective and superior compared to the modularity and CN-integrated neighbourhood-based RS in some of the datasets, as clearly seen from Table 13.3–Table 13.6. On the other hand, the performance of the LPA and Infomap-integrated neighbourhood-based RS is always better in almost all the datasets compared to other competitive. Thus, choosing the Infomap and LPA methods may sometimes be the best way to get better user neighbourhoods for a dataset. These neighbourhoods are then used by the adsorption algorithm to make better recommendations for the users. As a conclusion, we can infer that the probabilistic approaches to network community detection might be more effective for better neighbourhood generation, which could lead to more efficient and robust neighbourhood-based RSs.

TABLE 13.4
MAP and MAE Scores for the Amazon Photo Dataset

NBD	Subset	CN	Modu	Info	LPA	CA			NBC				
						t=0	t=0.2	t=0.3	t=0.4	t=0.6	t=0.8		
MAP													
5	s1	0.0121	0.0134	0.0227	0.0193	0.0112	0.0183	0.0196	0.0179	0.0173	0.0153		
	s2	0.0121	0.0133	0.0213	0.0216	0.0164	0.0173	0.0212	0.0182	0.0185	0.0165		
	s3	0.0113	0.0113	0.0215	0.0237	0.0173	0.0183	0.0211	0.0193	0.0186	0.0124		
	s4	0.0154	0.0182	0.0225	0.0216	0.0183	0.0195	0.0211	0.0182	0.0196	0.0133		
	Avg	0.0130	0.0140	**0.0220**	0.0215	0.0158	0.0183	0.0207	0.0184	0.0185	0.0143		
10	s1	0.0141	0.0145	0.0257	0.0231	0.0153	0.0256	0.0210	0.0193	0.0157	0.0162		
	s2	0.0128	0.0137	0.0225	0.0212	0.0156	0.0215	0.0201	0.0191	0.0191	0.0200		
	s3	0.0145	0.0154	0.0241	0.0219	0.0167	0.0223	0.0212	0.0202	0.0202	0.0182		
	s4	0.0144	0.0152	0.0235	0.0221	0.0188	0.0223	0.0213	0.0214	0.0211	0.0222		
	Avg	0.0139	0.0147	**0.0239**	0.0220	0.0166	0.0229	0.0209	0.0200	0.0190	0.0191		
15	s1	0.0131	0.0141	0.0238	0.0232	0.0194	0.0232	0.0221	0.0209	0.0190	0.0182		
	s2	0.0152	0.0176	0.0244	0.0231	0.0214	0.0222	0.0212	0.0201	0.0192	0.0198		
	s3	0.0113	0.0178	0.0241	0.0231	0.0195	0.0231	0.0215	0.0201	0.0191	0.0211		
	s4	0.0173	0.0178	0.0246	0.0228	0.0195	0.0236	0.0212	0.0204	0.0199	0.0182		
	Avg	0.0142	0.0168	**0.0242**	0.0230	0.0199	0.0230	0.0215	0.0203	0.0193	0.0193		
MAE													
5	s1	0.481	0.523	0.547	0.545	0.465	0.513	0.546	0.547	0.567	0.544		
	s2	0.475	0.539	0.567	0.546	0.456	0.513	0.554	0.564	0.524	0.515		
	s3	0.495	0.545	0.573	0.563	0.457	0.544	0.547	0.536	0.544	0.527		
	s4	0.466	0.524	0.573	0.575	0.468	0.536	0.544	0.534	0.546	0.535		

(Continued)

TABLE 13.4
(Continued)

NBD	Subset	CA				NBC					
		CN	Modu	Info	LPA	t=0	t=0.2	t=0.3	t=0.4	t=0.6	t=0.8
	Avg	0.479	0.532	**0.565**	0.557	0.461	0.526	0.547	0.545	0.545	0.530
10	s1	0.463	0.535	0.583	0.575	0.461	0.566	0.545	0.566	0.525	0.535
	s2	0.494	0.536	0.583	0.575	0.462	0.545	0.547	0.545	0.576	0.516
	s3	0.496	0.577	0.576	0.566	0.486	0.574	0.545	0.574	0.547	0.527
	s4	0.496	0.567	0.578	0.567	0.477	0.547	0.567	0.587	0.564	0.554
	Avg	0.487	0.553	**0.580**	0.570	0.471	0.558	0.551	0.568	0.553	0.533
15	s1	0.482	0.564	0.584	0.579	0.496	0.522	0.561	0.567	0.566	0.549
	s2	0.515	0.547	0.581	0.563	0.502	0.543	0.559	0.564	0.553	0.556
	s3	0.502	0.555	0.582	0.584	0.514	0.562	0.558	0.573	0.561	0.554
	s4	0.491	0.576	0.582	0.568	0.514	0.578	0.559	0.572	0.566	0.546
	Avg	0.497	0.560	**0.582**	0.573	0.506	0.551	0.559	0.569	0.561	0.551

The NBC approach used a threshold (t) on edge weight ranging from 0.0 to 0.8. The size of the neighbourhood (n) is changed between 5 and 15, and the number of recommendations, i.e., the value of k is set at 10.

Neighbourhood size (NBD); clustering approaches (CA); common neighbours (CN); modularity (modu); nodality-based clustering (NBC); Infomap (Info); label propagation (LPA).

TABLE 13.5
MAP and MAE Scores for the DBLP Dataset

NBD	Subset	CN	Modu	Info	LPA	CA					
						NBC					
						t=0	t=0.2	t=0.3	t=0.4	t=0.6	t=0.8
MAP											
5	S1	0.0173	0.0172	0.0181	0.0181	0.0177	0.0179	0.0181	0.0176	0.0169	0.0161
	s2	0.0153	0.0168	0.0184	0.0183	0.0177	0.0174	0.0180	0.0178	0.0162	0.0163
	s3	0.0167	0.0169	0.0183	0.0182	0.0176	0.0179	0.0179	0.0179	0.0169	0.0165
	s4	0.0177	0.0178	0.0183	0.0181	0.0173	0.0181	0.0178	0.0177	0.017	0.0166
	Avg	0.0167	0.0171	**0.0182**	0.0181	0.0175	0.0178	0.0179	0.0177	0.0167	0.0163
10	s1	0.0161	0.0176	0.0182	0.0179	0.0178	0.0182	0.0181	0.0178	0.0168	0.0167
	s2	0.016	0.0163	0.0183	0.0181	0.0179	0.0181	0.0182	0.0181	0.0177	0.0166
	s3	0.0163	0.0171	0.0182	0.0181	0.0177	0.0181	0.0183	0.0177	0.0172	0.0169
	s4	0.0161	0.0177	0.0183	0.0178	0.0176	0.0181	0.0182	0.0176	0.0174	0.0164
	Avg	0.0161	0.0171	**0.0182**	0.0179	0.0177	0.0181	**0.0182**	0.0178	0.0172	0.0166
15	s1	0.0158	0.0171	0.0184	0.0180	0.0179	0.0182	0.0182	0.0176	0.0173	0.0163
	s2	0.0158	0.0172	0.0184	0.0179	0.0178	0.0182	0.0181	0.0179	0.0172	0.0164
	s3	0.0156	0.0169	0.0182	0.0181	0.0177	0.0184	0.0181	0.0178	0.0173	0.0171
	s4	0.0157	0.0171	0.0184	0.0179	0.0179	0.0184	0.0184	0.0179	0.0171	0.0169
	Avg	0.0157	0.0170	**0.0183**	0.0179	0.0178	**0.0183**	0.0182	0.0178	0.0172	0.0166
MAE											
5	s1	0.529	0.523	0.567	0.569	0.502	0.562	0.582	0.528	0.519	0.496
	s2	0.522	0.531	0.585	0.565	0.523	0.563	0.553	0.563	0.527	0.485
	s3	0.513	0.542	0.596	0.575	0.514	0.565	0.545	0.526	0.555	0.516
	s4	0.512	0.534	0.567	0.556	0.525	0.564	0.554	0.528	0.524	0.483
	Avg	0.519	0.532	**0.578**	0.566	0.516	0.563	0.558	0.536	0.531	0.495
10	s1	0.514	0.545	0.573	0.594	0.514	0.593	0.556	0.549	0.515	0.515
	s2	0.514	0.526	0.619	0.589	0.534	0.596	0.547	0.549	0.514	0.506
	s3	0.514	0.527	0.586	0.583	0.494	0.594	0.547	0.534	0.528	0.513
	s4	0.517	0.526	0.595	0.596	0.526	0.592	0.575	0.554	0.533	0.484
	Avg	0.514	0.531	**0.593**	0.590	0.517	**0.593**	0.556	0.546	0.522	0.504
15	s1	0.515	0.527	0.592	0.579	0.523	0.587	0.559	0.544	0.524	0.504
	s2	0.504	0.537	0.602	0.588	0.526	0.596	0.559	0.546	0.515	0.514
	s3	0.514	0.531	0.596	0.586	0.517	0.593	0.561	0.545	0.526	0.513
	s4	0.516	0.524	0.589	0.614	0.513	0.599	0.561	0.555	0.537	0.516
	Avg	0.512	0.529	**0.594**	0.591	0.519	0.593	0.560	0.547	0.525	0.511

The NBC approach used a threshold (t) on edge weight ranging from 0.0 to 0.8. The size of the neighbourhood (n) is changed between 5 and 15, and the number of recommendations, i.e., the value of k is set at 10.

Neighbourhood size (NBD); clustering approaches (CA); common neighbours (CN); modularity (modu); nodality-based clustering (NBC); Infomap (Info); label propagation algorithm (LPA).

TABLE 13.6
MAP and MAE Scores for the MovieLens Dataset

						CA					
NBD	Subset	CN	Modu	Info	LPA				NBC		
						t=0	t=0.2	t=0.3	t=0.4	t=0.6	t=0.8
MAP											
5	s1	0.0154	0.0152	0.0151	0.0153	0.0145	0.0154	0.0157	0.0151	0.015	0.0147
	s2	0.0152	0.015	0.0159	0.0157	0.0146	0.0155	0.0153	0.0153	0.0151	0.0138
	s3	0.0152	0.0149	0.0159	0.0155	0.0144	0.015	0.0153	0.0152	0.0151	0.0132
	s4	0.0155	0.0151	0.0152	0.0156	0.0145	0.0151	0.0155	0.0151	0.0148	0.0139
	Avg	0.0153	0.0150	**0.0155**	**0.0155**	0.0145	0.0152	0.0154	0.0151	0.0150	0.0139
10	s1	0.0152	0.0153	0.0152	0.0157	0.0142	0.0153	0.0152	0.0151	0.0149	0.0141
	s2	0.0151	0.0154	0.0156	0.0155	0.0147	0.0154	0.0151	0.0151	0.0151	0.0142
	s3	0.0151	0.0152	0.0162	0.0155	0.0146	0.0151	0.0152	0.0151	0.0149	0.0139
	s4	0.0155	0.0153	0.0159	0.0157	0.0146	0.0152	0.015	0.0152	0.0151	0.0142
	Avg	0.0152	0.0153	**0.0157**	0.0156	0.0145	0.0152	0.0151	0.0151	0.015	0.0141
15	s1	0.0151	0.0153	0.0159	0.0158	0.0142	0.0155	0.0153	0.0151	0.0151	0.0142
	s2	0.0154	0.0153	0.0157	0.0157	0.0146	0.0155	0.0153	0.0151	0.015	0.0146
	s3	0.0151	0.0154	0.0158	0.0158	0.0143	0.0157	0.0155	0.0154	0.0152	0.0135
	s4	0.015	0.0156	0.0156	0.0157	0.0145	0.0152	0.0152	0.0149	0.0149	0.0143
	Avg	0.0151	0.0154	**0.0157**	**0.0157**	0.0144	0.0154	0.0153	0.0151	0.0150	0.0141
MAE											
5	s1	0.491	0.492	0.512	0.524	0.478	0.492	0.521	0.492	0.493	0.483
	s2	0.488	0.498	0.531	0.527	0.472	0.498	0.519	0.475	0.495	0.475
	s3	0.486	0.488	0.532	0.525	0.475	0.482	0.521	0.497	0.452	0.486
	s4	0.482	0.482	0.531	0.526	0.486	0.493	0.526	0.492	0.502	0.485
	Avg	0.486	0.490	**0.526**	0.525	0.477	0.491	0.521	0.489	0.485	0.482
10	s1	0.491	0.502	0.532	0.532	0.495	0.502	0.521	0.492	0.496	0.487
	s2	0.48	0.512	0.545	0.532	0.474	0.496	0.525	0.501	0.502	0.495
	s3	0.485	0.514	0.546	0.533	0.496	0.499	0.524	0.496	0.512	0.497
	s4	0.482	0.512	0.513	0.532	0.498	0.498	0.526	0.501	0.498	0.494
	Avg	0.484	0.510	**0.534**	0.532	0.490	0.498	0.524	0.497	0.502	0.493
15	s1	0.482	0.521	0.537	0.538	0.495	0.501	0.527	0.499	0.503	0.495
	s2	0.488	0.501	0.538	0.534	0.493	0.499	0.525	0.483	0.508	0.495
	s3	0.482	0.492	0.535	0.539	0.496	0.499	0.523	0.496	0.501	0.506
	s4	0.483	0.522	0.536	0.536	0.489	0.505	0.521	0.498	0.496	0.493
	Avg	0.483	0.509	**0.536**	**0.536**	0.493	0.501	0.524	0.494	0.502	0.497

The NBC approach used a threshold (*t*) on edge weight ranging from 0.0 to 0.8. The size of the neighbourhood (*n*) is changed between 5 and 15, and the number of recommendations, i.e., the value of *k* is set at 10.

Neighbourhood size (NBD); clustering approaches (CA); common neighbours (CN); modularity (modu); nodality-based clustering (NBC); Infomap (Info); label propagation algorithm (LPA).

13.11 CHALLENGES

No matter how widely applicable and usable a RS is in the real world on a daily basis, many RSs encounter a variety of difficulties or challenges when they are put into action in actual practice. Some of these important challenges are briefly explained in the following sections.

13.11.1 DATA SPARSITY

E-commerce RSs are facing challenges due to the presence of sparsity in the data. This is the issue that arises when there is insufficient information in the input data. [3] Only a small percentage of the total number of entries in a user-item matrix are evaluated by users.[69] Thus, the user-item matrix gets sparse for a sufficiently large item collection. This invariably results in the inability to find effective neighbours and, ultimately, the development of poor recommendations by RS. Techniques like dimensionality reduction,[70] probabilistic matrix factorization,[71] and more have been used to deal with this problem of sparse data, and they work.

13.11.2 SCALABILITY

Scalability has been a persistent issue and also an important challenge for RSs due to the nature of computing in the practical aspect. When the number of datasets is restricted, a recommendation approach that is efficient may fail to produce better recommendations as it grows.[1] The exponential growth of the database resulted in the algorithm performing poorly, as computer capabilities exceeded their realistic bounds. As a result, the performance of the majority of classic CF algorithms deteriorates when the number of users and items grows. Therefore, it would be essential to use the proper approach of RS so that it can scale up successfully as the database grows.

13.11.3 COLD START

The cold start problem may be referred to as an information deficit problem where a recommender does not have sufficient knowledge about a user or an object in order to generate meaningful recommendations. This is another important and significant concern impacting the performance of the RS. The information about a new user or item will be empty since the user has not rated any items, and as a result, the system will not be aware of his or her preferences.[72] It takes a significant amount of effort to entice a consumer and get them to know about your product. Many networks, on the other hand, encourage users to fill out information in order to provide them with additional possibilities to resolve cold starts.

13.11.4 SYNONYMS

Synonymy is another challenge in RSs that refers to the phenomenon of highly identical entities having dissimilar names or entries. The majority of RSs have difficulty distinguishing between closely similar items, such as the differences between baby wear and baby clothes. Many CF algorithms are typically unable to locate a match between two words in order to calculate their similarity.[73] Numerous techniques, including automated term expansion, the development of a thesaurus, and singular value decomposition (SVD), particularly latent semantic indexing, are capable of resolving the synonymy problem.

13.11.5 PRIVACY ISSUES

The RS frequently makes users' personal information available to the public. The "People You May Know" feature on Facebook is a wonderful example of this concept in action. When evaluating a customer, the question of trust comes up, and the system must make sure that it is well protected.[73]

13.11.6 BIASNESS

People are more likely to provide favourable comments or positive feedback on their own items than they are to provide negative feedback or bad reviews on the products of their competitors. It creates a biased situation or environment that generates poor recommendations.[74] This phenomenon should be taken care of by the RSs. On the other hand, the RS system must have some sort of safeguard in place to prevent this from happening.

13.12 APPLICATIONS

Personal, social, and corporate services are among the domains in which RSs are now being used in a range of applications. In the real world, all of these areas have applications in human life and have a substantial impact on it as well. The applicability of RSs includes recommending movies, music, television shows, books, websites, conferences, scenic areas, and instructional resources, among other things. As a consequence, the applications of the RS may be classified into the following major categories: e-business, e-governance, e-learning, e-commerce, and e-tourism, which will be discussed briefly in the following sections.

13.12.1 E-GOVERMENT RSs

The use of the internet and communication technologies to assist governments in providing better information and services to consumers and companies is known as electronic government (e-government). The fast rise of e-government has resulted in information overload and mismanagement of large amounts of growing data. Increases in information overload and data mismanagement might have a significant influence on the poor performance of e-government services. A proper RSs that has been used in e-government applications can solve this problem. A number of such RSs have been created to assist the government in its service to the public. An example of a recommendation system built by Lu et al. (2010) is BizSeeker,[75] which was created to assist the government in efficiently recommending the appropriate business partners to particular firms (such as overseas buyers and agents as well as distributors and retailers).

13.12.2   E-Business RSs

A lot of RSs have been made for e-business applications. Business-to-consumer (B2C) systems are systems that are designed to create recommendations for individual consumers. Business-to-business (B2B) systems are systems that are designed to deliver product and service suggestions to business users. Lee et al. (2006) proposed an ontology-based product RS that generates recommendations based on keyword, ontology, and Bayesian belief network methodologies.[76] Another RS was developed in Wang and Chiu (2008) to assist business customers in selecting reliable online auction vendors, and trade connections were utilised to generate recommendations.[77]

13.12.3   E-Commerce RSs

The term e-commerce RSs refers to RSs that work with B2C applications. Several novel e-commerce RSs have been created in recent years to provide guidance to online individual customers for their own benefit.[78, 79] e-shopping is a very specific type of ecommerce that is very popular. Numerous big e-commerce websites, like Amazon and eBay, currently employ RSs to assist their clients in locating their favourite things or products to purchase.[80, 81] e-commerce websites that sell goods to customers can show them products based on the best-selling items, customer demographics like age and gender, or an analysis of the customer's past buying habits as a predictor of what they'll do next. From an application standpoint, academics have created a variety of successful e-commerce platforms to test their unique algorithms. These systems give developers advice on how to use RSs for e-shopping in a practical way.

13.12.4   E-Learning RSs

e-learning RSs have grown in popularity among academic institutions in the last two decades. This sort of RS is typically used to aid students in selecting courses, subjects, learning resources, and other options to pursue. It also helps with the learning resources that they are interested in, as well as various learning activities such as in-class lectures or online group discussions, etc. Zaiane (2002) presented a method for developing a software agent that employs data mining techniques like association rule mining to build a model that describes online user behaviour and then uses that model to recommend activities.[82] Lu (2004) developed a system that recommends personalised e-learning materials (PLRS) in a similar fashion.[83] In digital library applications, recommendation algorithms can be used to assist users in finding and selecting appropriate materials and information sources.[84] CourseAgent is another e-learning RS developed by Farzan and Brusilovsky (2006) where students can submit feedback in both implicit and explicit ways.[85]

13.12.5 E-Tourism RSs

Tourists can use e-tourism RSs to get recommendations about the features of their destination. Some RSs concentrate on certain sites and locations, while others provide trip packages that include transportation, dining, and lodging. There are a number of restaurant RSs available in the literature. For example, Burke et al. (1996) created Entree, a RS based on knowledge-based techniques, to recommend eateries.[86] CATIS is another e-tourism RS that is a context-aware RS for tourist lodging, restaurants, and attractions.[87] Context information, such as location and device features used in CATIS, is dynamically collected by a context manager. REJA (Restaurants of JAen) is an e-tourism restaurant RS that combines the CF and KB techniques.[88] García-Crespo et al. (2009) developed a social pervasive e tourism advisor (SPETA) recommendation system that provides the kind of service that tourists expect from a human tour guide based on a user's present location, preferences, and the history of previous destinations.[89]

13.13 CONCLUSIONS

Our everyday life is enriched by the use of recommendation systems. The recommendation system contributes to the reduction of the problem of information overload and the facilitation of our daily lives. These RSs enable their users to access services and products that are unfamiliar to them or not readily available in their local area. At the moment, a variety of hybridization methodologies are available and being used to produce RSs that are customised to the specific demands of each individual user in the system. This chapter described a unique strategy in which ML techniques are incorporated into the neighbourhood-based RS to provide better and more efficient item recommendations to users. In this case, we incorporated and included various community identification methods to generate the nearest neighbours, which were then employed by the adsorption algorithm, a popular neighbourhood-based RS, to provide better recommendations. We have shown that different community detection techniques are acceptable for producing effective nearest neighbours corresponding to different datasets utilised here. Overall, the Infomap and LPA community detection methods performed better throughout the experiments corresponding to all the datasets. Thus, at the end of this chapter, we come to the conclusion that probabilistic approaches to network community detection may be more useful for generating better user neighbourhoods, which could help make better neighbourhood-based RSs. Our findings also suggest that community detection may be successful for sparse networks, and that the parameters governing a graph's sparsity might be significant in controlling the RS accuracy. People who study recommendations can use the methodology described in this chapter to learn more about and improve the way the RS works now. The performance of the RS continuously improves as new strategies are developed, incorporated, and implemented into the system. This understanding of diverse recommendation system methodologies will empower researchers and aid them in designing new, more effective solutions.

REFERENCES

[1] Greg Linden, Brent Smith, and Jeremy York. Amazon.com recommendations: Item-to-item collaborative filtering. *IEEE Internet Computing*, 7(1):76–80, 2003.

[2] Prem Melville, Raymond J Mooney, Ramadass Nagarajan, et al. Content boosted collaborative filtering for improved recommendations. *Aaai/iaai*, 23:187–192, 2002.

[3] Robin Burke. Hybrid recommender systems: Survey and experiments. *User Modeling and User-Adapted Interaction*, 12(4):331–370, 2002.

[4] Michael JA Berry and Gordon S Linoff. *Data mining techniques: For marketing, sales, and customer relationship management*. John Wiley & Sons, 2004.

[5] Yehuda Koren, Robert Bell, and Chris Volinsky. Matrix factorization techniques for recommender systems. *Computer*, 42(8):30–37, 2009.

[6] Vivek Sembium, Rajeev Rastogi, Lavanya Tekumalla, and Atul Saroop. Bayesian models for product size recommendations. In *Proceedings of the 2018 world wide web conference*, pages 679–687, 2018.

[7] Shuai Zhang, Lina Yao, Aixin Sun, and Yi Tay. Deep learning based recommender system: A survey and new perspectives. *ACM Computing Surveys (CSUR)*, 52(1):1–38, 2019.

[8] John S Breese, David Heckerman, and Carl Kadie. Empirical analysis of predictive algorithms for collaborative filtering. *arXiv preprint arXiv:1301.7363*, 2013.

[9] Guy Shani, David Heckerman, Ronen I Brafman, and Craig Boutilier. An mdp-based recommender system. *Journal of Machine Learning Research*, 6(9), 2005.

[10] Ruslan Salakhutdinov, Andriy Mnih, and Geoffrey Hinton. Restricted boltzmann machines for collaborative filtering. In *Proceedings of the 24th international conference on Machine learning*, pages 791–798, 2007.

[11] Urszula Kuzelewska. Advantages of information granulation in clustering algorithms. In *International conference on agents and artificial intelligence*, pages 131–145. Springer, 2011.

[12] Nir Friedman, Dan Geiger, and Moises Goldszmidt. Bayesian network classifiers. *Machine Learning*, 29(2):131–163, 1997.

[13] Johan AK Suykens and Joos Vandewalle. Least squares support vector machine classifiers. *Neural Processing Letters*, 9(3):293–300, 1999.

[14] Grégoire Montavon, Wojciech Samek, and Klaus-Robert Müller. Methods for interpreting and understanding deep neural networks. *Digital Signal Processing*, 73:1–15, 2018.

[15] Xavier Amatriain, Nuria Oliver, Josep M Pujol, et al. Data mining methods for recommender systems. In *Recommender systems handbook*, pages 39–71. Springer, 2011.

[16] Mark EJ Newman. Modularity and community structure in networks. *Proceedings of the National Academy of Sciences*, 103(23):8577–8582, 2006.

[17] Vincent D Blondel, Jean-Loup Guillaume, Renaud Lambiotte, and Etienne Lefebvre. Fast unfolding of communities in large networks. *Journal of Statistical Mechanics: Theory and Experiment*, 2008(10):P10008, 2008.

[18] Usha Nandini Raghavan, Réka Albert, and Soundar Kumara. Near linear time algorithm to detect community structures in large-scale networks. *Physical Review E*, 76(3):036106, 2007.

[19] Martin Rosvall and Carl T Bergstrom. Maps of random walks on complex networks reveal community structure. *Proceedings of the National Academy of Sciences*, 105(4):1118–1123, 2008.

[20] Swarup Chattopadhyay, Tanmay Basu, Asit K Das, Kuntal Ghosh, and Late CA Murthy. Towards effective discovery of natural communities in complex networks and implications in e-commerce. *Electronic Commerce Research*, 21(4):917–954, 2021.

[21] Badrul M Sarwar, George Karypis, Joseph Konstan, and John Riedl. Recommender systems for large-scale e-commerce: Scalable neighborhood formation using clustering. In *Proceedings of the fifth international conference on computer and information technology*, volume 1, pages 291–324. Citeseer, 2002.

[22] Shumeet Baluja, Rohan Seth, Dharshi Sivakumar, Yushi Jing, Jay Yagnik, Shankar Kumar, Deepak Ravichandran, and Mohamed Aly. Video suggestion and discovery for youtube: Taking random walks through the view graph. In *Proceedings of the 17th international conference on World Wide Web*, pages 895–904, 2008.

[23] Rohit Parimi and Doina Caragea. Community detection on large graph datasets for recommender systems. In *2014 IEEE international conference on data mining workshop*, pages 589–596. IEEE, 2014.

[24] Network dataset. Dblp computer science bibliography. *KONECT*, 2022.

[25] Network dataset. Bookcrossing (implicit). *KONECT*, 2022.

[26] Oleksandr Shchur, Maximilian Mumme, Aleksandar Bojchevski, and Stephan Günnemann. Pitfalls of graph neural network evaluation. *CoRR*, abs/1811.05868, 2018.

[27] Network dataset. MovieLens 20m. *Kaggle*, 2022.

[28] Shahab Saquib Sohail, Jamshed Siddiqui, and Rashid Ali. Feature extraction and analysis of online reviews for the recommendation of books using opinion mining technique. *Perspectives in Science*, 8:754–756, 2016.

[29] Pearl Pu, Li Chen, and Rong Hu. A user-centric evaluation framework for recommender systems. In *Proceedings of the fifth ACM conference on Recommender systems*, pages 157–164, 2011.

[30] Djallel Bouneffouf, Amel Bouzeghoub, and Alda Lopes Ganarski. Riskaware recommender systems. In *International conference on neural information processing*, pages 57–65. Springer, 2013.

[31] Long-Sheng Chen, Fei-Hao Hsu, Mu-Chen Chen, and Yuan-Chia Hsu. Developing recommender systems with the consideration of product profitability for sellers. *Information Sciences*, 178(4):1032–1048, 2008.

[32] Jian Wang and Yi Zhang. Opportunity model for e-commerce recommendation: Right product; right time. In *Proceedings of the 36th international ACM SIGIR conference on research and development in information retrieval*, pages 303–312, 2013.

[33] Bruno M Veloso, Fátima Leal, Benedita Malheiro, and Juan Carlos Burguillo. On-line guest profiling and hotel recommendation. *Electronic Commerce Research and Applications*, 34:100832, 2019.

[34] Hao Wang, Xingjian Shi, and Dit-Yan Yeung. Relational stacked denoising autoencoder for tag recommendation. In *Twenty-ninth AAAI conference on artificial intelligence*, 2015.

[35] Dingqi Yang, Daqing Zhang, Zhiyong Yu, and Zhu Wang. A sentiment enhanced personalized location recommendation system. In *Proceedings of the 24th ACM conference on hypertext and social media*, pages 119–128, 2013.

[36] Dhoha Almazro, Ghadeer Shahatah, Lamia Albdulkarim, Mona Kherees, Romy Martinez, and William Nzoukou. A survey paper on recommender systems. *arXiv preprint arXiv:1006.5278*, 2010.

[37] Shulong Chen and Yuxing Peng. Matrix factorization for recommendation with explicit and implicit feedback. *Knowledge-Based Systems*, 158:109–117, 2018.

[38] Hartmut Döhner, Elihu Estey, David Grimwade, Sergio Amadori, Frederick R Appelbaum, Thomas Büchner, Hervé Dombret, Benjamin L Ebert, Pierre Fenaux, Richard A Larson, et al. Diagnosis and management of aml in adults: 2017 eln recommendations from an international expert panel. *Blood, the Journal of the American Society of Hematology*, 129(4):424–447, 2017.

[39] Markus Zanker and Markus Jessenitschnig. Case-studies on exploiting explicit customer requirements in recommender systems. *User Modeling and User-Adapted Interaction*, 19(1):133–166, 2009.

[40] Folasade Olubusola Isinkaye, Yetunde O Folajimi, and Bolande Adefowoke Ojokoh. Recommendation systems: Principles, methods and evaluation. *Egyptian Informatics Journal*, 16(3):261–273, 2015.

[41] Daniel T Larose and Chantal D Larose. *Discovering knowledge in data: An introduction to data mining*, volume 4. John Wiley & Sons, 2014.

[42] Bamshad Mobasher, Xin Jin, and Yanzan Zhou. Semantically enhanced collaborative filtering on the web. In *European web mining forum*, pages 57–76. Springer, 2003.

[43] Gediminas Adomavicius and Alexander Tuzhilin. Toward the next generation of recommender systems: A survey of the state-of-the-art and possible extensions. *IEEE Transactions on Knowledge and Data Engineering*, 17(6):734–749, 2005.

[44] Shahab Saquib Sohail, Jamshed Siddiqui, and Rashid Ali. Classifications of recommender systems: A review. *Journal of Engineering Science & Technology Review*, 10(4), 2017.

[45] Mehrbakhsh Nilashi, Othman Bin Ibrahim, and Norafida Ithnin. Hybrid recommendation approaches for multi-criteria collaborative filtering. *Expert Systems with Applications*, 41(8):3879–3900, 2014.

[46] Tulasi K Paradarami, Nathaniel D Bastian, and Jennifer L Wightman. A hybrid recommender system using artificial neural networks. *Expert Systems with Applications*, 83:300–313, 2017.

[47] Alexander Felfernig, Ludovico Boratto, Martin Stettinger, and Marko Tkalčič. *Group recommender systems: An introduction*. Springer, 2018.

[48] Derek Bridge, Mehmet H Göker, Lorraine McGinty, and Barry Smyth. Case-based recommender systems. *The Knowledge Engineering Review*, 20(3):315–320, 2005.

[49] John K Tarus, Zhendong Niu, and Abdallah Yousif. A hybrid knowledge based recommender system for e-learning based on ontology and sequential pattern mining. *Future Generation Computer Systems*, 72:37–48, 2017.

[50] Shang H Hsu, Ming-Hui Wen, Hsin-Chieh Lin, Chun-Chia Lee, and ChiaHoang Lee. Aimed-a personalized TV recommendation system. In *European conference on interactive television*, pages 166–174. Springer, 2007.

[51] Christina Christakou, Spyros Vrettos, and Andreas Stafylopatis. A hybrid movie recommender system based on neural networks. *International Journal on Artificial Intelligence Tools*, 16(05):771–792, 2007.

[52] Liu Xin, Junde Song, Meina Song, Junjie Tong, et al. Book recommendation based on community detection. In *Joint international conference on pervasive computing and the networked world*, pages 364–373. Springer, 2013.

[53] Mushtaq Hussain, Wenhao Zhu, Wu Zhang, and Syed Muhammad Raza Abidi. Student engagement predictions in an e-learning system and their impact on student course assessment scores. *Computational Intelligence and Neuroscience*, 2018, 2018.

[54] Amal Trifa, Aroua Hedhili, and Wided Lejouad Chaari. Knowledge tracing with an intelligent agent, in an e-learning platform. *Education and Information Technologies*, 24(1):711–741, 2019.

[55] Masahiko Mikawa, Soichi Izumi, and Kazuyo Tanaka. Book recommendation signage system using silhouette-based gait classification. In *2011 10th international conference on machine learning and applications and workshops*, volume 1, pages 416–419. IEEE, 2011.

[56] Hao Ma, Tom Chao Zhou, Michael R Lyu, and Irwin King. Improving recommender systems by incorporating social contextual information. *ACM Transactions on Information Systems (TOIS)*, 29(2):1–23, 2011.

[57] Ian Goodfellow, Yoshua Bengio, and Aaron Courville. *Deep learning*. MIT Press, 2016.

[58] Chong Zhang, Kay Chen Tan, Haizhou Li, and Geok Soon Hong. A cost sensitive deep belief network for imbalanced classification. *IEEE Transactions on Neural Networks and Learning Systems*, 30(1):109–122, 2018.

[59] Jia Lina, Mao Zhiyong, et al. The application of book intelligent recommendation based on the association rule mining of clementine. *Journal of Software Engineering and Applications*, 6(7):30, 2013.

[60] Gui-Rong Xue, Chenxi Lin, Qiang Yang, WenSi Xi, Hua-Jun Zeng, Yong Yu, and Zheng Chen. Scalable collaborative filtering using cluster-based smoothing. In *Proceedings of the 28th annual international ACM SIGIR conference on research and development in information retrieval*, pages 114–121, 2005. https://www.researchgate.net/publication/221300626_Scalable_collaborative_filtering_using_cluster-based_smoothing

[61] Subhash K Shinde and Uday Kulkarni. Hybrid personalized recommender system using centering-bunching based clustering algorithm. *Expert Systems with Applications*, 39(1):1381–1387, 2012.

[62] Mustansar Ali Ghazanfar and Adam Prügel-Bennett. Leveraging clustering approaches to solve the gray-sheep users problem in recommender systems. *Expert Systems with Applications*, 41(7):3261–3275, 2014.

[63] Kyoung-Jae Kim and Hyunchul Ahn. A recommender system using ga k-means clustering in an online shopping market. *Expert Systems with Applications*, 34(2):1200–1209, 2008.

[64] Shristi Shakya Khanal, PWC Prasad, Abeer Alsadoon, and Angelika Maag. A systematic review: Machine learning based recommendation systems for e-learning. *Education and Information Technologies*, 25(4):2635–2664, 2020.

[65] Andrea Lancichinetti and Santo Fortunato. Community detection algorithms: A comparative analysis. *Physical Review E*, 80(5):056117, 2009.

[66] Xiaojin Zhu and Zoubin Ghahramani. *Learning from labeled and unlabeled data with label propagation*. Technical Report, 2002. https://www.researchgate.net/publication/2475534_Learning_from_Labeled_and_Unlabeled_Data_with_Label_Propagation.

[67] Henry Small. Co-citation in the scientific literature: A new measure of the relationship between two documents. *Journal of the American Society for Information Science*, 24(4):265–269, 1973.

[68] Jonathan L Herlocker, Joseph A Konstan, Loren G Terveen, and John T Riedl. Evaluating collaborative filtering recommender systems. *ACM Transactions on Information Systems (TOIS)*, 22(1):5–53, 2004.

[69] Deuk Hee Park, Hyea Kyeong Kim, Il Young Choi, and Jae Kyeong Kim. A literature review and classification of recommender systems research. *Expert Systems with Applications*, 39(11):10059–10072, 2012.

[70] Serdar Sali. Movie rating prediction using singular value decomposition. *Machine learning project report by University of California*, Santa Cruz, 2008.

[71] Hao Ma, Haixuan Yang, Michael R Lyu, and Irwin King. Sorec: Social recommendation using probabilistic matrix factorization. In *Proceedings of the 17th ACM conference on information and knowledge management*, pages 931–940, 2008. https://www.researchgate.net/publication/221615498_SoRec_Social_recommendation_using_probabilistic_matrix_factorization

[72] Iván Cantador, Peter Brusilovsky, and Tsvi Kuflik. Second workshop on information heterogeneity and fusion in recommender systems (hetrec2011). In *Proceedings of the fifth ACM conference on Recommender systems*, pages 387–388, 2011.

[73] Min Gong, Zhaogui Xu, Lei Xu, Yanhui Li, and Lin Chen. Recommending web service based on user relationships and preferences. In *2013 IEEE 20th international conference on web services*, pages 380–386. IEEE, 2013.

[74] Paul Resnick and Hal R Varian. Recommender systems. *Communications of the ACM*, 40(3):56–58, 1997.

[75] Jie Lu, Qusai Shambour, Yisi Xu, Qing Lin, and Guangquan Zhang. Bizseeker: A hybrid semantic recommendation system for personalized government-to-business e-services. *Internet Research*, 2010. https://www.researchgate.net/publication/220147028_BizSeeker_A_hybrid_semantic_recommendation_system_for_personalized_government-to-business_e-services

[76] Taehee Lee, Jonghoon Chun, Junho Shim, and Sang-goo Lee. An ontology based product recommender system for b2b marketplaces. *International Journal of Electronic Commerce*, 11(2):125–155, 2006.

[77] Jyun-Cheng Wang and Chui-Chen Chiu. Recommending trusted online auction sellers using social network analysis. *Expert Systems with Applications*, 34(3):1666–1679, 2008.

[78] Raymond J Mooney and Loriene Roy. Content-based book recommending using learning for text categorization. In *Proceedings of the fifth ACM conference on digital libraries*, pages 195–204, 2000. https://www.cs.utexas.edu/users/ml/papers/libra-sigir-wkshp-99.pdf

[79] Richard D Lawrence, George S Almasi, Vladimir Kotlyar, Marisa Viveros, and Sastry S Duri. Personalization of supermarket product recommendations. In *Applications of data mining to electronic commerce*, pages 11–32. Springer, 2001.

[80] Ron Kohavi and Foster Provost. Applications of data mining to electronic commerce. In *Applications of data mining to electronic commerce*, pages 5–10. Springer, 2001.

[81] Zan Huang, Wingyan Chung, and Hsinchun Chen. A graph model for e-commerce recommender systems. *Journal of the American Society for Information Science and Technology*, 55(3):259–274, 2004.

[82] Osmar R Zaiane. Building a recommender agent for e-learning systems. In *International conference on computers in education, 2002 proceedings*, pages 55–59. IEEE, 2002.

[83] Jie Lu. A personalized e-learning material recommender system. In *International conference on information technology and applications*. Macquarie Scientific Publishing, 2004.

[84] Carlos Porcel and Enrique Herrera-Viedma. Dealing with incomplete information in a fuzzy linguistic recommender system to disseminate information in university digital libraries. *Knowledge-based Systems*, 23(1):32–39, 2010.

[85] Rosta Farzan and Peter Brusilovsky. Social navigation support in a course recommendation system. In *International conference on adaptive hypermedia and adaptive web-based systems*, pages 91–100. Springer, 2006.

[86] Robin D Burke, Kristian J Hammond, and Benjamin C Young. Knowledge based navigation of complex information spaces. In *Proceedings of the national conference on artificial intelligence*, volume 462, page 468, 1996.

[87] Ariel Pashtan, Remy Blattler, Andi Heusser Andi, and Peter Scheuermann. *Catis: A context-aware tourist information system*, 2003. https://www.researchgate.net/publication/228742147_CATIS_A_Context-Aware_Tourist_Information_System.

[88] Luis Martinez, Rosa M Rodriguez, and Macarena Espinilla. Reja: A georeferenced hybrid recommender system for restaurants. In *2009 IEEE/WIC/ACM international joint conference on web intelligence and intelligent agent technology*, volume 3, pages 187–190. IEEE, 2009.

[89] Angel García-Crespo, Javier Chamizo, Ismael Rivera, Myriam Mencke, Ricardo Colomo-Palacios, and Juan Miguel Gómez-Berbís. Speta: Social pervasive e-tourism advisor. *Telematics and Informatics*, 26(3):306–315, 2009.

14 Recommendation Systems for Choosing Online Learning Resources
A Hands-On Approach

Arkajit Saha, Shreya Dey, Monideepa Roy,
Sujoy Datta, and Pushpendu Kar

CONTENTS

DOI: 10.1201/9781003319122-14

14.1 INTRODUCTION

Nowadays, online learning has become a significant part of the education system. Numerous online courses and learning materials are being offered on web-based platforms to benefit users. To promote e-learning, many colleges, universities, businesses and organizations worldwide like MIT open courseware, Learndirect. com, NPTEL and MOOC are providing students distance learning courses, online certifications and online degrees. So personalization is a necessary approach for enabling a smoother user experience. However, in expanding to this new level of customization, education systems increase the amount of data that customers must process before they are able to select which courses or certifications meet their needs.

Recommendation systems are one of the essential solutions to this information overload problem and help in delivering relevant and correct information to the learners. Two paradigms of recommendation systems are content-based recommendation systems, which try to recommend items similar to those a given user has interacted with in the past, and systems designed according to the collaborative recommendation paradigm, which try to identify users whose preferences are similar to those of the concerned user and recommend items they have liked. Content-based recommenders analyze item descriptions and/or attributes formerly browsed by a user and build a structured representation of user interests adopted to recommended interesting items by matching attributes of the user profile to that of a content or object in the form of user profile.[1] A profile that correctly meets user needs and likings proves tremendously advantageous for an effective information access process. For example, it could be used to filter search results by determining if a user is interested in a specific item or not and, in the negative case, then preventing it from being displayed.

For understanding content-based recommender systems and implementing them for course recommendation, we have presented a comprehensive study and interpretation of recommender systems in the following sections of the chapter, which show the intention:

- to provide an overview of previously used state-of-the-art systems, while highlighting the most effective and widely adopted techniques, and the domains in which they have been adopted and applied

- to provide a deep dive into the problem statement and the planning behind the features or requirements needed during our project work to propose a solution to the problem; the approximate time analysis required to meet all the requirements; and the various types of assumptions, dependencies and constraints to be considered while developing the solution or software
- to show how a recommendation system has been used and implemented in this project work to suggest relevant courses with respect to a user and the visualization and analysis of the results obtained from the implementation
- to explore recommended practices for the project design, coding and testing followed during this project
- to present future research scope and trends, which could steer the subsequent generation of content-based recommender systems.

14.2   BACKGROUND/BASIC CONCEPTS

In this chapter, we explore and highlight how a content-based recommendation engine has been implemented for course recommendation. But before that, we explore some of the previously used state-of-the-art systems, while highlighting the most effective and widely adopted content-based techniques, and the domains in which they have been adopted and applied.

Some of the original ideas of usage of content-based filtering started back in 1960s and were known as "selective dissemination of information".[2] At the time, the aim was to match latest information items with presumed interests of the recipients that were stored in user profiles and to distribute the information based on it. Another source of content-based filtering systems can be traced back to the concept of information retrieval (IR). Content-based approaches, for instance, primarily bank on document encodings, which in turn were developed in field of IR.[3] Gradually, with the advent of Web era, content-based filtering techniques came to be applied successfully in diverse fields, for instance, to formulate personalized recommendations of appealing web pages.[4]

Soon it was discovered that pure content-based filtering approaches had quite a few limitations, especially when compared to collaborative filtering approaches. The main problem was insignificant consideration of quality of items for recommendation, for example, the unintelligible and restricted movie recommendations delivered by content-based recommendation system, which used to be similar to those preferred by the user in the past.

Till the last few decades, researchers found it difficult to find high performing content-based models to be used for boosting collaborative systems, e.g., in cold-start situations.[5] Recently, due to the obtainability of modern and superior structured and unstructured knowledge sources such as user-generated content, hybrid systems are being widely proposed, which aim to make better recommendations. What's more is that content-based item recommendations are gaining more importance in some application scenarios.[6] To conclude, content-based data helps to deliver better descriptions,[7] which is becoming ever more an important characteristic for future recommender systems to be fair and transparent.

14.3 PROBLEM STATEMENT/REQUIREMENT SPECIFICATIONS

In recent times, online learning has been adopted as one of the prime education systems. As a result, a wide variety of online courses and learning materials are being offered on web-based platforms in extensively personalized ways. Therefore, finding courses that are in accordance with their interests from a large collection of available courses and certifications is one of the major problems users encounter while browsing through the options at their disposal.

Recommender systems offer a solution to this information overload problem as the users will get recommendations using a system of smart searches.[8] The challenge is to create or develop a system that can be used by learners to promptly discover items of interest in a digital space containing a large collection of items.

14.4 DESIGNING THE RECOMMENDATION ENGINE

As this framework includes non-biased sorting of courses as per their similarity score with the course inputted by user, we implemented a simple user interface for showing the course recommendations. The steps to be taken in consideration when building the base code followed by deployment of a shareable web app can be represented using a list of features to be developed as follows in the next sections.

14.4.1 MENU

Description: When the user enters the Streamlit web app, a menu for navigation with options to choose from appears.

Input: The app has to be opened and the dropdown box titled "Menu" on the top-left side of the web app is to be clicked, which will help the user to toggle the navigation menu.

Output: The navigation menu options appear as "Home", "Recommend" and "About". By default, the menu is set to Home when any user enters the web app.

14.4.2 HOME

Description: The Home menu option allows the user to get a sneak peek at the various attributes that are available in the dataset for every course for their viewing.

Input: The users can freely scroll through the first 20 courses available in the dataset.

Output: On exploration of the data frame representation of the first 20 courses in the dataset, the users can see the course ID (course_id), course title (course_title), link to course website (URL), number of subscribers (num_subscribers), number of reviews (num_reviews), number of lectures (num_lectures) and cost price of the course (price) for every course.

Processing: The data frame showing the course details of first 20 courses in the dataset acts as an interactive table as the courses displayed can be sorted in ascending or descending order based on any column attributes' values; with a single click on the column name for ascending order and two clicks on column name, it shows the courses in descending order.

14.4.3 RECOMMEND

Description: The main outcome page of our project, which will show recommendations of courses with similarity scores of courses in the dataset with the one inputted by the user.

Input: Choose the Recommend option from Menu dropdown to navigate to Recommend page.

Output: The Recommend page opens with left side having the box for "Number" input and the "Search" box on the right side for desired course input by user.

Input: A number should be set by the user between 5 and 40 (10 being the default value) for the number of recommended courses they would like to see in the Number box.

Output: After the Number and Search box is set, the recommendations up to that count are shown.

Input: The user enters the desired topic they are searching courses for in the Search box.

Output:

- If a course name in the dataset matches exactly with the input of the user, a list of recommended courses immediately appears with similarity score, course title, link to website and price for each of the courses; and the number of recommendations rendered is equal to the previous input in Number field.
- If the input of the user does not match exactly with any course's name in the dataset, "Not Found" is displayed and a list of suggested options is displayed containing the words inputted by the user. The user is free to scroll and copy and paste any course title which seems fitting in the search box to get the output as described in previous pointer.

14.4.4 ABOUT

Description: A page which shows brief information about how the web app is built.

Input: From the dropdown box in the top-left hand side of the web app, About is selected.

Output: The user is directed to the About page, which show some information about the Streamlit web app.

14.4.5 SHARE

Description: This feature helps to share the Streamlit web app with people.

Input: The user has to:

Click on the Share button or click on the hamburger menu and choose "Share this app".

Output:

- On clicking the Share button, the user gets to see a pop-up where other users can be invited via emails, or the app can be made public by using a toggle and the link can be copied and shared.
- On clicking "Share this app", the option to share the app through Twitter, LinkedIn, Hacker News, email and the Streamlit discuss forum is displayed on the screen.

14.5   SYSTEM DESIGN DETAILS

14.5.1   DESIGN AND IMPLEMENTATION CONSTRAINTS

- Python language is used for writing the script for implementation of course recommendation app.
- Streamlit user interface (UI) is used to deploy and share the course recommendation app with some features fixed by including HTML, CSS and JavaScript in the previously mentioned Python script only.
- Streamlit UI must be toggled such so that every time a new element is added to the script, the app reruns itself on its own and the changes can be seen immediately.

14.5.2   OPERATING ENVIRONMENT

The web app is suitable for the following operating environments:

- Operating System: Windows 10/11, Linux
- Platform: Google Chrome/Edge/Firefox

14.5.3   ASSUMPTIONS AND DEPENDENCIES

It is assumed that the database design for this web app will work appropriately, and the speed of the internet used by the user is efficient enough to load the data from the dataset uploaded on GitHub to the user system or browser. The browser is also assumed to be up-to-date and able to handle that much heavy data.

14.5.4   USER INTERFACES

- The user interface created with the help of Streamlit elements shall be supported by any browser like Google Chrome, Microsoft Edge and Mozilla Firefox.
- The user interface comprises Home, Recommend and About pages.

14.5.5 HARDWARE INTERFACES

As the web app must run using internet, the hardware interface comprises the following:

- Network interface
- Device having valid and fast internet connection—Wi-Fi or 4G/5G to support the features of the app

14.5.6 SOFTWARE INTERFACES

- Python language is used to create the base script for the course recommendation app. Python in-built modules and libraries are also used for loading data and executing required functions on it to get the desired UI as the final outcome.
- Streamlit also uses open-source Python to create the final user interface and helps to deploy the app directly by connecting to GitHub repository.
- The course recommendation web app uses following as communications interface:
  - Stable internet connection
  - HTTP protocol.

14.5.7 BLOCK DIAGRAM

In this section, an overview of content-based recommender systems along with block diagram is explained before jumping into its implementation in the form of the course recommendation system and app in the next section[9, 10].

Content-based filters involve data provided, either explicitly (rating) or implicitly (clicking on a link), by specific users instead of a group of similar users. Based on personalized interests, the algorithm picks items with similar content and recommends them to the users. When the user takes actions on the recommendations or searches for new items, the system is able to improve its accuracy over time. Though the diversity in recommendations is less, this relieves the users of the dependence on other users' rating to discover an item which might be of substantial benefit to them [11, 12].

As there can be multiple subject-related products on which similarity can be calculated, in the case of courses, our own recommender system based on course titles was planned, though content description or subject or other attributes/tags can also be included.

In this type of system, the recommendations are made in the form of following steps as shown in Figure 14.1:

- Content descriptions of items are first processed by the content analyzer wherein features are extracted from unstructured text and a structured item description is extracted and displayed in a systematic way to users.

- The feedback—implicit or explicit reactions mapped with the item descriptions—are sent for profile learning of distinct users through the profile learner.
- As the model learns and gets trained differently for each distinct user, it gains the ability to accurately predict and recommend only those items from the database that would interest each unique user.
- This feedback-induced learning cycle keeps iterating and allows the recommender system to dynamically filter user preferences in a customized manner.

The adoption of a content-based recommender helps encourage user independence, transparency on the explanation behind the recommendation of particular items and recommendations of new items remaining unaffected from first-rater problem.

14.6 IMPLEMENTATION

This section provides an overview of content-based recommender systems with the aim of highlighting the different aspects involved in their design and implementation in the form of a course recommendation app [13].

14.6.1 COURSE RECOMMENDATION SYSTEM

Course recommender system maximizes similarity scores between different courses in the database and those courses or their related field of courses searched, browsed

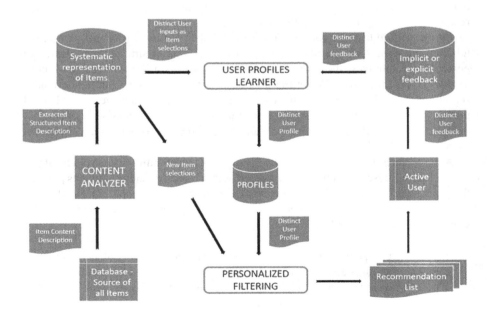

FIGURE 14.1 Basic structure and mechanism of a content-based recommender system.

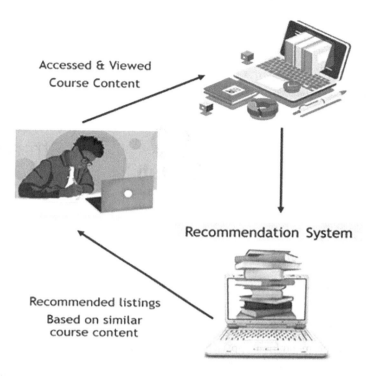

Accessed & Viewed
Course Content

Recommendation System

Recommended listings
Based on similar
course content

FIGURE 14.2   Logical illustration of a course recommendation system.

through or enrolled in by the learner; and it makes suggestions accordingly, as can be seen in Figure 14.2.

The system includes the following major processes:

- To begin, features are extracted from the data and vectorized for better understanding
- Then, the similarity between the courses is computed, considering cosine similarity as the metric
- Next, the recommendation function is built to recommend selected relevant and similar courses to the one inputted by the user
- The course IDs/indexes are obtained, and the similarity scores are sorted according to the cosine similarity scores
- Lastly, on the basis of these preliminary processes, the recommendation function is built to recommend selected relevant and similar courses to the one inputted by the user

These base concepts of the system have been implemented and highlighted in the following sections in the further development of the course recommendation app (Figure 14.3).

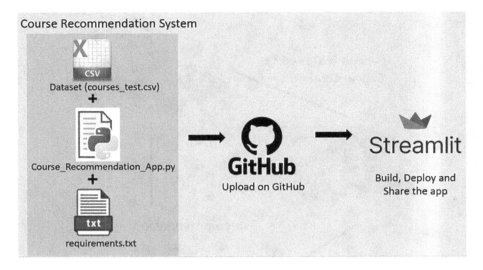

FIGURE 14.3   Logical illustration of a course recommendation app.

14.6.2   COURSE RECOMMENDATION APP

The course recommendation app is based on the basic concepts and components of a course recommendation system, which we have included in the Course_ Recommendation_App.py file that is elaborated on the next section (Figure 14.3). The python file (.py) and dataset (requirements.txt) containing information about all the libraries, modules and packages on which our project is dependent or requires to run are uploaded on the GitHub repository.

The app includes the following processes:

- To begin, features are extracted from the dataset and vectorized for better understanding
- Then, functions for vectorization of these features and for computation of similarity between the courses, considering cosine similarity as the metric, are developed
- Next, the course IDs/indexes are obtained, and the similarity scores are sorted according to the cosine similarity scores; our recommendation function is built on the basis of these preliminary processes
- Lastly, the functions developed in previous steps are applied along with addition of cascading style sheets (CSS) to get recommendations of selected relevant and similar courses to the one inputted by the user, in the form of a presentable web app using Streamlit. The web app is deployed and shared.

14.6.3   DATASET

A manually merged dataset containing 4000+ courses containing course details from massive open online course provider Udemy and derived from datasets available on Kaggle were used and loaded using the function displayed in Figure 14.4.

Our approach was to use course titles to make recommendations while keeping in mind that the features could be extended to course description, subject details, etc. as they provide much more information regarding courses for mapping. As the format of these attributes were in text format (string) and we needed to use natural language processing (NLP) [14], it was important to tokenize and convert them into numbers to calculate the cosine similarities for the course recommender [15, 16].

14.6.4 Functions for Vectorization and Cosine Similarity

14.6.4.1 Vectorization of Dataset

We also imported CountVectorizer of the sklearn library, which was used to convert the data obtained from a previous code snippet execution to a vector of token counts. We have used CountVectorizer's fit.tranform as shown in Figure 14.5 to count the number of texts as every word in our data, which is important to detect similarity.

14.6.4.2 Cosine Similarity

Similarity between two items is measured using the distance metric where similarity and relevance is highest when distance between the points is least. During computation of distance between unrelated dimensions/features, caution must be exercised and relative values of elements must be normalized.

```python
# Load Our Dataset
def load_data(data):
        df = pd.read_csv(data)
        return df
```

FIGURE 14.4 Code showing function for loading dataset.

```python
# Fxn
# Vectorize + Cosine Similarity Matrix

def vectorize_text_to_cosine_mat(data):
        count_vect = CountVectorizer()
        cv_mat = count_vect.fit_transform(data)
        # Get the cosine similarity matrix
        cosine_sim_mat = cosine_similarity(cv_mat)
        return cosine_sim_mat
```

FIGURE 14.5 Code showing usage of CountVectorizer() and generation of cosine similarity matrix.

For our work, we used cosine similarity from sklearn library as our distance metric, which calculates similarity in the form of normalized dot product shown in Figure 14.6. It measures the cosine of the angle between two vectors such that an angle of 0 degree has cosine value as 1 meaning the data points are 100% similar and an angle of 90 degrees means data points are dissimilar.

Firstly, the course details are transformed as vectors in a geometric space, and to find cosine of the angle between course titles vectors as seen in Figure 14.7, we use cosine_similarity to generate a NumPy array, cosine_sim_mat matrix, with calculated cosine similarity scores as implemented in Figure 14.5.

14.6.5 RECOMMENDATION FUNCTION

14.6.5.1 Getting Course Indexes and Scores

Now, we extract the indices of course titles in the variable course_indices, while drop_duplicates helped us to train our model only on unique titles as shown in the code snippet in Figure 14.8.

$$similarity = cos(\theta) = \frac{u \cdot v}{\|u\|\|v\|} = \frac{\sum_{i=1}^{n} u_i v_i}{\sqrt{\sum_{i=1}^{n} u_i^2} \sqrt{\sum_{i=1}^{n} v_i^2}}$$

FIGURE 14.6 Calculation of similarity in the form of normalized dot product.

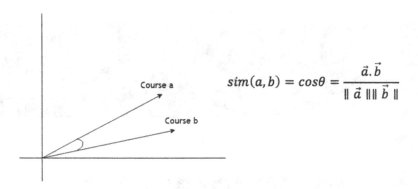

FIGURE 14.7 Cosine of the angle between course titles vectors a and b.[17]

```
# Get Course ID/Index
course_indices = pd.Series(df.index,index=df['course_title']).drop_duplicates()
```

FIGURE 14.8 Code to obtain course indices.

```
# Look into the cosine matr for that index
sim_scores =list(enumerate(cosine_sim_mat[idx]))
```

FIGURE 14.9 Code to obtain list of scores from iteration of cosine_sim_mat.

Next aim was to distinguish the top similar courses having highest similarity scores, and for this we add a counter to the iterable list cosine_sim_mat by using the enumerate method as implied in Figure 14.9 to get desired output list.

Then, we sorted the courses' indices and scores obtained by executing previously mentioned code snippets, w.r.t the list scores we just obtained. To do this, we included the parameter reverse=True as shown in Figure 14.10 so that it will render the results in descending order, clearly citing the most similar courses at the head of the output.

sim_scores = sorted(sim_scores, key = lambda x: x[18], reverse=True)

14.6.5.2 Building the Recommendation Function

The groundwork for building the recommendation function has been done on the basis of previously mentioned modularized concepts like storing the title input by user in variable IDX, searching and sorting of similarity scores and indices from similarity matrix and storing the final result in a data frame and incorporating in the merged function as shown in Figure 14.11.

14.6.6 Applying Functions to Get Recommendations, Display the Streamlit Web App in Desired Style, Deploy and Share It

Since we are building a content-based recommendation system, knowledge of users' interests is vital to predict a similar course. Therefore, the next step is to take as

```
# Sort our scores per cosine score
```

FIGURE 14.10   Code to sort the courses as per descending order of their cosine scores while omitting individual courses in their rows.

```
# Recommendation System
@st.cache
def get_recommendation(title,cosine_sim_mat,df,num_of_rec=10):
    # Get Course ID/Index
    course_indices = pd.Series(df.index,index=df['course_title']).drop_duplicates()
    # Index of course
    idx = course_indices[title]

    # Look into the cosine matr for that index
    sim_scores =list(enumerate(cosine_sim_mat[idx]))
    sim_scores = sorted(sim_scores,key=lambda x: x[1],reverse=True)
    selected_course_indices = [i[0] for i in sim_scores[0:]]
    selected_course_scores = [i[1] for i in sim_scores[0:]]

    # Get the dataframe & title
    result_df = df.iloc[selected_course_indices]
    result_df['similarity_score'] = selected_course_scores
    final_recommended_courses = result_df[['course_title','similarity_score','url','price','num_subscribers']]
    return final_recommended_courses.head(num_of_rec)
```

FIGURE 14.11   Code of recommendation function.

input a course title that the user likes in the search box and apply the functions for vectorization, cosine similarity and recommendation to get the required number of courses (the value of which is obtained from num_of_rec) as output from the courses database similar to the one inputted [16, 9].

14.6.6.1 Handling Exceptions and Iterating through Results

If we enter some random text as search_term, a course with exactly that course_ title might not exist. In that case, an exception occurs, and a warning message "Not Found" is displayed. But if we enter an existing course_title, the various courses similar to the searched one are displayed in different rows due to iterations highlighting their title, similarity score, link to course webpage, price and number of subscribers. The recommendations and details are also available for display in JavaScript Object Notation (JSON) format for better readability of data interchange. Its execution from user perspective, all with the help of code, is shown in Figure 14.12

The exception of course "Not Found" is handled by the display of a warning message and by using the function search_term_if_not_found as shown in Figure 14.12 and Figure 14.13.

```
elif choice == "Recommend":
    st.subheader("Recommend Courses")
    cosine_sim_mat = vectorize_text_to_cosine_mat(df['course_title'])
    search_term = st.text_input("Search")
    num_of_rec = st.sidebar.number_input("Number",5,35,10)
    if st.button("Recommend"):
        if search_term is not None:
            try:
                results = get_recommendation(search_term,cosine_sim_mat,df,num_of_rec)
                with st.expander("Results as JSON"):
                    results_json = results.to_dict('index')
                    st.write(results_json)

                for row in results.iterrows():
                    rec_title = row[1][0]
                    rec_score = row[1][1]
                    rec_url = row[1][2]
                    rec_price = row[1][3]
                    rec_num_sub = row[1][4]

                    # st.write("Title",rec_title,)
                    stc.html(RESULT_TEMP.format(rec_title,rec_score,rec_url,rec_price,rec_num_sub),height=270)

            except:
                results= "Not Found"
                st.warning(results)
                st.info("Suggested Options include")
                result_df = search_term_if_not_found(search_term,df)
                st.dataframe(result_df)
```

FIGURE 14.12   Printing a list of recommended courses.

```
# Search For Course
@st.cache
def search_term_if_not_found(term,df):
    result_df = df[df['course_title'].str.contains(term)]
    return result_df
```

FIGURE 14.13   Printing a list of recommended courses.

14.6.6.1.1 Using Streamlit and Adding CSS

Streamlit, a free, open-source, all-Python framework, is used to quickly build an interactive web app for our project. Streamlit has the ability to rerun the entire Python script whenever code is changed or any user interacts with the app. We are also able to tap into the caching mechanism of Streamlit, thus allowing our app to stay performant when loading, reading or manipulating the large amount of data in our dataset that may cause expensive computation with every user interaction with the help of st.cache(). As shown in Figure 14.14, st.cache() helps to read and display the suggested courses efficiently and quickly when the user enters a course not in our database; as data is only loaded into app once.

Apart from the basic app look and feel created with the help of Streamlit, we also created a result CSS template as shown in Figure 14.15 to change the way a user will see the course recommendations, similar to the ones they input on the basis of cosine similarity scores.

```
# Search For Course
@st.cache
def search_term_if_not_found(term,df):
        result_df = df[df['course_title'].str.contains(term)]
        return result_df


def main():

        #st.title("Course Recommendation App")
        menu = ["Home","Recommend","About"]
        choice = st.sidebar.selectbox("Menu",menu)
        stc.html(HTML_BANNER)
```

FIGURE 14.14 Streamlit elements in use (st.cache, st.sidebar, stc.html).

```
RESULT_TEMP = """
<div style="width:90%;height:100%;padding:5px;position:relative;border-radius:5px;border-bottom-right-radius: 60px;
box-shadow:0 0 15px 5px #ccc; background-color: #ffffff;
  border-left: 8px solid #3399ff;">

<p style="color: black; font-size:20px; margin-left:10px;"><b>{}</b></p>

<p style="color:blue; font-size:16px; margin-left:20px;"><span style="color:black;">
<img src="https://drive.google.com/uc?export=view&id=1PDcoERVospHnqIdMZiKh2VksEEz1Ayaw" width="22px" height="22px"> Score: </span>{}</p>

<p style="color:blue; font-size:16px; margin-left:20px;"><span style="color:black;">
<img src="https://drive.google.com/uc?export=view&id=16q4pgIpzH1IA9jYQvfV534PKf9Ko_hXm" width="22px" height="22px"> </span>
<a href="{}", target="_blank"> Link</a></p>

<p style="color:blue; font-size:16px; margin-left:23px;"><span style="color:black;">
<img src="https://drive.google.com/uc?export=view&id=1pTUXJAFFpMrX_OPqZOXK9UWwe1Cd29SF" width="12px" height="15px">      Price: </span>{}</p>

<p style="color:blue; font-size:16px; margin-left:20px;"><span style="color:black;">
<img src="https://drive.google.com/uc?export=view&id=1nRLRvBKOOpvw-Wq7MItD8MjPG0TEk2aS" width="30px" height="22px"> No. of Subscribers: </span>{}</p>
</div>
"""
```

FIGURE 14.15 CSS template for displaying the recommended courses in a desired style.

14.6.6.1.2 Deploy and Share the Web App

We first login to Streamlit (https://share.streamlit.io/) using a GitHub profile and reach a screen of our apps as shown in Figure 14.16.

In the home page, we click on "New app" and are directed to the "Deploy an app" page as seen in Figure 14.17. Here, we need to set the repository and path in GitHub

FIGURE 14.16 Home page of Streamlit apps.

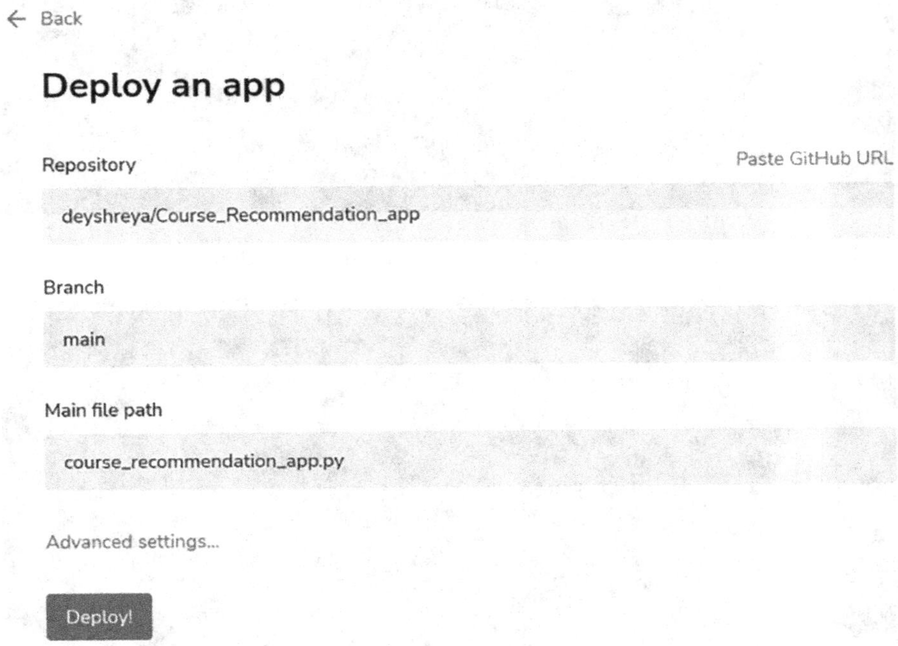

← Back

Deploy an app

Repository   Paste GitHub URL

deyshreya/Course_Recommendation_app

Branch

main

Main file path

course_recommendation_app.py

Advanced settings...

Deploy!

FIGURE 14.17 Deploy our app using Streamlit.

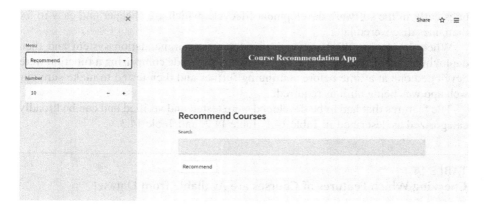

FIGURE 14.18 Home page of course recommendation app.

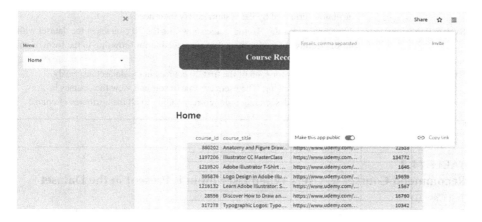

FIGURE 14.19 Share our app using Streamlit.

where we have uploaded our dataset, Python script and requirement file as mentioned previously and select the "Deploy!" button.

The course recommendation web app is thus deployed and is available for use as shown in the screenshot in Figure 14.18.

Finally, we click on the "Share" button on top of the screen and then on "Make this app public" as shown in Figure 14.19. We can thus copy the link of our public course recommendation app and share it for use.[19]

14.7 TESTING AND VERIFICATION

Unit testing is a type of white box testing and is carried out on each block of code as the software is developed by the developer. It helps in identifying the majority of the bugs early in the software development lifecycle, which are cheaper and easy to fix than ones discovered later.

When developing the basic logic for course recommendation system and then deploying it in the form of a web app, a few lines of code comprising a function were developed one at a time before continuing further and then tested to make sure our web app was being built as required.

The features that had to be developed were tested and verified and can be broadly categorized as described in Table 14.1, Table 14.2, and Table 14.3.

TABLE 14.1
Checking Which Features of Courses are Available from Dataset

Test Case ID	1
Test Case Title	Checking which features of courses are available from dataset
Test Condition	The features or attributes of courses in dataset should be made available for users to explore easily. The users should be able to interact with the features of the courses and see if they choose to get recommendations; will all the attributes furnished by the system satisfy their needs.
System Behaviour	The function for the "Home" page shows the top 20 courses in the dataset with all the features of each course that are available for browsing in the form of an interactive data frame.
Expected Result	All the features for each of the first 20 courses in the dataset are easily available for viewing. The users are free to sort and view the courses in ascending and descending order corresponding to all the attributes of course.

TABLE 14.2
Recommend Courses to Users When User Input is Present in the Dataset

Test Case ID	2
Test Case Title	Recommend courses to users when user input is present in the dataset
Test Condition	The user inputs any topic or subject of their interest matching the title of an existing course in the dataset and finds recommendations of courses similar to the user input.
System Behaviour	The user inputs a topic of interest in the search box and the function with condition for page "Recommend"; searches if a course exists with the same title as that entered by the user. Considering both matches, a list of recommendations of the count entered by the user in number box is generated.
Expected Result	If the user input matches with any course title in the dataset, a list of recommended courses is generated with the default number of recommendations being 10, though the total number of recommendations can be adjusted to 40. The recommendations' major highlights are the course title, the website link for the course, similarity score, price and number of subscribers. The first recommendation has a course title matching with the user input with the highest similarity score; other courses follow suit in a descending order of similarity scores.

TABLE 14.3
Recommend Courses to Users When User Input is not Present in the Dataset

Test Case ID	3
Test Case Title	Recommend courses to users when user input is not present in the dataset
Test Condition	The user inputs any topic or subject of their interest not matching exactly with the title of an existing course in dataset and finds recommendations of courses similar to the user input.
System Behaviour	The user inputs a topic of interest in the search box and the function with condition for page "Recommend", searches if a course exists with the same title as that entered by the user.
	Considering that both don't match exactly, a list of suggested options is generated in the form of an interactive data frame, the same as the one on the "Home" page.
Expected Result	If the user input does not match with any course title in the dataset, a list of suggested courses is generated with the help of the "search if not found" function in the form of an interactive data frame where the user can sort the suggestions according to any feature they need. The user can choose any course title that grabs their attention according to their requirement and paste it in the search box. The recommendations' list will be generated as mentioned in Table 14.2's expected result.

14.8 RESULTS

The course recommendation web app developed using Streamlit was successfully deployed and the screenshots of the same are presented in Figure 14.20, Figure 14.21, Figure 14.22 and Figure 14.23 with suitable explanations of the output.

In Figure 14.20, the screenshot shows how a user will be welcomed to the web app by the default web page and menu "Home". When menu is toggled to "Home", the user sees the head of the dataset or first 20 courses of the dataset with details like course ID, course title, URL (website link), number of subscribers, number of reviews, number of lectures and price for each course. The user will also have the option to sort these courses in any order corresponding to any of the displayed attributes as it is an interactive data frame.

Figure 14.21 shows if the word/phrase entered by the user such as "cryptocurrency" is not the name of a course in the dataset, then the message "Not Found" is displayed and "Suggested Options" are displayed for the user to browse from containing the string "cryptocurrency". These options are also displayed to the user in the form of an interactive data frame so that the user can sort according to any attribute and discover a course title that interests them.

From the options displayed in Figure 14.21, the user might find "Cryptocurrency Fundamentals: Buy, Sell, Trade Cryptocurrency", a title suitable to their need, and paste it in the search box. On searching for a title present in dataset, the app recommends courses with similarity scores for the user to choose from as shown in Figure 14.22. The recommendations are also available as JSON for better readability, which is shown in Figure 14.23.

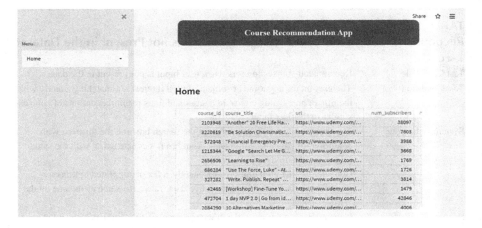

FIGURE 14.20 "Home" page of the course recommendation app gives a sneak peek into course attributes available for user browsing.

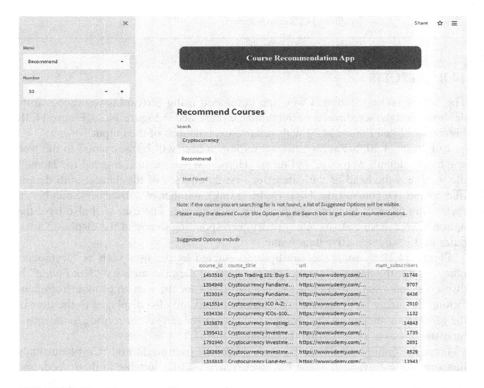

FIGURE 14.21 "Recommend" page used to suggest courses to users when user input is not present exactly in the dataset.

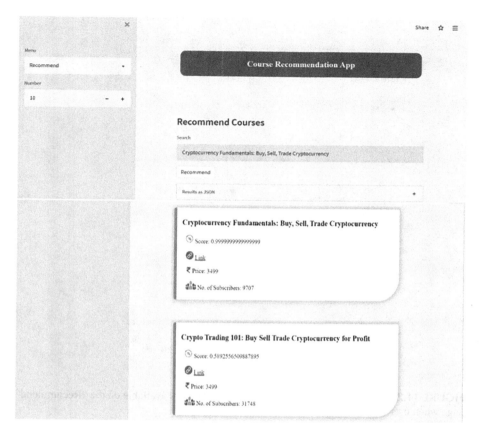

FIGURE 14.22 "Recommend" page used to recommend courses to users when user input is present in the dataset.

14.9 CONCLUSION AND FUTURE SCOPE

In this chapter, we have presented a course recommender system that uses content-based filtering, which is a specialized recommender system that we have used for suggesting relevant courses.

We have taken a close look at its components and demonstrated the results of various design choices. We built on previous approaches for content-based, hybrid recommendation systems and integrating our results and analysis with it. Focusing primarily on the course titles and content descriptions distinguishes our method from other recommender systems [20, 21]. This chapter further discusses future research scope and trends, which could steer the subsequent generation of content-based recommender systems.

Recommender systems can benefit a large range of businesses by prioritizing user-generated content and delivering serendipitous recommendations to the concerned users. With applications in multiple industries, recommendation systems are not only

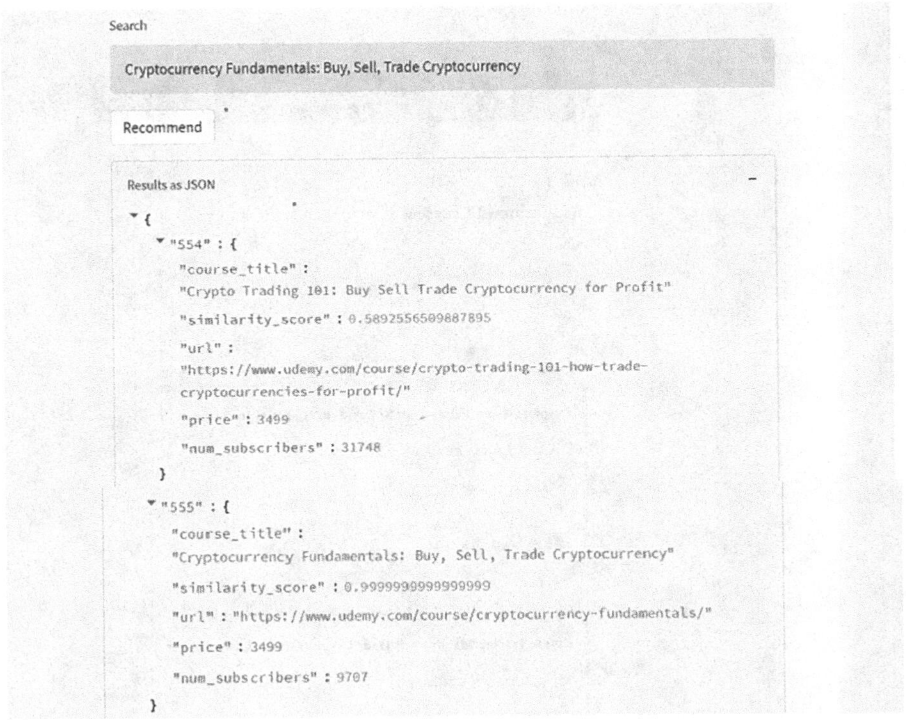

Search

Cryptocurrency Fundamentals: Buy, Sell, Trade Cryptocurrency

Recommend

Results as JSON   —

{
    "554" : {
        "course_title" :
        "Crypto Trading 101: Buy Sell Trade Cryptocurrency for Profit"
        "similarity_score" : 0.5892556509887895
        "url" :
        "https://www.udemy.com/course/crypto-trading-101-how-trade-
        cryptocurrencies-for-profit/"
        "price" : 3499
        "num_subscribers" : 31748
    }
    "555" : {
        "course_title" :
        "Cryptocurrency Fundamentals: Buy, Sell, Trade Cryptocurrency"
        "similarity_score" : 0.9999999999999999
        "url" : "https://www.udemy.com/course/cryptocurrency-fundamentals/"
        "price" : 3499
        "num_subscribers" : 9707
    }
}

FIGURE 14.23 Results as JSON for recommended courses available on the "Recommend" page when user input is present in the dataset.

benefitting companies with increased sales without increased marketing effort but are also increasing customer satisfaction. The following are some of the industries that stand to gain from recommender systems.

- Educational requirements differ from one student to another based on their career objectives and skills gap. The recommender systems add a significant amount of value to the educational sector by allowing students to learn more easily by suggesting to them quality online degrees and certifications as per their areas of interest.
- Recommendation systems were first widely used in the e-commerce industry. It helps drive traffic on the e-commerce websites through personalized emails and helps the companies gather more data for each customer's profile. It also helps analyze the customers' browsing history and suggest relevant products in real-time. Recommendation engines thus help increase profits while reducing workload and overhead.
- Through data-enabled product recommendation engines, retailers can distinguish patterns in traffic, be it online or in-store, which are used to design store layouts or customize user profiles on their websites that helps maximize sales. In the retail industry, a huge amount of shopping data is

generated daily for which a reliable recommendation system should be at the forefront of companies making accurate recommendations.[17]

- Media businesses jumped into recommendations very early. News sites or entertainment sites widely use recommendation systems. They have become a powerful helping hand in predicting user ratings before users explicitly provide one by using specialized algorithms and techniques that have the ability to support large product catalogues.

- In competitive sectors such as banking, customer experience is an indispensable lever. An abundant number of suppliers have made it very easy for any displeased customer to quickly switch to other providers.[22] Recommender systems provide assistance to banks to assess transaction data and decide upon college loans or real estate investment. It aims to boost banks' revenues and enable improved personalization to the customer. Knowledge regarding a customer's current financial situation, their past preferences, and the same type of data of thousands of other similar users helps in building a powerful recommendation service.

- Due to a significant increase in prevailing services in the telecom domain, more choices are being made available to the end users. Such extensive offers cannot be completely assessed by the user, which might lead some useful services to go unobserved. The usage of recommender systems in the telecom industry is rising as it promptly notifies the users about the wide range of services and offers that might interest them.[22]

REFERENCES

[1] Pasquale Lops, Dietmar Jannach, Cataldo Musto, Toine Bogers, Marijn Koolen. "Trends in Content-Based Recommendation." *User Modeling and User-Adapted Interaction*, 29 (2019), 239–249. https://doi.org/10.1007/s11257-019-09231-w

[2] C.B. Hensley. "Selective Dissemination of Information (SDI): State of the Art in May, 1963." In *The Proceedings of the 1963 Spring Joint Computer Conference*, Detroit, Michigan, 1963, May.

[3] G. Salton, M.J. McGill. *Introduction to Modern Information Retrieval*. New York: McGraw-Hill Inc, 1986.

[4] M. Pazzani, J. Muramatsu, D. Billsus. "Syskill & Webert: Identifying Interesting Web Sites." In *The Proceedings of the Thirteenth National Conference on Artificial Intelligence*, Portland, Oregon, 1996, August.

[5] P. Melville, R.J. Mooney, R. Nagarajan. "Content-Boosted Collaborative Filtering for Improved Recommendations." In *The Proceedings of the Eighteenth National Conference on Artificial Intelligence*, Edmonton, Alberta, 2002, July.

[6] Y. Yao, F.M. Harper. "Judging Similarity: A User-centric Study of Related Item Recommendations." In *The Proceedings of the 12th ACM Conference on Recommender Systems*, Vancouver, British Columbia, 2018, October.

[7] F. Gedikli, D. Jannach, M. Ge. "How Should I Explain? A Comparison of Different Explanation Types for Recommender Systems." *International Journal of Human-Computer Studies*, 72 (2014), 367–382.

[8] Simon Philip, P.B. Shola, Abari Ovye John. "Application of Content-Based Approach in Research Paper Recommendation System for a Digital Library." *International Journal of Advanced Computer Science and Applications*, 5(10) (2014).

[9]   https://builtin.com/data-science/recommender-systems

[10] https://www.analyticsvidhya.com/blog/2021/07/recommendation-system-understanding-the-basic-concepts/

[11] https://medium.com/genifyai/recommender-systems-and-applications-in-banking-f0cef8f87fa6

[12] Jian Yu, Paolo Falcarin, Antonio Vetro. "A Recommender System for Telecom Users: Experimental Evaluation of Recommendation Algorithms." In *Proceedings of 2011, 10th IEEE International Conference on Cybernetic Intelligent Systems, CIS 2011*, 2011. https://www.researchgate.net/publication/235732705_A_Recommender_System _for_ Telecom_Users_Experimental_Evaluation_of_Recommendation_Algorithms

[13] https://towardsdatascience.com/intermediate-streamlit-d5a1381daa65

[14] https://towardsdatascience.com/how-to-build-from-scratch-a-content-based-movie-recommender-with-natural-language-processing-25ad400eb243

[15] https://www.geeksforgeeks.org/movie-recommender-based-on-plot-summary-using-tf-idf-vectorization-and-cosine-similarity/?ref=rp

[16] https://www.analyticsvidhya.com/blog/2015/08/beginners-guide-learn-content-based-recommender-systems/

[17] https://towardsdatascience.com/using-cosine-similarity-to-build-a-movie-recommendation-system-ae7f20842599

[18] Pasquale Lops, Marco de Gemmis, Giovanni Semeraro. "Content-based Recommender Systems: State of the Art and Trends." In *Recommender Systems Handbook*. Springer, 2011. http://doi.org/10.1007/978-0-387-85820-3

[19] https://share.streamlit.io/deyshreya/course_recommendation_app/main/course_ recommendation_app.py

[20] https://medium.com/analytics-vidhya/understanding-simclr-a-simple-framework-for-contrastive-learning-of-visual-representations-d544a9003f3c

[21] https://indiaai.gov.in/article/cosine-similarity-the-metric-behind-recommendation-systems

[22] https://research.aimultiple.com/recommendation-system/

Index

Printed in the United States
by Baker & Taylor Publisher Services